Fog of War

THE SECOND WORLD WAR AND
THE CIVIL RIGHTS MOVEMENT

Edited by

Kevin M. Kruse

and

Stephen Tuck

OXFORD
UNIVERSITY PRESS

OXFORD
UNIVERSITY PRESS

Oxford University Press, Inc., publishes works that further
Oxford University's objective of excellence
in research, scholarship, and education.

Oxford   New York
Auckland   Cape Town   Dar es Salaam   Hong Kong   Karachi
Kuala Lumpur   Madrid   Melbourne   Mexico City   Nairobi
New Delhi   Shanghai   Taipei   Toronto

With offices in
Argentina   Austria   Brazil   Chile   Czech Republic   France   Greece
Guatemala   Hungary   Italy   Japan Poland   Portugal   Singapore
South Korea   Switzerland   Thailand   Turkey   Ukraine   Vietnam

Published by Oxford University Press, Inc.
198 Madison Avenue, New York, New York 10016

www.oup.com

Oxford is a registered trademark of Oxford University Press

Library of Congress Cataloging-in-Publication Data
Fog of war : the Second World War and the civil rights movement / edited
by Kevin M. Kruse and Stephen Tuck.
p.   cm.
Includes index.
ISBN 978-0-19-538241-9 (alk. paper)—ISBN 978-0-19-538240-2 1. World War, 1939–1945—Social aspects—
United States. 2. World War, 1939–1945—African Americans. 3. African Americans—Civil
rights—History—20th century. 4. African Americans—Social conditions—20th century. 5. Civil rights
movements—United States—History—20th century. 6. United States—Social conditions—1933–1945.
7. United States—Race relations—History—20th century. 8. War and society—United States—History—
20th century. I. Kruse, Kevin Michael, 1972– II. Tuck, Stephen G. N.
D744.7.U6F64   2012
940.53089'96073—dc23   2011017614

1 3 5 7 9 8 6 4 2

Printed in the United States of America
on acid-free paper

{ CONTENTS }

{ ACKNOWLEDGMENTS }

We would very much like to thank the contributors to this volume—each of whom brought their expertise to bear on the question of race and war, and some of whom rewrote their chapter several times in order to integrate wider themes as the project developed.

We are also grateful to the scholars who offered critiques and contributed to the discussion along the way, especially Tony Badger, Gareth Davies, Mary Dudziak, Desmond King, Wilson Moses and Jay Winter.

This project is the result of a partnership between the Oxford Centre for Research in U.S. History and the Princeton History Department. Both universities awarded this project very generous grants so that we could bring the contributors together. The Rothermere American Institute provided us with an excellent venue for our main workshop.

Finally, our thanks to Susan Ferber, our editor at OUP, who gave us outstanding support throughout the process—as is her custom.

{ CONTRIBUTORS }

Elizabeth Borgwardt is Associate Professor of History at Washington University in St. Louis. She is the author of *A New Deal for the World: America's Vision for Human Rights* (Belknap Press of Harvard University Press, 2005).

Jane Dailey is Associate Professor of American History at the University of Chicago. She is the author of *Before Jim Crow: The Politics of Race in Post-Emancipation Virginia* (University of North Carolina Press, 2000).

Kevin M. Kruse is Associate Professor of History at Princeton University. He is the author of *White Flight: Atlanta and the Making of Modern Conservatism* (Princeton University Press, 2005).

Kimberley L. Phillips is Frances L. and Edwin L. Cummings Associate Professor of History and American Studies at the College of William and Mary. She is the author of *Alabama North: African American Migrants, Community, and Working-Class Activism in Cleveland* (University of Illinois Press, 1999).

James T. Sparrow is Assistant Professor of History at the University of Chicago. He is the author of *Warfare State: World War II Americans in the Age of Big Government* (Oxford University Press, 2011).

Thomas Sugrue is David Boies Professor of History and Sociology at the University of Pennsylvania. He is the author of *Sweet Land of Liberty: The Forgotten Struggle for Civil Rights in the North* (Random House, 2008).

Patricia Sullivan is Professor of History at the University of South Carolina. She is the author of *Lift Every Voice: The NAACP and the Making of the Civil Rights Movement* (The New Press, 2009).

J. Mills Thornton III is Professor Emeritus of History at the University of Michigan. He is the author of *Dividing Lines: Municipal Politics and the Struggle for Civil Rights in Montgomery, Birmingham, and Selma* (University of Alabama Press, 2002).

Stephen Tuck is University Lecturer in American History at Oxford University. He is the author of *We Ain't What We Ought To Be: The Black Freedom Struggle from Emancipation to Obama* (Belknap Press of Harvard University Press, 2010, with accompanying web site, www.weaintwhatweoughttobe.com).

Penny Von Eschen is Professor of History and American Culture at the University of Michigan. She is the author of *Satchmo Blows Up the World: Jazz Ambassadors Play the Cold War* (Harvard University Press, 2004).

Jason Morgan Ward is Assistant Professor of History at Mississippi State University. He is the author of *Defending White Democracy: The Making of a Segregationist Movement and the Remaking of Racial Politics, 1936–1965* (University of North Carolina Press, 2011).

Julian E. Zelizer is Professor of History and Public Affairs at Princeton University. He is the author of *Arsenal of Democracy: The Politics of National Security: From World War II to the War on Terrorism* (Basic Books, 2009).

Fog of War

Introduction

THE SECOND WORLD WAR
AND THE CIVIL RIGHTS MOVEMENT

Kevin M. Kruse and Stephen Tuck

The Second World War remade the world and transformed much of American society. But what of its impact on the struggle for racial equality—and in turn, what does that tell us about the connection between war and rights, the nature of African American protest, and the origins of the civil rights movement?

Because of the thoroughly revolutionary character of the war, and the fact that civil rights protests came to such prominence barely a decade after the Allies' victory, some scholars have assumed that the war must have been the transformational moment in the long struggle for black equality—the moment when the structures of Jim Crow began to crack and crumble and a nascent civil rights movement started to take shape. On the face of it, there is plenty of evidence to support this interpretation. On the international stage, of course, Adolf Hitler gave racism a bad name, while American policymakers discovered that domestic racial discrimination could harm their diplomatic overtures to non-white nations, as black leaders connected the Allies' war against fascism to their own fight against colonialism. In the United States, the black press championed a "Double V" campaign, demanding a victory for democracy at home as well as abroad; the largest black protest organization of the era, the National Association for the Advancement of Colored People (NAACP), saw its membership grow eightfold; and a new civil rights organization, the Committee (later the Congress) of Racial Equality (CORE), employed nonviolent direct action protests that would become the hallmark of the civil rights movement. In national politics, labor leader A. Philip Randolph used his March on Washington Movement to secure a presidential order against racial discrimination in the defense industries and the creation of a Fair Employment Practices Committee (FEPC), which together represented the most meaningful federal intervention in the realm of black civil rights since Reconstruction. In the courts, the NAACP won key victories, notably the landmark 1944 Supreme Court ruling against the whites-only political primary, *Smith v. Allwright*, that heralded a rapid rise in black voting in the South. And at the grass roots, African Americans demanded equal rights in return for their contribution to the defense economy, their loyalty to the war effort, and their sacrifices as soldiers—and as mothers and wives of soldiers. When the conflict came to an end, black veterans returned home, many drilled in combat and all suffused with entitlement, eager to wage a new struggle for equal rights on the home front.

In the late 1960s—with the heyday of the civil rights movement barely past—historian Richard Dalfiume took note of these facts and first called attention to the war's importance as "the forgotten years of the Negro revolution." "The seeds" of the civil rights movement, he asserted, "were indeed sown in the World War II years." It quickly became commonplace to refer to the war years as the "watershed" of civil rights activism. "These were the years when American Negroes began for the first time to fight for their rights effectively and independently," argued Geoffrey Perrett in the early 1970s. "Here was when the modern civil rights movement began; here was where it scored its first important victories."[1] The assumption of the war's importance informed—and was reinforced by—the next generation of civil rights historians who focused on the struggle for equality at the grass roots. As scholars turned their attention from national leaders and organizations to local people, they unearthed countless stories of wartime militancy in which black Americans confronted white supremacy head on—from voting campaigns to brawls on buses and fights outside army bases. John Dittmer, for instance, began his path-breaking 1994 study of the civil rights movement in Mississippi by detailing the unprecedented postwar belligerence of veterans in a chapter entitled "We Return Fighting."[2]

In recent years, historians have pushed the chronology of strident, and sometimes successful, challenges to white supremacy back before the Second World War.[3] Writing long histories of black protest, dating back to emancipation and beyond,[4] such scholars have emphasized, among other things, black defiance and nationalism during the First World War, aggressive labor protests at the end of the nineteenth century, and the bold advances made during the Civil War and Reconstruction eras. Meanwhile, some scholars have focused in particular on the left-leaning protests of the New Deal era, when biracial labor organizing promised a reorientation of the South along both class and race lines. Elegantly summarizing this scholarship, Jacquelyn Dowd Hall has theorized "a 'long civil rights movement' that took root in the liberal and radical milieu of the late 1930s." But if such scholars no longer find the *origins* of more militant protest in the war years, most still assert that the movement, in Hall's words, "accelerated during World War II." The "good war," in their telling, was still clearly good for the fight for racial equality.[5]

Yet, if many scholars now see the Second World War as a point of origin, an important prelude, or a period of marked progress toward the civil rights movement, others have disputed the notion that the war mobilized

African Americans to protest. Perhaps most notably, Harvard Sitkoff—who originally played a prominent role in advancing the "militancy-watershed" thesis—reversed course and rejected the argument he had once championed. "It is comforting to think that the destructiveness of mass warfare can have redeeming virtues; it is good to have forebears to admire and emulate," he noted. "But if by a watershed in militancy we mean a crucial turning point in the aggressiveness of black actions, a far greater combativeness than previously exhibited, then the evidence to prove this argument conclusively has yet to appear; and major questions concerning this interpretation remain unanswered."[6]

Indeed, closer inspection shows that evidence of a widespread mobilization of the civil rights struggle during the war years is thinner than it may initially appear. First and foremost, much of the "watershed" argument rested to a great extent on vague estimates of black attitudes and aspirations, rather than concrete accomplishments. Dalfiume asserted, for instance, that the war "stimulated the race consciousness and the desire for change among Negroes."[7] But "race consciousness" is a slippery term and an unreliable metric. Anecdotal evidence suggests there were many African Americans who were roused to a new militancy during the war, but there were countless others—including plenty of influential black leaders—who went into the war already outraged by race discrimination.[8] Moreover, the "Double V" campaign did not herald a lasting change in black attitudes. The Pittsburgh *Courier*, the paper that popularized the motto in early 1942, largely abandoned the rallying cry by the end of that same year. In any case, the vast majority of black newspapers shelved their complaints about racial issues and rallied around the war effort. "The hour calls for a closing of ranks, for joining of hands," the influential Chicago *Defender* argued after Pearl Harbor, "not for a widening of the racial gap."[9] Indeed, Lee Finkle has argued that the "Double V" campaign was actually a conservative effort to co-opt widespread black militancy and channel it to patriotic ends.[10]

As for the actual accomplishments of African American activists during the war, they were thin on substance—a fact that many wartime activists pointed out in frustration. The Fair Employment Practices Committee, for example, certainly had symbolic significance, especially compared with government indifference to, or even support for, discriminatory policies in previous generations. But in practice it was a toothless agency.[11] The most successful civil rights organization of the decade, the NAACP, did grow dramatically in the early 1940s, but questions remain as to just what its new membership represented. Was the NAACP more militant, mobilizing new support, or simply well-organized, adroitly adopting a non-threatening protest position that garnered small annual dues—but little more—from middle-class African Americans? Meanwhile, CORE's nonviolent direct action techniques were, in fact, neither innovative nor inspirational. CORE's actions were closely modeled and named after the "sit-down strikes" of late 1930s labor unions. And few of the student "sit-in" activists of the 1960s realized that they were echoing CORE's wartime example.

Indeed, recent scholarship of strident pre-war and more moderate postwar protest might suggest that the war actually marked a *downturn* in black militancy.[12] Thus it was a "watershed" in a negative sense, because it was followed by the "bad" years of the Cold War, when anti-communist paranoia at home served to restrict not just the movement of civil rights activists, but their vision for reform itself. The nature of wartime protest—with its emphasis on securing equal employment opportunities and workplace conditions, its anti-colonial vision, and its embrace of black self-defense—made it more of a piece with the economically driven militant campaigns of the Great Depression than a stepping stone to the postwar civil rights movement, with its rather different emphasis on legal rights and middle-class respectability. In the late 1930s heyday of Popular Front politics, African Americans had engaged in boycotts that emphasized their identities as producers rather than just as consumers. Meanwhile, rapidly growing urban black communities had flexed their increasing muscle as consumers and asserted a form of nationalism through "Don't-Buy-Where-You-Can't-Work" campaigns across the country. All these economic campaigns of the late 1930s collapsed once the nation entered the war. So too did the March on Washington Movement. Randolph forced Roosevelt to act on the eve of war, but his calls for mass demonstrations *during* the war were heeded only by members of his union—and, even then, only by some of them. By the end of the war, the movement's headquarters in Harlem had become a bookshop.[13]

Thus this collection is a timely reconsideration of the intersection between two of the dominant events of twentieth-century American history, the upheaval wrought by the Second World War and the social revolution brought about by the African American struggle for equality. Recognizing the long-running nature of black protest, the essays in this volume do not simply seek to assess the role of wartime changes in fomenting the civil rights and Black Power movements of the 1950s and 1960s; they also address the ways in which the war years changed the direction of existing protest in the early twentieth century. Rather than seeking a single answer, the contributors consider the question of race and war from a wide variety of angles, from the rural South to the urban North, from grassroots activism to national politics, from courts of law to fields of battle, from domestic upheaval to global concerns, from popular culture to federal policy, from the question of civil rights to that of human rights, and from the perspective of those seeking racial equality and those defending racial hierarchy, not to mention those whose primary aim was just to win a war.

What is immediately clear is that the impact and legacy of war were decidedly ambiguous, at times empowering black activists, at times constraining them, at times emboldening those seeking to preserve racial hierarchies, and at times making surprisingly little difference at all. For the most part, though, the upheaval of wartime did indeed reshape the battleground and tactics of the black freedom struggle. That it did so in such a variety of ways was, in part, because there were so many diverse activists seeking to use the war for their own ends. Moreover, the war meant different things to different people; there was not even agreement over how long it lasted. For African Americans who understood their freedom in global terms, the war started in 1935 with Italy's invasion of Ethiopia. For those demanding full integration in the army, the war did not end until withdrawal from Korea in 1953.

As a starting point, several of the contributors frame the struggle for black equality by considering the impact of the war on the racial practices and policies of the United States government. Power in American politics was divided and distributed in uneven ways, scattered across disparate offices at the local, state, and federal levels and, within the upper level of government, fractured once more as federal responsibilities were distributed through the executive, legislative, and judicial branches. The complexity of American government was exacerbated by the demands and duration of the war. The conflict reshuffled the citizens of the United States, and it reordered their political system as well. Countless new agencies were created, while old ones took on new purposes and expanded reach. In the end, the multiplicity of governments during this era meant that the war did not have one impact on the black freedom struggle, but many.

In the first chapter, James Sparrow considers how the growing capacities of a federal government preoccupied by the urgent need to mobilize its citizens for total war provided an opportunity for those groups seeking full rights of citizenship. A heightened wartime sense of national citizenship and responsibility—encouraged by the sudden surge of influence of the Army and Navy, as well as the new proliferation of power of federal agencies—enabled activists, in return, to demand new rights from the federal government. This would, in due course, lead to the so-called "rights revolution" of the 1960s, a revolution that underpinned, and was expedited by, the civil rights movement. Yet during the war, the state's need to foment nationalism and preempt unrest prevented groups that were seeking consumer rights and civil rights from making much headway. After all, the state's concern was not with minority rights, but maintaining morale. To do so, federal agencies co-opted African American officials, giving them a semblance of influence but constraining their freedom to dissent. Ironically, it was precisely because African American morale—in other words, their willingness to work and fight without disruption—could not be taken for granted that African American officials had any power to shape policy at all.

If federal officials in the executive branch spoke the language of rights, a majority in the legislative branch most certainly did not. Despite the crucial part that Congress would play in the eventual passage of landmark legislation like the Civil Rights Act of 1964 and the Voting Rights Act of 1965, its role during the war has traditionally been overshadowed by a focus on the steps toward racial equality taken by the Supreme Court and (more tentatively) the White House. As Julian Zelizer demonstrates in chapter 2, the war years did not pave the way for those later developments but instead represented a period of conservative retrenchment in Congress. Southern Democrats tightened their grip on the reins of power during the war. Inside key committees, they used their seniority to crush many nascent efforts at reform; on the floors of the House and Senate, they worked with conservative Republican allies to stop the rest. In the end, Southern Democrats succeeded in stalling all efforts at meaningful civil rights legislation. As a result, congressional conservatives emerged from the war more confident in their abilities to prevent change and more determined to use them to defend white supremacy in the postwar era. Yet there was one unexpected legacy of conservative defiance: incoming young liberal Democrats learned the importance of controlling congressional machinery, lessons they would put to good use in decades to come.

Turning away from Washington, J. Mills Thornton in chapter 3 considers the impact of war on Southern communities. Because the lived experience of African Americans in the Alabama countryside, like politics itself, was intensely local, few of the changes experienced in national government actually affected their daily lives. Conditions at the local level witnessed little, if any, change prompted by the new national discussion on citizenship and rights. They instead took direction from more immediate sources, varying from place to place. While cities tended to implement a codified system of segregation by statute, rural areas instead relied on an informal and flexible system of white supremacy based upon custom and rooted in local economic dependencies. Thus even seemingly abrupt changes in racial policies in successive state administrations during the course of the war did not shake the stubborn continuity of race relations at the local level. Direct challenges to white supremacy would come slowly to Alabama, a result of much longer term economic and demographic trends rather than the short-term impact of war. And when challenges did come, they would be shaped by the peculiar circumstances of individual towns and counties, and would not simply be a response to a state or regional movement.

The chapters in this volume also offer new perspectives on the nature of black activism during the conflict. Patricia Sullivan in chapter 4 chronicles the ways in which NAACP officers tried to harness wartime militancy in the South—their work with veterans and voting campaigns, their lobbying and litigation, and their policies and personalities. Advancing in a number of directions at once, the NAACP achieved some notable successes, but experienced just as many frustrations. Director of Branches Ella Baker worked tirelessly, and to good effect, to ensure that the much-publicized growth in NAACP membership translated into meaningful protest. But at the end of the war she resigned, deeply frustrated by the unwillingness of national leaders to support her efforts fully. Others—such as the veteran activist W.E.B. Du Bois—would be forced out by the organization's postwar turn against any hint of communist entanglement. Ultimately it would be the "legal insurgency" that took hold in the South that would provide the greatest legacy of the NAACP's wartime work in the region—an insurgency dependent not just upon the organization's dedicated legal team, but also upon the new infrastructure of branches and the heightened aspirations and militancy generated by the war.

Thomas Sugrue, meanwhile, shifts the perspective in two ways in chapter 5—from the NAACP's national offices to the local work of grassroots activists, and from the South to the North. Focusing on the wartime struggle against segregated education in Hillburn, New York, he demonstrates the ways in which militant activists, in a newly revived branch of the NAACP, framed their local struggle for a national and international audience by marshalling the rhetoric of the wartime era and advancing it to their own ends. Rather than just advocating the "Double V" call for democracy at home and abroad, though, Northern activists deployed a much more powerful rhetorical weapon: the connection between fascism at home and abroad. Black Americans had learned the language of anti-fascism during the Ethiopian war, a language disseminated by the proliferation of black newspapers. But the Second World War gave black anti-fascism wider traction in American society, allowing Northern activists to launch an assault on segregation. Meanwhile, defense employment gave African Americans—particularly women—the economic security to fight for their rights. That they won the battle against state-sponsored segregation in Hillburn highlights the opportunities of the war. That white parents quickly removed their children from the newly desegregated school shows the limits of wartime gains, and portended the resistance to integration that would so stymie the Northern civil rights movement a generation later.

While many African Americans claimed new rights as citizens and fought for their rights in everyday life, some activists—including the leadership of the NAACP—sought to improve the black image in popular culture. As Stephen Tuck explains in chapter 6, these activists saw popular culture as a central battleground in the wartime fight for equality, believing that the black image shaped the place of black men and women in the white mind, and by extension, in American society. With the involvement of black soldiers in the war effort, the inclusion of black advisors in the federal information bureaus, and the opportunities for leading black cultural figures to display patriotism, the war provided black leaders with an unprecedented opportunity to launch a propaganda campaign. They campaigned with vigor. Yet, for the most part, they campaigned in vain. The indifference of state officials and media moguls and the opposition of Southern censors and politicians meant that—with a few tantalizing exceptions—African Americans did not break into mainstream popular culture as either good soldiers or everyday men and women. The only wartime breakthrough came as entertainers, which had decidedly ambiguous implications. The major legacy of the war with regard to popular culture, then, was not an improved place for African Americans, but the lessons that black leaders learned about the importance of manipulating the black image—lessons that would be remembered both in the civil rights and Black Power movements.

If black activists mobilized during the war, so too did white segregationists. As Jason Ward demonstrates in chapter 7, Southern conservatives developed their own "Double V" campaign—in their case, victory for democracy at home meant a staunch defense of Jim Crow in the name of states' rights and individual freedom. In part, Southern white resistance was a response to assertive behavior by black troops and black domestics on Southern streets and in Southern homes. In part, it grew out of concern about the growing influence and liberal outlook of the New Deal government as the war progressed. But this was not simply a rearguard action by rustic racists whose time had come. Rather, a coalition of conservatives at the grass roots and in state and national politics won significant victories—and, in some cases, maintained white supremacy with renewed violence. The ways in which segregationists used the war for their ends shaped wartime black activism as much as it reacted to it. The power of white segregationists at the end of the war meant that a breakthrough civil rights movement seemed far from inevitable. It provided a reminder, if one were needed, that any future black activism or federal interference could expect massive resistance.

Turning the focus from white Southern conservatives to Southern moderates, Jane Dailey shows in chapter 8 that the war rent asunder the New Deal alliance between white and black reformers. Central to the split was the wartime prominence of a perennial white panic—interracial sex. Reformers, black and white, had ducked the "social equality" issue during the New Deal, but the advent of war brought the issue front and center. The Nazis' ugly attempts to create racial purity undermined the case against intermarriage at home, while winning the right to fight made a strong case for African Americans to win the full rights of citizenship—including freedom to marry across the color line. Meanwhile, wartime contact between black men and white women at United Service Organization canteens and outside Southern army bases ratcheted up sexual tensions. As black leaders and white segregationists found themselves broaching the once taboo topic of "social equality" from opposite directions, white reformers found their position untenable. The war meant that their vision for gradual reform in the South would not be realized. Confrontation was in store.

Placing the domestic struggle for civil rights in a global framework, meanwhile, Penny Von Eschen in chapter 9 challenges conventional views that the war was a catalyst for the expansion of civil rights at home and anti-colonial movements abroad. Despite the horrors of the Holocaust and the faltering of Europe's empires under the pressures of war, colonialism was reinstated after the war, just as returning veterans were forced back to their subordinate place in Southern society. Ideas of race were made and remade during the war, but the practice of racism continued. The postwar extension of American power depended on the social production of new forms of racial thinking as well as the unthinking "commonsense" employment of previously held assumptions. By considering race, civil rights, and colonialism from a global perspective, Von Eschen suggests that the war be de-centered from the story of the twentieth-century struggle for racial freedom and instead situated within the longer context of colonial conquest and anti-colonial struggle.

The quest for civil rights must be placed in the context of human rights, too, much as activists did immediately after the war and at the height of the civil rights movement. Elizabeth Borgwardt in chapter 10 takes a closer look at the 1945 San Francisco conference to negotiate the charter for the United Nations. In doing so, she rejects one of the founding narratives inaugurating the postwar efflorescence of nongovernmental organizations (NGOs), namely, that American grassroots civic groups "spoke truth to power" in their official consulting role to the U.S. State Department by insisting on strengthening the human rights–related provisions in the charter. By and large, white American activists tended to fall in line behind State Department positions that elided, downplayed, or simply contradicted the obvious race-related implications of such additional language, whether for the domestic Jim Crow regime, for the so-called "dependent areas" to be administered as trusteeships under the UN Charter, or for the politics of decolonization generally. From the perspective of African American activists, this "mainstream" NGO advocacy illuminated the disappointingly thin relationship of international human rights rhetoric to a more robust and racialized vision of domestic civil rights.

Finally, Kimberley Phillips in chapter 11 takes the story of racial integration in the armed services through to the Korean War. It was only on the battlefields of Korea that African Americans finally won the right to fight. NAACP leaders were delighted, and revising the rhetoric of the Second World War, they believed that rights of combat would lead to wider citizenship rights. But for many black Americans, such rhetoric was outdated—they were concerned by the obligation to fight in what they considered to be an imperialist venture. Phillips shows that African American attitudes to global racial politics, and their commitment to nonviolent protest strategies at home, were profoundly impacted by this changing context of military service.

Taken together, these essays confirm that the turmoil and rhetoric and bloodshed of war did indeed provide a far-reaching challenge to Southern, national, and global systems of race. But that challenge did not push racial systems in a single direction, and certainly not one moving inexorably toward greater equality. Ideas of race were reformulated and the practices of racism were remade in many different, often contradictory, ways. Activists on both sides—those demanding equality and those defending inequality—could draw strength from some aspects of war, but found themselves vulnerable on other measures. At the end of the war, anti-racist activists faced a new battleground in the long-running struggle for a meaningful freedom, but it was a battle-ground nonetheless.

That the war had both a far-reaching and an ambiguous impact should perhaps come as no surprise. The struggle for (and against) racial equality was intimately interconnected with any number of different aspects of society and politics, in the United States and beyond—as the wartime experience of black protest makes abundantly clear. A simple, linear story of progress might suit American public memory, but it does a disservice to the myriad twists and turns of African American protest, and to the sacrifices of so many who suffered as well as succeeded. This complexity is compounded by the fact that war itself, as the Prussian military analyst Carl von Clausewitz famously noted, presents a "peculiar difficulty" of "great uncertainty"—an uncertainty that is even more pronounced in a world war fought across so many fronts. In war, Clausewitz argued, "all action must, to a certain extent, be planned in a mere twilight, which . . . not unfrequently—like the effect of a fog or moonshine—gives to things exaggerated dimensions and an unnatural appearance." If historians search for the roots of the civil rights movement in the wartime struggle, they will doubtlessly find something in the discordant record resembling the evidence they seek. But if they stop to appreciate the Second World War as it was experienced at the time—in multiple ways, by multiple Americans—they can avoid giving those years exaggerated dimensions and an unnatural appearance.

Notes

1. Richard Dalfiume, "The 'Forgotten Years' of the Negro Revolution," *Journal of American History*, Vol. 55, No. 1 (June 1968): 106; Geoffrey Perrett, *Days of Sadness, Years of Triumph: The American People 1939–1945* (Madison, 1973): 323; James A. Nuechterlein, "The Politics of Civil Rights: The FEPC, 1941–46," *Prologue: The Journal of the National Archives*, Vol. 10 (1978): 171. For a sense of the historical consensus of that era locating the origins of the civil rights movement in the Second World War, see Richard Polenberg, *War and Society: The United States, 1941–1945* (Philadelphia, 1972); John Morton Blum, *V Was for Victory: Politics and American Culture During World War II* (New York, 1976); Neil A. Wynn, *The Afro-American and the Second World War* (New York, 1976); A. Russell Buchanan, *Black Americans in World War II* (Santa Barbara, 1976).

2. John Dittmer, *Local People: The Struggle for Civil Rights in Mississippi* (Urbana, 1994), 1–18.

3. In fact, there has been a long-standing tradition in black historical writing to survey the history of African Americans, to quote the title of John Hope Franklin's classic text, *From Slavery to Freedom*. In this tradition, though, it was the civil rights movement that represented, to quote Franklin again, the moment when African Americans first began "resorting to direct and more drastic action to secure [their] rights." John Hope Franklin, *From Slavery to Freedom: A History of African Americans* (New York, 1994), 492. In Franklin's interpretation, the war was not a key watershed—not least because the first edition of his

book was published in 1947, a decade before the civil rights movement.

4. What distinguishes the newer scholarship of the long history of black protest has been the recognition of such "direct and drastic action" well before the Second World War. See, for example, Steven A. Reich, "Soldiers of Democracy: Black Texans and the Fight for Citizenship, 1917–1921," *Journal of American History*, Vol. 82, No. 4 (March 1996): 1478–1504; Robin Kelley and Earl Lewis, *To Make Our World Anew: A History of African Americans* (New York, 2000); Adam Fairclough, *Better Day Coming: Blacks and Equality, 1890–2000* (New York, 2001); Mark R. Schneider, *We Return Fighting: The Civil Rights Movement in the Jazz Age* (Boston, 2002); Robert J. Norrell, *The House I Live In: Race in the American Century* (New York, 2005); Stephen Tuck, *We Ain't What We Ought to Be: The Black Freedom Struggle from Emancipation to Obama*, (Cambridge, Mass., 2010).

5. Jacquelyn Dowd Hall, "The Long Civil Rights Movement and the Political Uses of the Past," *Journal of American History*, Vol. 91, No. 4 (March 2005): 1235; Jane Dailey, Glenda Elizabeth Gilmore, and Bryant Simon, eds., *Jumpin' Jim Crow: From Civil War to Civil Rights* (Princeton, 2000); Robert Korstad, *Civil Rights Unionism: Tobacco Workers and the Struggle for Democracy in the Mid-Twentieth-Century South* (Chapel Hill, 2003); Glenda Elizabeth Gilmore, *Defying Dixie: The Radical Roots of Civil Rights, 1919–1950* (New York, 2008).

6. For the evolution of Sitkoff's thoughts, see Harvard Sitkoff, "Racial Militancy and Interracial Violence in the Second World War," *Journal of American History*, Vol. 58, No. 3 (December 1971): 661–681; Harvard Sitkoff, "American Blacks in World War II: Rethinking the Militancy-Watershed Hypothesis," in James Titus, ed., *The Home Front and War in the Twentieth Century* (Washington, D.C., 1984): 147–155; and Harvard Sitkoff, "African American Militancy in the World War II South," in Neil R. McMillen, *Remaking Dixie: The Impact of World War II on the American South* (Jackson, Miss., 1997): 70–92 [quotation from 71]. Some other prominent scholars who advanced the idea of the civil rights movement's origins in the Second World War have also had second thoughts. See, for instance, Richard Polenberg, "The Good War'?: A Reappraisal of How World War II Affected American Society," *The Virginia Magazine of History and Biography*, Vol. 100, No. 3 (July 1992): 295–322; Neil A. Wynn, "The 'Good War': The Second World War and Postwar American Society," *Journal of Contemporary History*, Vol. 31, No. 3 (July 1996): 463–482.

7. Dalfiume, "The 'Forgotten Years' of the Negro Revolution," 104.

8. Tuck, *We Ain't What We Ought to Be*, 210.

9. Sitkoff, "American Blacks in World War II," 151; *Chicago Defender* cited in Sitkoff, "African American Militancy," 72.

10. Lee Finkle, "Conservative Aims of Militant Rhetoric: Black Protest During World War II," *Journal of American History*, Vol. 60, No. 3 (December 1973): 692–713.

11. Merl Reed, *Seedtime for the Modern Civil Rights Movement: The President's Committee on Fair Employment Practice, 1941–1946* (Baton Rouge, 1991).

12. For excellent accounts of pre-war militancy see, for example, Harvard Sitkoff, *A New Deal for Blacks: The Emergence of Civil Rights as a National Issue* (New York: Oxford University Press, 1978); Aldon D. Morris, *The Origins of the Civil Rights Movement: Black Communities Organizing for Change* (New York: Free Press, 1984); Robin D.G. Kelley, *Hammer and Hoe: Alabama Communists in the Great Depression* (Chapel Hill: UNC Press, 1990); John Egerton, *Speak Now Against the Day: The Generation Before the Civil Rights Movement in the South* (New York: Knopf, 1994); Patricia Sullivan, *Days of Hope: Race*

and Democracy in the New Deal Era (Chapel Hill: UNC Press, 1996); Mark I. Solomon, *The Cry Was Unity: Communists and African Americans, 1917–36* (Jackson: University of Mississippi Press, 1998).

13. August Meier and Elliott Rudwick, *Along the Color Line: Explorations in the Black Experience* (Champaign, 1976): 314–316; Sitkoff, "American Blacks in World War II," 153.

1

Freedom to Want

THE FEDERAL GOVERNMENT AND POLITICIZED
CONSUMPTION IN WORLD WAR II

James T. Sparrow

A riddle characterized state-building and national citizenship during the 1940s. These were years of retrenchment, when the social citizenship of the New Deal welfare state withered under conservative fire, while the multilateral promises of Rooseveltian diplomacy fatefully gave way to the realpolitik of unilateral containment. Yet this was also a time when a profusion of rights movements pressed for guarantees of expanded citizenship at home and throughout the world. Workers' rights, consumers' rights, civil rights, human rights—these were banners held aloft by vibrant social movements whose memberships grew and often overlapped throughout the period. Most of these movements generally failed to accomplish their loftiest objectives. Instead, they straggled into the 1950s with a left vanguard decimated by anti-communism and supplanted by cold war liberalism. For this reason, the early rights movements of the 1940s were long overlooked or discounted. More recently they have been recovered, with the greatest rediscoveries occurring for civil rights outside the South.[1] Yet the underlying reasons for the efflorescence of these movements—and, by the end of the decade, their abeyance—remain largely unexplored.

After decades of agitation by rights groups, an effusion of rights talk finally gained traction in World War II due to the growing needs and capacities of a federal government preoccupied by the economic, military, and ideological mobilization of the citizenry for total war. Americans encountered the national government in everyday life during the war, and consequently began to think of their contributions—the obligations that balanced and thus justified their mounting sense of entitlement—as having national and even international ramifications. They did so in various roles: as everyday GIs elevated to the hero status of the "combat soldier"; as "soldiers of production" whose factory work provided the materiel so vital to winning a war of machines; as patriotic consumers who "backed the attack" by conserving and rationing scarce goods, while diverting inflationary dollars into taxes and bonds to fund the war; and as voters who supported food aid and societal reconstruction for war-torn foreigners—even if they recently had been enemies.

As they encountered federal authority at the grass roots, Americans began to translate an incipient sense of national citizenship into claims aimed at the federal government. New Dealers had begun to cultivate this process among their core constituencies in the 1930s, but by the end of the decade their agenda was embattled domestically, while developments in foreign affairs further sapped any residual momentum for reform. Only the overwhelming mobilization of society and the popular mentality—occasioned by American entry into the Second World War, and sustained by the continuing prospect of total war thereafter—made it possible to cement the legitimacy of national citizenship. This was the critical development that encouraged diverse groups to press for expanded rights guaranteed by the federal government, while simultaneously making their claims recognizable (if not always acceptable) to other Americans. Over the course of a generation, it would foster the "rights revolution," a political transformation that would underpin the African American civil rights movement.

Yet during the war and its immediate aftermath, rights talk was insufficient in itself to preserve, much less advance, rights in practice. Nationalism overrode the rights of the individual in countless ways. The most basic civil liberties were routinely denied not only to African Americans in the South, but also to Mexican agricultural workers in the Southwest, Filipino guest workers on the West Coast, and with the passage of the Smith Act in 1940, to political radicals in all regions. The mass imprisonment of nearly the entire population of citizens and residents of Japanese descent served as unforgettable proof that the Constitution could be revoked summarily, regardless of individual merit, simply on the grounds of racial suspicion. Internment was a reminder, as well, that the defense of democratic ideals prompted by Nazi barbarities did not cancel out the greater priority that most Americans accorded to the goal of prosecuting a race war in the Pacific. Thus, even though wartime propaganda placed the full authority of the federal government behind the language of rights— heralding a major opportunity for African Americans in pursuit of equality— the assurances offered by war propaganda fell quickly when they clashed with, or merely inconvenienced, reasons of state.

This chapter examines popular encounters with the war government in order to explore the interplay between rights and reasons of state that provided the opening within which civil rights activism finally found room to maneuver in the 1940s. It does so first by considering the broad demographic and structural changes that gave rights traction during the war. The limitations of that traction are the concern of the remainder of the chapter, which considers how the "morale management" practiced by the Treasury Department and the Office of Price Administration in their outreach to black consumers demonstrated both the fragile and consequential aspects of rights talk in these years.

One reason that full citizenship seemed so imminent during World War II was the substantial, if temporary, loosening of the social structure at all levels. Mass conscription and economic mobilization for total war fostered dramatic personal mobility with great suddenness. Two of the "Four Mobilities"— geographic and social—that tend to corrode local solidarities accelerated during World War II.[2] As the war propelled millions to escape the confines of their local circumstances and pursue broader horizons, it also placed them in new contact with the federal government, whose ideological guarantees suddenly had concrete ramifications for their everyday lives.

Geographic mobility was the most immediate and vividly experienced form of personal freedom fostered by the war. Over 25 million Americans, or roughly a fifth of the nation, moved across county lines between 1940 and 1947, with half of them doing so in order to relocate to other states. Just under 16 million men and a quarter of a million women traveled to the far corners of the nation and the globe for military service. Millions more civilians followed jobs or their drafted spouses into war centers, where they encountered the burgeoning opportunity, frenetic confusion, and unsupervised freedom that was fostered by U.S. history's greatest economic boom.[3]

Freedom of movement had often been taken for granted, especially by white male migrants, but thanks to the recent appointment of New Dealers to the Supreme Court, freedom of movement across state lines, regardless of economic status, was reaffirmed as a constitutional right with the ruling in *Edwards v. California* (1941).[4] Even so, African Americans, who suffered the petty tyranny of local authority more acutely than most other groups of Americans due to their concentration in the Jim Crow South, often had to claim "freedom of movement" before chasing the "Four Freedoms" promised by FDR. Despite the concerted efforts of Southern planters and other large employers to keep black workers on the farm with debt peonage laws and selective service classifications, among other measures, millions of African Americans were able to claim their freedom of movement because of the unprecedented demand for labor in the war economy.[5] Over 1 million of the roughly 10 million African Americans living in the South in 1940 moved North or West during the war, the latest and one of the greatest chapters of migration in a long history of mass movement for freedom dating back to emancipation. Additionally, more than 1.1 million black men from around the country entered military service, leaving their hometowns for boot camp, followed by troop assignment stationed, more often than not, overseas. Awaiting these black migrants were under-employment, job discrimination, and relegation to segregated "Negro" troop units in the segregated armed forces. Even so, departure from the South represented relative advancement for the vast majority of migrants.

Social mobility, like its geographic counterpart, flowed directly from the unprecedented demand for labor created by the war mobilization. After a decade of depression in which the incomes of full-time employees had remained largely stagnant while as much as a quarter of the labor force fell unemployed, the personal opportunities of ordinary Americans suddenly improved dramatically, starting in the middle of 1940. The GDP rose from $101 billion that year to $223 billion in 1945, an increase of almost 73 percent after inflation. With this rise in the general prosperity of the country came a staggering 30 percent increase in real disposable personal income, an improvement that buoyed the entire labor force. Underwriting the vast improvement of economic fortunes was the federal government, whose annual expenditures for national defense reached nearly $83 billion by 1945, accounting for 37 percent of the GDP and two-thirds of all industrial production.[6]

Rising earnings made life easier for workers. Two other developments—full employment and declining inequality—transformed this prosperity into something more. With industry groaning at full capacity by 1943–1944, unemployment rates fell to 1.2 percent, or 670,000 in a labor force that had grown by 17.8 percent since 1940 to 66 million.[7] An explosion of largely unionized industrial employment represented a considerable expansion of better-paying jobs providing new opportunities for personal advancement, which workers often pursued by leaving jobs, quitting at the astronomical rate of over 5 percent a month by the war's end. As many as 15 million workers shifted jobs for higher pay or better working conditions during the war, reflecting a confident optimism.[8]

Not only were more jobs available to those who sought them, but income disparities were shrinking along some of the most salient lines of social inequality: class, occupation, and race. Families in the bottom quintile of the national income distribution saw their average annual incomes rise from $450 in 1941 to $982 by 1946, twice the proportional improvement of those in the top quintile.[9] Wartime income redistribution did not amount to a social revolution, but a 3 percent shift in the income structure of a nation as vast and prosperous as the United States in the 1940s still represented a palpable opening of opportunity among those citizens whose economic horizons had been severely constricted in the previous decade. Furthermore, the shift in incomes was accompanied by a permanent and significant flattening in the distribution of *wealth*—a far more intractable source of economic inequality. Between 1939 and 1945, the richest one percent of Americans dropped their share of wealth by 8.9 percentage points, from 35.9 to 27 percent of all assets. (Their share continued to drop after the war, falling as low as 17.3 percent by 1976.) As the national structures of income and wealth shifted, ordinary workers could sense that their lot was improving. The hard numbers that ruled the family budget told them so with each growing paycheck.[10]

Just as important as these shifts in the larger tiers of class were the narrowing gaps between groups of workers who worked (and lived) in close proximity, where even minor variations in income seemed glaring. The difference in median wage rates between skilled and unskilled manufacturing workers narrowed during the war, decreasing the pay premium for skilled labor from

65 percent above unskilled wage rates in 1937–1940, to a 55 percent premium in 1945–1947.[11] The flattening of the wage structure also occurred among workers at the same skill level, cutting by 30 percent the wage disparities that prevailed among ordinary laborers in different industries during this period.[12]

As demand for labor skyrocketed and semiskilled positions proliferated, even the most marginalized workers improved their relative positions within the economy. Black and other minority workers did not enjoy full employment until almost a year into the war, when labor scarcity began to threaten war production. But even with this late start, their economic fortunes improved dramatically during the war. Nearly 1 million African Americans entered the wartime workforce, bringing the total number of black workers to 5.3 million by the spring of 1944, and raising the average annual earnings of black urban workers from $400 to over $1,000. The average income of African Americans rose faster in the period 1940–1950 than in any other decade during the twentieth century. Black men also made relative advances. Over the course of the war, their earnings went from a third to a half of what white men earned. These figures reflected a doubling of the jobs available for black skilled craftsmen, foremen, and semi-skilled operatives between 1940 and 1944, a rise in black union membership from 200,000 to over a million between 1940 and 1945, and to a lesser extent the influence of the Fair Employment Practices Committee, which President Franklin D. Roosevelt had created in response to black demands. The racial differential for women also improved, if less dramatically, with white women earning 2.1 times as much as black women in 1946, down from a multiple of 2.5 in 1939.[13]

The opening of opportunity only made persistent discrimination all the more galling. White workers clung fiercely to their race-based privileges, fighting black advancement into skilled jobs at every step by resorting to intimidation, union control over the hiring hall, and even collusion with management. When these channels failed, hate strikes erupted in war plants around the country, often sparked by efforts to upgrade just a few black workers to jobs formerly reserved for whites.[14]

As Americans left the comforts of home and struck out across the nation and the world, they encountered a federal government that had grown far more centralized—and yet also more locally present—than ever before. Wartime mobilization transformed the political economy, state capacity, and citizenship practices of the New Deal, shifting the foundations of the state from welfare to warfare. The war government quickly dwarfed New Deal agencies that had seemed gargantuan only a few years earlier, absorbing a federal budget that was more than ten times greater than it had been during the peak of New Deal spending in 1939.[15] War agencies were also far less beholden to state and local political interests than had been the case in the 1930s, thanks to the Second

War Powers Act of 1942, one of the greatest grants of executive discretion in U.S. history.

As the war government grew to unprecedented size, it touched the lives of more citizens than ever before: over 85 million war bond holders (in a total population of 140 million by 1945); 42 million new income taxpayers; nearly all of the nation's 17 million industrial workers employed by war industry, and further millions in supporting white-collar jobs; over 16 million servicemen and women. Rationing was so widespread that registration for ration books was used as a proxy for census information in 1943. Only the Civil War touched Americans' daily lives more thoroughly than World War II did.

The parts of the war mobilization most vital to the government—military service, industrial work, fiscal expansion, inflationary controls—were also those that relied most fundamentally on mass participation. The war agencies in charge of each of these policy areas inserted federal authority into the power relationships that mattered most to ordinary Americans. Prerogatives of class, gender, and race were negotiated in the social spaces infiltrated by the war government: on shop floors, at store counters, in households with draft-age boys, and in family budgets making room for income taxes and war bonds. Without legitimacy, the warfare state would have collapsed for lack of compliance. Administrators realized this and so commissioned hundreds of classified studies of "morale" to monitor acceptance of war measures and identify potential problem areas for compliance.

African Americans were especially vulnerable to "low morale" due to their continued exclusion from good war jobs and relegation to segregated military units. War administrators did not help things when they sought to paint a bright face on things. The Office of War Information's pamphlet, "Negroes and the War" struck Lester Granger, Executive Secretary of the National Urban League, as "kicking a man who is down, and congratulating him because he is not yet dead."[16] The psychologist Kenneth Clark observed in mid-1943 that the fundamental challenge was to find some way to overcome the bitter memories of World War I, and its betrayal of W.E.B. DuBois's promise that African Americans' willingness to "close the ranks" behind the war effort would be rewarded. This time around, it would not be possible to spur black identification with a government-run war effort through appeals to "loyalty and patriotism, as if these were entities which could be subjectively divorced from their conditions of life."[17] A contemporaneous survey of federal agencies concerned with "Negro morale" presented a similar assessment, claiming that the nation's very survival hinged on the "effectiveness with which it rights the wrongs which prevail on the home front"—and in the long run, on addressing the global problem of the "minorities of the world."[18] If morale demanded the adjustment of personal and racial grievances to the requirements of national interest, it also, conversely, pointed the way from frustration with meliorism to ever-broader realms of redress.

Race relations were too threatening to economic, military, and ideological mobilization to leave to episodic damage control. They required a systematic approach.[19] Consequently, nearly every major war agency retained a race relations advisor drawn from the ranks of the interwar civil rights movement. Like the appointees of the "black cabinet" who had preceded them in the New Deal, these men and women entered government in a display of the influence that black voters and organizations were gaining within the Democratic Party outside the South. But they also found themselves placed in the position of the claims adjustor, highlighting some complaints for redress while neglecting others, according to calculations of what was politically feasible. For this reason race managers often found their ambitions for leverage thwarted and their careers in jeopardy. The race relations advisor operated on the ground where rights defined by social justice and entitlements allowed by bureaucratic logic met.

The efforts that the Treasury made to reach out to the black community revealed the problems that were posed by asking African Americans to take on the obligations of citizenship when they could not enjoy many of its rights. In 1941 the Treasury asked William Pickens to leave his post as field director for the NAACP to join the Defense Savings Staff, where he became the head of the Interracial Section in early 1942, the first black official appointed to the department since the Wilson administration. Pickens, the son of former slaves, had risen to prominence late in the progressive era as an orator, educator and author of books on emancipation, segregation, and the New Negro. He had taken part in the Niagara Movement, helped establish the officers' Training Camp for Negroes during World War I, then worked on the field staff of the NAACP for most of the interwar period. By the late 1930s he had served as a forum leader for the Interior Department while working for the NAACP. In 1940 Pickens caught the attention of James Houghteling, the director of the National Organizations Division of the Treasury. Pickens "speaks the language, thinks the thoughts, lives the lives of his own people," Houghteling believed, concluding that "Negroes believe in him." His long experience with many black civic organizations, including the AME Church and the YWCA, served the War Savings Program's efforts to inculcate an ideology of voluntarism by relying almost exclusively on private associations to conduct bond promotions, drives, and other sales of the "E" bond.[20]

Before the war Pickens had not hesitated to highlight the unfair treatment of black citizens by emphasizing how little they got for their tax dollars. Responding to a ban on black employment at the Hoover Dam construction project in the 1930s, Pickens had traveled to Las Vegas and made a well-publicized speech to a largely black audience, reminding them that "this is taxpayer money that you're spending." Not long afterward, a token group of forty-four black laborers were hired at the dam. Pickens bluntly claimed in one essay that the supposed delicacies of the "race problem" simply served as "the sheep's clothing of economic exploitation":

> The colored American has never enjoyed full democracy in the public schools, although he pays his full share of the taxes. He does not get his share of the tax receipts, because of the peculiar arrangements of our economic system.[21]

By the end of the decade Pickens had grown so frustrated with New Deal tokenism and Roosevelt's appeasement of Southern Democrats that he personally set about organizing the Colored Citizens Committee for Wendell Willkie, the Republican candidate for president in 1940. This move caused him considerable difficulty within the NAACP.[22]

Around the same time, Pickens vented his anger at the South in an editorial on his recent visit to Texas. It opened by asking the reader, "How would you feel if you went to plead for civilization in a place that was hardly half civilized, and where you were barely tolerated?" Black Southerners had to "pay taxes without getting receipts" necessary to establish voting eligibility, even as the same taxes funded segregated schools, buses, and other amenities. The poor man "pays everything," he observed. Pickens concluded with a foreboding thought: "Whoever would destroy our democracy, would find it most vulnerable in this part of our geography."[23]

Pickens changed his tune once he became head of the Interracial Section. In the foreword to the Interracial Section's annual report for 1943, Pickens wrote of the pride he felt "in having been privileged to serve as the agents or media through which the Government and its Negro citizens and some of their friends, have got together on this job." Rather than bemoan the systemic exclusion from equal accommodation that black taxpayers still experienced, he flipped the meaning of citizens' obligations and observed, "In our democracy any citizen of any race or color has the privilege of buying his bonds through all the issuing agencies."[24] If rights were not yet equal, obligations were becoming so.

An air of over-the-top patriotism suffused the promotional work that Pickens directed, as if he sought to reassure the Office of War Information (OWI) analysts who warned of dangerously low black morale, or the FBI field agents who saw radical conspiracies around every corner. (Indeed, such thoughts may have occurred to him; the charges of "un-Americanism" that had tarnished his confirmation never quite dissipated.) In April 1942 he commended the editor of the Richmond *Times-Dispatch* for a recent "high-minded" editorial. "We are going to hang together in this country," he wrote—"over racial lines, religious lines, economic lines, political-party lines, and all other lines. When we face a foreign foe, we are all AMERICANS."[25] The Interracial Section's report for 1944 opened with an approving quotation from Ted Gamble, the white national director of bond sales, who invoked the black media's Double V campaign for democracy at home as well as abroad:

"When the record of this war effort shall have been written, it will show that Negroes not only fought the enemy in the front lines of the battle overseas, but met him on the homefront on the assembly lines and the bond-purchasing lines."[26]

Every trace of Pickens's impatience with the administration had evaporated. When his former NAACP colleague Pauli Murray wrote him in the summer of 1944, proposing that the Treasury offer a "peace gift" for the postwar reconstruction of liberated countries that pacifists such as herself might purchase, Pickens responded with condescension bordering on contempt. He observed that everyone within the United States would have to pay for the war with their taxes, whether they believed in war or not. To that he added an argument for self-interest, observing that the "depositing of money by the colored people in the safest bank in the world is to insure them against the effects of the great war, whether they like the war or not." Provoked, Murray replied with a long exegesis on the futility of using violence to overcome violence. The "bombs dropping on innocent people in Germany today" were a "fine way to get rid of human hatred." She went on: "Would you want to see the entire population of the South, white and black, wiped out to get rid of Jim Crow? Would you, Mr. Pickens?" He left no record of an answer to her question in his files.[27]

Many black Americans were willing to indulge Pickens's patriotic suspension of disbelief. Pickens drew on the vast web of black civic connections he had spun as field secretary for the NAACP, and channeled their aspirations for national recognition of black contributions to the war effort. The 1944 annual report was a virtual catalog of boosterism. It celebrated the outstanding initiative taken by individual black citizens to promote the sale of bonds, like the "elderly colored widow, with no sons or daughters to fight or join the armed services," who sold her home for $15,000 and converted the proceeds into war bonds. A listing of the most productive promotions also included high-profile events that were the bread and butter of the War Savings program, such as the National Baptist Convention, which raised $10 million in August. Even the Board of Directors of the NAACP, with whom Pickens still had strained relations, played along by investing $40,000 of its trust funds in bonds, thereby urging "all Negro organizations and individuals to invest to the limit in democracy while they work to make that democracy real for all, irrespective of race, creed, color or national origin."[28]

Although mass participation in the fiscal state provides a window onto the dilemmas of "Negro morale" and racial brokerage, it is ultimately a limited one, in part because the Treasury liked to think of itself as operating on a civic plane that transcended race. Tellingly, it refused to keep any official records of bond holders' racial background. Pickens captured the spirit of this refusal when he corrected the *Survey Graphic* in 1941 for mistakenly identifying him as the head of a "Negro Division" in the Treasury. He chided that the Treasury had never had such a division—and, he concluded, "I sincerely hope that it never will."[29]

If bonds and taxes could be couched only in the language of patriotism and racial boosterism, the larger realm of inflation control permitted a much less elevated tone, and a much more conflicted politicization of mass encounters with the state. As a direct consequence of its efforts to encourage popular compliance with rationing and price control, the Office of Price Administration (OPA) inadvertently cultivated an expectation of fair treatment guaranteed by the federal government, even though it was essentially in the business of saying "no" to consumer entitlement. Here, too, the rhetoric of rights was both inflated and contained by overriding reasons of state.

Roosevelt spoke frequently of the "American standard of living"—nowhere more eloquently than in his "economic bill of rights" speech of January 11, 1944, which defined the liberal vision of full national citizenship for the postwar period. The OPA followed his lead, adopted a similar approach, portraying compliance with rationing and price control as both patriotic common sense and self-interest. Paying only ceiling prices and using rationing coupons without indulging the black market were cast as the only sure-fire ways in which the standard of living could be protected from inflation. Other propaganda portrayed illicit consumption as jeopardizing the well-being of soldiers on the fighting front. A typical war-minded advertisement presented civilian consumers with the image of a determined GI striding across the battlefield with a wounded comrade slung over his shoulder. "Will he" make it back home to enjoy "home-made apple pie, or the nine o'clock show at the Colonial with his girl friend?" it asked. Yes, it answered, "if you do these things"—"buy only what you need," "pay no more than ceiling prices," among other anti-inflationary measures. "You'll be fixing it," the ad closed, "so that the boy up there will come back to a country where he and you can work and live happily."[30]

Consumers of all races appropriated these themes, and as with their responses to other kinds of propaganda, they reworked them to suit their outlook on the war and its impact on their lives. In polls, a solid majority indicated that price control and rationing were legitimate and even desirable, and that participating in the black market was unpatriotic. Yet actions betrayed a more complicated reality lurking beneath the surface. By the end of the war, well over a fifth of all business transactions involved black market activities.[31]

African American views of the OPA were particularly ambivalent, fueled by long-simmering anger about unfair treatment within a Jim Crow marketplace. Accordingly, the OPA appointed Frances Williams as the agency's race relations advisor, a position she held until the OPA's demise. In that position Williams, a member of the NAACP's Citizens' Committee, drew on the connections and civic organizations within the interwar civil rights movement she had cultivated as secretary of interracial education for the YWCA between 1935 and 1940.[32] Mary McLeod Bethune, president and founder of the National

Council of Negro Women, checked in on Williams in late 1945, encouraging her to "continue to give representation to our Cause there."[33] Claude Barnette, founder and president of the Associated Negro Press, wrote in around the same time to prod her to share information on black participation in the OPA, and to affirm that the "agency has done a good job and I hope some time you can brag about it unrestrainedly."[34]

The OPA's national staff took pains to lessen the injuries of race as part of a larger effort to democratize the wartime political economy—a commitment that reflected the influence of labor economists, union leaders, consumer advocates, and allied liberals. Although the OPA was well-known—indeed, almost notorious—for its liberal approach to race relations, this stance was also a function of its pragmatic need to secure compliance with an anti-inflation program essential to maximum production. As Williams herself later put it when summarizing the contributions of the OPA to race relations, her position "was designed to avoid criticism of the OPA's relations to Negro citizens, to insure reasonable and fair participation of Negroes in the OPA program, and to take all possible steps to enlist their support and cooperation." Still, the value of the troubleshooting that Williams performed should not be underestimated. According to her boss, OPA head Chester Bowles, she deserved much of the credit for the OPA's relatively strong record of employing black employees, who constituted 14 percent of its national staff, versus a mere one percent of all other government employees during the war.[35]

Letters streamed into Williams's office, as they did into that of Pickens, asking her to adjust particular inequities over which she might exercise leverage. When the NAACP sent a telegram to President Roosevelt asking for "immediate action" to prevent the eviction of a black tenant living in Chester, Pennsylvania, by a landlord who wanted to collect the rent without making repairs mandated to comply with OPA regulations, it was routed to Williams.[36] So too was a complaint from Lester Granger, executive secretary of the National Urban League, about politicized resistance encountered by the racially mixed Harlem Price Panel.[37] When Harlem congressman Adam Clayton Powell forwarded a suggestion by the Bronx Consumer Coordinating Council that the OPA prevent butchers from refusing black customers when they presented sufficient money and valid rationing points, Williams worked with Chester Bowles to draft a diplomatic reply, pleading insufficient local enforcement capacity.[38]

The OPA also received letters from less prominent correspondents who demonstrated that the wartime language of rights and democracy was not simply a rhetorical flag waved about by interest groups as they jockeyed for position. On the day that the second atomic bomb was dropped over Nagasaki, a letter arrived in Washington, D.C., for Chester Bowles, who passed it to Williams. It protested injustices perpetrated by a local rationing board in Willoughby, Ohio. "Just what do 'Four Freedoms' mean?" it began. "My . . . Board thinks that a man should crawl on his hands and knees in order to get what other people get—but we Jews are not liked in this KKK and German-American Bund County."[39] Black housewife Inex Avery of Abron, Ohio, wrote to Eleanor Roosevelt directly (her secretary promptly forwarded it to the OPA) to express her feeling that it was "unfair that I can't get my house fixed or rent lowered" even though she had 16 percent of her salary invested in war bonds (well above the 10 percent recommended by the Treasury).[40] Like her Jewish fellow Ohioan, Avery had been habituated by the OPA and other war agencies to look to the federal government to guarantee fairness in the economic transactions that marked her everyday life, whether they involved war bonds, rent control, or employment. Little wonder, then, that very high percentages of African Americans surveyed—79 percent of black housewives in one national study in early 1945—felt that price control would continue to be "necessary" even after V-E Day.[41]

A similar expectation of fair treatment within the consumer marketplace, guaranteed by the OPA, surfaced in scouting reports conducted in spring of 1943 by field staff in Chicago.[42] Typed up on the backs of WPA payroll forms—an indication of the scouts' institutional, and perhaps political, background—these transcripts captured a range of reactions, notably confusion about the workings of the rationing point system, frustration over red tape and bureaucratic bungling, and outright criticism of "those people in Washington." Despite these varied responses, a common theme emerged of basic faith in the government, and in the fairness of rationing (at least in principle), to avoid or counteract the inequities that beset poor citizens. One middle-aged married man captured this view when he explained why he thought rationing was necessary:

> That's the only way to be sure that all of us get our fair share of things. That's been the trouble all along. People that had all of the money could buy up all the things and people like you and me had to try to save for so many years . . . I think they might have to ration things even after the war is over because it might be a pretty good while before this country can start producing the things like they did before the war started.[43]

For African Americans this class sentiment carried an added racial valence because the consumers whose privileges had so often disadvantaged them were white. One interviewee alleged that the family she worked for was using the excuse of rationing to feed her less than they should—a common complaint among domestic workers whose employers often took over their rationing "points" and then scrimped egregiously on their board.[44]

Despite the strong progressive impulses that attracted many African Americans to the OPA, its decentralized structure and the enemies it made doomed its consumerist agenda, restricting civil rights activism to bureaucratic meddling around the edges of a government and a marketplace that were still, in the 1940s, organized around racial privilege. If black support for the OPA was strong, consistent, and suffused with expectations of national citizenship, it was also headed off the edge of a cliff. Just as black consumers had been galvanized by the prospect of the federal government acting as a guarantor of fair market transactions, so too were small businessmen alarmed by the same experience, which had brought price panel "consultants" snooping around their shops, and the threat of sanctions imposed by their neighbors' wives. Together with other conservative opponents, including trade associations, Southern Democrats, and business lobbies, the Republicans took back both houses of Congress in the "beefsteak election" of 1946, bringing down the OPA in the process.[45]

Food relief demonstrated the logic by which new rights were elevated by official ideology, even as they remained circumscribed by reasons of state, particularly when they touched on race. If neither consumer rights nor civil rights saw decisive victories within the OPA or the Treasury during World War II, expectations of both were powerfully inculcated by popular participation in the wartime state. These expectations converged in the early postwar years on one basic right to consume: the right to a subsistence diet, which represented only the faintest echo of Roosevelt's "Freedom from Want." But even this right was only feebly and partially tendered to black citizens, in stark contrast with what taxpayers underwrote for whites—even those who very recently had been enemies.

In January of 1943, 81.6 percent of poll respondents said they would be willing to have the United States remain on a rationing basis for five years to "help starving people in other countries."[46] Even as late as the spring and summer of 1946, when support for the OPA began to decline precipitously in the face of conservative assaults, as many as 70 percent of respondents still said they would be willing to return to the recently suspended system of food rationing in order to send food to people of other nations.[47] In reality, though, the OPA was too central to conservative mobilization in Congress and the press to allow it to revive rationing, which had been abandoned soon after V-J Day.[48]

Given the intensity of prewar isolationism, support for food aid was surprising. It reflected an admixture of humanitarian concern and national interest unique to the 1940s, the matrix within which support for the United Nations and other human rights institutions persisted, even as cold war tensions progressively reoriented U.S. international commitments toward global containment of communism. Church groups like the United Christian Council for Democracy advocated the continuation of U.S. financial support for the United Nations Relief and Rehabilitation Agency (UNRRA), asking "How can we lead the world toward peace if we refuse to meet desperate human needs?"[49] More mainstream voters either agreed with this sentiment or tolerated it sufficiently to continue supporting massive amounts of food relief and other forms of aid into the first years of the 1950s.

In this larger climate of support for collective security and humanitarianism, African Americans had some reasons to be hopeful about foreign relations in the postwar period. Ralph Bunche, a black scholar of Africa, had played an important role in the State Department's planning for the founding of the UN, followed by a prominent role in the United Nations Organization as the director of the Trusteeship Department. Robert Weaver, a member of the New Deal's "black cabinet," found a position at UNRRA, in the mission to the Ukraine. But these hopeful developments came up hard against the emerging fact that the Truman Administration's aid program would increasingly be designed in deference to conservative critics and their loud claims that the UNRRA, and subsequent aid programs, would be mismanaged and waste vital food resources on the limitless needs of desperate nations. Food relief would be extended only to starving Europeans, not to Africans.

Black organizations on the Left, like the Council on African Affairs, denounced the extension of the color line even to starvation. In May 1946, the *Pittsburgh Courier* published a long op-ed piece by Kumar Goshal, "As an Indian Sees It," whose subtitle, "Preserving a Peace That Doesn't Exist for Millions Who'll Never Live to Enjoy It," made clear the implications of the administration's Eurocentric definition of refugee relief. "People in India find it significant," reported Goshal, that American and British sympathies had been exercised by the prospect of Germans subsisting on a daily diet of a mere 2,000 calories, when "Indians are getting less than 960 calories a day." The Indian government warned that as many as 20 million might die from famine that year, yet as of the editorial's writing, it had received "no aid whatsoever" from UNRRA. According to Dorothy Norman of the *New York Post*, USDA officials felt that India was "overpopulated, accustomed to famine and disease, and . . . will just have to get along as best she can."[50] These bitter protests were made to no avail.

Even at home, freedom from hunger eluded many African American citizens well into the twentieth century. When Truman sought to make permanent the New Deal school lunch program that had expanded dramatically during World War II, Dixiecrats and their conservative allies in Congress guaranteed that the strings tied to the funding did not force Southern schools to guarantee black students lunches. Black students in the North had better luck in this, as in other matters, at least until the end of the 1970s, but they remained dependent on the political vagaries of matching funds.[51] Over the course of the postwar period, even the pittance afforded by Aid to Families with Dependent Children (AFDC), Food Stamps, and the school lunch program became poisoned fruit, as the war on poverty devolved into a war on the poor.

Beginning in World War II, rights claims directed at the federal government became an increasingly pervasive, even paradigmatic feature of politics because national power rested more firmly than ever on a state that obscured the sources of its power—unleashing the growth of the mixed economy while branding it the "free market"; concentrating national and global power in a military establishment disarmingly named the "Department of Defense" and authorized to safeguard "the free world"; constantly surveilling the loyalty of citizens to preempt internal subversion of a "free society." The pervasive imagery of freedom, which abetted this early rights revolution, obscured the nature of public power by individualizing it. Rights—even precious rights to enlist, vote, work, or consume without discrimination—were the coin of that realm, more payment than prize in the 1940s. But they provided ways to conceptualize public benefits and claim political leverage that gained a critical toehold in both society and government, opening an approach to national citizenship that a later generation of black activists would claim as their prize.

Notes

Thanks are due to Cybelle Fox, Timothy Gilfoyle, Michael Khodarkovsky, Robert Lieberman, William Link, and the Loyola History Department's Faculty Seminar for their helpful criticisms of this essay in its earlier iterations.

1. See Robert Korstad and Nelson Lichtenstein, "Opportunities Found and Lost: Labor, Radicals, and the Early Civil Rights Movement," *Journal of American History* Vol. 75, No. 3 (December 1988): 786–811, the fountainhead from which this new literature has sprung.

2. Michael Walzer, "The Communitarian Critique of Liberalism," in *Thinking Politically: Essays in Political Theory*, ed. Walzer (New Haven, 2007), 101–105. The other two kinds of mobility, marital and political, also increased dramatically for African Americans during the war, although they are beyond the scope of this chapter.

3. Susan B. Carter et al., eds., *Historical Statistics of the United States, Earliest Times to the Present: Millennial Edition* (New York, 2006), series Ac424–6, Ed1, Ed27. <http://hsus.cambridge.org>;; (hereafter cited as *HSUS—ME*).

4. *Edwards v. California*, 314 U.S. 160 (1941). The right to move was first affirmed in *Crandall v. Nevada*, 73 U.S. 35 (1868), but subsequently fell into neglect, along with much of Reconstruction-era jurisprudence.

5. Charles Chamberlain, *Victory at Home: Manpower and Race in the American South During World War II* (Athens, 2003), 69–96.

6. *HSUS—ME*, Ca9–10, Ea705; U.S. Department of Labor, *Industrial Disputes and Wage Stabilization in Wartime*, vol. I of *The Termination Report of the NWLB* (Washington, D.C.: USGPO, [1948]), 547–559, esp. Tables 2 and 5, Chart 3, and 551.

7. W. S. Woytinsky et al., *Employment and Wages in the United States* (New York, 1953), 398–399, Fig. 31 and Tables 169–170.

8. "Wartime Expansion of the Labor Force," *Monthly Labor Review,* Vol. 61, No. 2 (August 1945): 234–236.

9. John W. Jeffries, *Wartime America: The World War II Home Front* (Chicago, 1996), 61–64.

10. Carole Shammas, "A New Look at Long-Term Trends in Wealth Inequality in the United States," *American Historical Review,* Vol. 98, No. 2 (April 1993): 412–431, esp. 425, Table 5.

11. Lloyd G. Reynolds and Cynthia Taft, *The Evolution of the Wage Structure* (New Haven, 1956), 323, Table 12–13; Woytinsky et al., *Employment and Wages in the United States*, 473–474, 760, Table 116.

12. Reynolds and Taft, *The Evolution of the Wage Structure*, 336–337, esp. Table 12–6c.

13. Woytinsky et al., *Employment and Wages in the United States*, 452–453, Table 204; Neil A. Wynn, *The Afro-American and the Second World War* (New York, 1975; 2nd ed., 1993), 55–57; Jacqueline Jones, *Labor of Love, Labor of Sorrow: Black Women, Work and the Family from Slavery to the Present* (New York, 1985), 235–253.

14. Bruce Nelson, "Organized Labor and the Struggle for Black Equality in Mobile During World War II," *Journal of American History,* Vol. 80, No. 3 (December 1993): 952–988.

15. *HSUS—ME*, Ea698, Ca149.

16. *New York Amsterdam News,* March 20, 1943.

17. Kenneth B. Clark, "Morale of the Negro on the Home Front: World War I and II," *Journal of Negro Education,* Vol. 12, No. 3 (Summer 1943): 417–428, quote on 428.

18. Mary A. Morton, "The Federal Government and Negro Morale," *Journal of Education,* Vol. 12, No. 3 (Summer 1943): 452–463, quote on 463.

19. Daniel Kryder, *Divided Arsenal: Race and the American State During World War II* (Cambridge, 2000).

20. Sheldon Avery, *Up from Washington: William Pickens and the Negro Struggle for Equality, 1900–1954* (Newark, 1989); Lawrence R. Samuel, *Pledging Allegiance: American Identity and the Bond Drive of World War II* (Washington, 1997), 127–151; Houghteling press release on 127.

21. William Pickens, "The Economic Basis of the 'Race Problem,'" n.d. typescript [late 1930s], 6, box 3, microfilm R994, William Pickens MS, Schomburg Center, NYPL (hereafter cited as Pickens MSS).

22. Avery, *Up from Washington*, 154–155.

23. William Pickens, "How Would You Feel?" n.d. typescript for editorial; "Dean William Pickens Announces Support of Wendell Willkie," Republican National Committee press release, 8/23/1940; both in reel 2, microfilm R993–997, Pickens MS; Avery, *Up from Washington*, 154–158; Claytee White, "The March That Never Happened: Desegregating the Las Vegas Strip," in *Pursuing Justice in the West, Nevada Law Journal* Vol. 5, No. 71 (Fall 2004): 71–83, quote on 74.

24. "Report of the Interracial Section for 1943," box 19, Microfilm R-4463, Pickens MSS.

25. Pickens to editors of the Richmond *Times-Dispatch*, April 27, 1942, box 19, Microfilm R-4463, Pickens MSS.

26. "Report of the Interracial Section—1944," box 19, Microfilm R-4463, Pickens MSS.

27. Pauli Murray to Pickens, July 15, 1944; Pickens to Murray, July 21, 1944; Murray to Pickens, July 25, 1944, box 19, Microfilm R-4463, Pickens MSS.

28. "Report of the Interracial Section—1944," 80–87.

29. Pickens to Kathryn Close, *Survey Graphic*, September 14, 1941, box 19, Microfilm R-4463, Pickens MSS.

30. Acushnet Process Company, "All Right, What *Is* He Fighting For," *Saturday Evening Post* (1944), item W0279 in Ad*Access, Duke University Library Digital Collections, http://library.duke.edu/digitalcollections/adaccess.W0279/;.

31. Marshall Clinard, *The Black Market: A Study of White-Collar Crime* (New York, 1952), 28–50, 89–94.

32. "Williams, Frances Harriet," *Who's Who in Colored America* [1950], 556; Judith Weisenfeld, *African-American Women and Christian Activism: New York's Black YWCA, 1905–1945* (Cambridge, 1997), 197–198.

33. Mary McLeod Bethune to Williams, n.d. [September 1945], in "Analysis of Reports on Negro Participation, War Price and Rationing Boards" folder, box 1, Records of the Race Relations Advisor, OPA Records, RG 188, NA-CP. (Hereafter cited as "OPA-RRA.")

34. Claude A. Barnette to Williams, September 12, 1945, in "Analysis of Reports on Negro Participation, War Price and Rationing Boards" folder, box 1, OPA-RRA.

35. Chester Bowles, *Promises to Keep: My Years in Public Life, 1941–1969* (New York, 1971), 63–64; Frances Williams, "Minority Groups and OPA," *Public Administration Review* Vol. 7, no. 2 (Spring 1947): 123–128, quote on 126.

36. George Raymond, President of NAACP, Chester, PA Branch, to F D Roosevelt, telegram, July 1, 1943, in "Complaints" folder, box 12, OPA-RRA.

37. Lester Granger to Chester Bowles, June 2, 1945, in "Price Panels" folder, box 7, OPA-RRA.

38. "For Congressman Powell," memorandum, March 22, 1945; Chester Bowles to Adam Clayton Powell, May 8, 1945; both in "Powell, Congressman Adam C." folder, box 7, OPA-RRA.

39. Geo[rge] Miller of Noble, Ohio, to Chester Bowles, n.d. [processed 8/9/1945]; Williams to Miller, August 9, 1945; both in "Complaints" folder, box 2, OPA-RRA.

40. Mrs. Index Avery of Abron, Ohio, to Mrs. F D Roosevelt, n.d.; Avery to "Susie Warriels" [Susie S. Warrick], n.d. [probably spring 1945]; both in "Rent" folder, box 8, OPA-RRA.

41. Williams to James Soully, assistant to the administrator, memorandum October 11, 1945, "Third Consumer Compliance Survey—Negro Sample," box 2, OPA-RRA.

42. "Negro Rationing" folder, box 2, Bureau of Agricultural Economics, Department of Agrigulture, RG 83, NA-CP.

43. Interview no. 3, March 29, 1943, "Negro Rationing" folder.

44. Interview marked "Rec'd 5/13/43," "Negro Rationing" folder.

45. Meg Jacobs, *Pocketbook Politics: Economic Citizenship in Twentieth-Century America* (Princeton, 2005), 179–200.

46. Hadley Cantril, *Public Opinion 1935–1946* (Princeton, 1951), 909, #31.

47. NORC, "Where UNESCO Begins: The Climate of Opinion in the United States and Other Countries," report no. 34 (1947), 47.

48. "Summary of American Opinion on Relief," report no. 18 (April 12, 1946), 2, in box 50, Schuyler Foster Files, State Department, RG 59, NA-CP.

49. "Weekly Summary of U.S. Opinion on Food and Relief-VIII" (covering October 20–26, 1945), 2, in box 50, Schuyler Foster Files.

50. Kumar Goshal, "As an Indian Sees It," *Pittsburgh Courier,* May 11, 1946, 7.

51. Susan Levine, School Lunch Politics: The Surprising History of America's Favorite Welfare Program (Princeton, 2008), 82–88.

2

Confronting the Roadblock

CONGRESS, CIVIL RIGHTS, AND WORLD WAR II

Julian E. Zelizer

In certain respects, World War II had a transformative effect on the United States. The wartime mobilization vastly expanded the scale and scope of the federal government in ways that were sometimes greater than the expansion achieved by the New Deal. As the nation squared off against fascism in Germany, Japan, and Italy, more Americans found themselves paying income taxes, consuming within a system of rationing and price regulations, and working in factories that produced the weapons needed for war. When millions of Americans left their homes to join the army, old social norms were challenged. Soldiers were forced to live and serve with people who were very different from those in their hometown communities. As the government tried to maintain domestic tranquillity, officials extended federal efforts to calm racial and labor tensions, sometimes creating the expectation of new rights among citizens. When African Americans returned from the war, many insisted that the government should provide them with the same rights that they had been fighting for abroad.

The U.S. Congress, however, was difficult to change. More than almost any other part of the political system, Congress demonstrated how resilient political institutions could be, even during periods of national crisis and social change. The procedures and folkways of the House and Senate were deeply entrenched. The major political coalitions on Capitol Hill were dug into their trenches. The conservative coalition of Southern Democrats and Republicans that had emerged in Congress in the 1930s—a bipartisan coalition that targeted civil rights and unionization—maintained tight control over the committee system and was determined to ward off pressures from the executive branch and social activists to liberalize policies related to race.[1]

World War II tested the resiliency of the congressional committee system and the political strength of those who were demanding a new era of civil rights. The result was a contentious struggle in Congress between 1941 and 1945 about race relations and the role of the federal government in achieving equality. This chapter explores how the wartime mobilization encountered a formidable force on Capitol Hill and examines the ways in which the political battles of this period influenced the up-and-coming generation of liberal legislators.

Before the Committee Process was Conservative

The major obstacle that civil rights proponents in the 1950s and the 1960s would need to overcome in the legislative branch was the conservative coalition of senior Democrats and Republicans who dominated both chambers of Congress. While Southern Democrats, the more powerful members of this relationship, were deeply divided about most policy issues, they were unanimously opposed to measures that would benefit organized labor and civil rights. One notorious member of the coalition, Senator James Eastland (D-MS), enjoyed bragging that as chair of the Subcommittee on Civil Rights, he single-handedly blocked legislation from passing: "Why, for three years I was chairman, that committee didn't hold a meeting. I had special pockets in my pants, and for years I carried those bills around in my pockets everywhere I went and every one of them was defeated."[2]

The power of the conservative coalition rested on the committee system that had taken form at the turn of the twentieth century. In the committee system, power emanated from a larger infrastructure organized around autonomous, insular, seniority-based committees and congressional districts that privileged rural voters. The media usually refrained from aggressive investigative stories, technocratic expertise enjoyed unprecedented authority, and campaigns revolved around a secretive process that favored large contributors. In the Senate, where individual legislators possessed more tools to cause trouble, committee chairs relied on the filibuster as the ultimate insurance against undesired legislation.[3]

The House and Senate had adopted the norm of seniority after the Civil War, and it became the mechanism through which legislators were promoted.[4] As a result of seniority, legislators improved their position on a committee by remaining in office rather than because they followed the demands of party leaders or due to their skills as legislators. Southerners thrived under seniority, given that they tended to enjoy safe seats. In their one-party region, competitive elections were rare. Democrats who could survive the primaries—which a large number did because of the advantages of incumbency—counted on holding their seats for many decades. Southern incumbents drew on an enormous pool of campaign finance money from large commercial planters and local businessmen. For Southerners in the House, inequitably drawn districts that were slanted toward rural voters further ensured political stability.

Before civil rights became a major issue in Congress, Southern Democrats were nearly impossible to characterize politically. By the early 1930s, there were some Southern Democrats who certainly fulfilled the caricature of the crusty old Dixiecrat who opposed all new federal initiatives. Yet a large number of Southerners understood that, regardless of their inclinations, it was in their political interest to follow Roosevelt, given his enormous popularity in the region. Many Southerners also genuinely supported federal programs on issues such as agriculture and rural electrification that benefited their region. During the 1920s, Alabama's George Huddelston lined up at the forefront of a legislative coalition pushing for federal unemployment relief. The following decade, the federal government sent Southern states approximately $2 billion in relief.[5] One example of the bifurcated Southern mind was the ardent racist Senator Theodore Bilbo, who was known among his constituents in Mississippi as a champion of New Deal welfare for poor white Southerners. Georgia senator Richard Russell served as a loyal foot soldier for most of the New Deal. He was a strong champion of agricultural supports and rural electrification. Then there were liberals such as Hugo Black of Alabama and Claude Pepper of Florida, powerful figures in the New Deal, who put Midwestern progressives to shame.[6]

Before 1937, there was no inherent conflict between the committee system, dominated by Southern Democrats, and New Deal liberalism. The political diversity of Southern Democrats was great enough that the president and Northern legislators could form coalitions that produced important expansionary domestic initiatives. Roosevelt proved enormously successful at working with Southern chairmen throughout his first term to pass significant bills that ranged from a new federal commitment to welfare to Social Security for the elderly. To be sure, the key to this bargain was that Northern Democrats usually left civil rights off the agenda while Southern Democrats (often with the support of Northern liberals) shaped programs that relied on local and state administration, and excluded from Social Security the occupations in which most African Americans worked.[7] When civil rights proposals were floated before 1937, such as with the anti-lynching bill from Missouri Republican Leonidas Dyer, who represented an African American district, Southerners moved forward with full force to block such measures by using a filibuster.

Northern liberals and Southerners in the early New Deal also designed bills that relied on local and state administration—as well as certain occupational exclusions—which did not cause Southern Democrats to worry about federal involvement in the racial hierarchy of local labor markets. Policymakers and elected officials across the political spectrum preferred programs that were incremental and that favored local, not federal, control. Arguments against nationalization often resonated with progressive voices. Moreover, the impetus behind occupational exclusions, such as domestic and agricultural workers, often emanated from Northern policymakers who were not interested in dealing with racial discrimination and the non-industrial work force, while some Southern legislators were more eager to include these groups under coverage. In 1935, Southern Democrats were divided and confused over whether to include farm workers. Some powerful segments of the regional economy understood that they would benefit from having these groups covered. White businesses often depended on African American purchasing power, which would increase as a result of the government funds.

The Creation of a Conservative Coalition, 1937–1940

The relationship between New Deal liberalism and the committee system began to sour in Roosevelt's second term. The election of 1936 and its immediate aftermath made many Southern Democrats wary of supporting the Roosevelt administration and more willing to join congressional Republicans in a voting coalition.

There were several incidents that caused Southerners concern. During the Democratic Convention in 1936, Democrats had abandoned a rule that required candidates to obtain two-thirds of the delegate vote. Southerners had depended on this rule to protect their interests as their numbers in the party were starting to decline. In the election, which witnessed a smaller percentage of Southern votes in the Democratic total than ever before and in which Roosevelt demonstrated how it was possible to win the presidency without depending on Southern states, the tone of the administration seemed to have changed dramatically. The growing political strength of the African American community, progressive labor forces under the leadership of the CIO, and increasing numbers of Northern liberals in Congress created immense pressure on Southern Democrats. The Great Migration had also brought more African Americans into the pool of voters located in swing states in the Electoral College and thus gave them the power to effect change.

Southern Democrats sensed a change in tone within the White House when Roosevelt proposed expanding the number of Supreme Court Justices. The plan, which was defeated and caused a massive backlash against the president, further distanced Southern Democrats from the administration. The Supreme Court had been a bulwark to Southerners in the defense of states rights and the fight against racial equality. Roosevelt's loss in this controversy, as well as in a plan to reorganize the executive branch, emboldened legislative opponents of the New Deal and alienated many allies. North Carolina senator Josiah Bailey warned, "We are engaged in a great battle in America. The lines are drawn. The socialistic forces of America are not confined to the Socialist Party."[8]

As the tensions mounted, Southern committee chairs started to use legislative procedure more frequently against the administration. After 1937, the House Rules Committee became a burial ground for progressive initiatives. Chairman John O'Connor (D-NY), a political conservative, worked with a coalition of five Democrats and four Republicans on the Rules Committee to bottle up progressive legislation. Eugene Cox of Georgia and Howard Smith of Virginia (a younger member from Virginia who had joined the committee in 1933) co-ordinated strategy with Republicans Joseph Martin (MA) and William Colmer (MS). The committee relied on its power to control the rules used to debate leg-islation to force major compromises. The coalition, for example, made certain that maximum hours and minimum wage legislation passed in 1938 excluded agricultural, domestic, and service workers. Southerners insisted on a broad exclusion so that the regulations would not undermine their economy, which depended on low-cost (and African American) workers. "Liberals," Roosevelt administration official Harold Ickes noted in 1938, were "rapidly more and more dispirited."[9]

Civil rights was the area of greatest concern for Southern Democrats. For example, the NAACP had been pushing for anti-lynching legislation for several years, with increasing congressional support.[10] Their initial efforts in the 1920s had been defeated by Southern Democrats, but a rise in the number of lynch-ings in the 1930s forced the issue back onto the legislative agenda. In 1935, Democratic senators Robert Wagner (NY) and Senator Edward Costigan (CO) co-sponsored legislation to criminalize lynching. When it failed, they tried again in 1937, hoping that the new political climate following the post-1936 election would improve their chances. President Roosevelt, warning that coming out in favor of the legislation would cost him support for essential domestic bills, had consistently refused to support it. Even Eleanor Roosevelt had refused to speak to the NAACP about one version of the bill, writing that "President says this is dynamite."[11]

Growing black voting power in Northern states as a result of migration had increased support for this legislation.[12] Lead NAACP lobbyist Walter White conducted a masterful campaign to sway public opinion. The NAACP orga-nized mass demonstrations in Northern cities, and drew attention to polls in 1937 that revealed that a majority of Southerners favored federal anti-lynching legislation. House Democrats were able to force the bill out of the Judiciary Committee by obtaining 218 signatures on a petition, and the bill passed.

But in the Senate, Southern Democrats mounted a thirty-day filibuster that forced the Democratic leadership to shelve the legislation. Russell called fed-eral anti-lynching legislation "skunk meat."[13] Senator Bilbo of Mississippi said that the bill would "open the floodgates of hell in the South. . . ."[14] Coalition members tended to dismiss Northern liberalism as an attempt to cater to Afri-can American voters or lobbyists. Senator James Byrnes of South Carolina said, "The South may just as well know . . . that it has been deserted by the Democrats of the North. . . . If Walter White . . . should consent to have this bill laid aside, its advocates would desert it as quickly as football players un-scramble when the whistle of the referee is heard."[15] During a different debate over the poll tax, Ellison "Cotton Ed" Smith of South Carolina argued that the real aim of the legislation was for Democrats to purchase African Ameri-can votes.[16]

Roosevelt refused to support the legislation. He did not think that it would be politically possible for him to pass the legislation, given Southern power in Congress. When speaking with White, the president famously explained that "I did not choose the tools with which I must work. . . . The Southerners by reason of the seniority rule in Congress are chairmen or occupy strategic places on most of the Senate and House committees. If I come out for the anti-lynching bill now, they will block every bill I ask Congress to pass to keep America from collapsing."[17] Indeed, the president was annoyed with the Northern legislators pushing for this bill, which was causing severe fissures with Southern Democrats who were otherwise hesitant to oppose him. Conservatives such as Georgia senator Walter George were more comfortable condemning the president for his position on lynching than they would have been criticizing the legitimacy of New Deal programs.[18] According to Montana senator Burton Wheeler, the once-united Democratic Party had disintegrated into "bitterly opposed factions." Looking back at the year, Wheeler explained that "we might as well face the fact that great numbers of Southern Democrats are being alienated because of administration approval of so-called anti-lynching legislation."[19]

The growing factionalism within the Democratic Party exploded in the congressional elections, when Roosevelt actively campaigned against eight Democrats—seven of whom were Southerners—in the 1938 primaries in an effort to "purge" his Southern opponents from the party. The most publicized campaigns focused on Walter George, Ellison Smith, Millard Tydings, and John O'Connor. Administration officials believed that the outcome of the conflict would dictate the future of the Democratic Party. "The Democratic Party," Harold Ickes wrote to Maury Maverick, a populist Democrat from Texas, "is engaged in a great struggle against reaction within the party as well as without the party."[20] In one of the most dramatic moments of this midterm election, Roosevelt appeared at a campaign event with Senator George. When the president took to the stage, he implored the audience to vote against the senator in the upcoming election, while a visibly furious George sat on his hands.

The campaign did not work out well for the president. All but one of the legislators whom Roosevelt had opposed (including George) were victorious. Additionally, Republicans gained several seats, as did conservative Southerners who replaced New Deal liberals in several elections.[21] Following the attempted purge, the atmosphere was tense. According to James Murray, a Democrat from Montana, "There was a time when I would have bled to have any more dealings with him [the president] and I just intend to stay away from him and he can do as he pleases."[22]

Despite being a congressional minority, Republicans were able to influence committee work by allying with these Southerners. Although they had much less interest in opposing civil rights, the GOP counted on Southern Democratic votes on labor issues or tax policies. Southern Democrats refused to enter into a formal coalition with the GOP, but they were willing to work informally since Republicans were not an electoral force in the region.[23] "The Republican-Southern Democratic coalition was an unnatural alliance that existed only because the Southerners were prisoners of the race issue," Lyndon Johnson's advisor recalled.[24]

The coalition would include a number of prominent figures. Democratic representative Cox would work through the House Rules Committee, along with Howard Smith, to protect coalition interests. Carter Glass, Harry Byrd, and Josiah Bailey, who had been voting against Roosevelt since 1933, were the veterans in the group. Ellison Smith and James Byrnes moved away from their support of the New Deal to emerge as stalwart opponents of the president.[25] Some of the lesser known members, such as Clifton Woodrum of Virginia or William King of Utah, could be counted on to vote relatively consistently on the high-profile issues facing the coalition. Race remained their core concern. As Bailey said: "The catering by our National Party to the Negro vote . . . is not only extremely distasteful to me, but very alarming to me. Southern people know what this means and you would have to be in Washington only about three weeks to realize what it is meaning to our Party in the Northern states."[26]

The Coalition Emboldened, 1941–1945

The push for civil rights continued to grow stronger in Washington during the war, including in the halls of Congress as more Northern legislators promoted these measures. The mobilization to fight for democracy abroad gave civil rights activists the space to make more demands within the United States. The need for African American workers in wartime production and as soldiers, moreover, heightened expectations for domestic race relations. The massive growth of unions in the North, and much smaller but still noticeable gains in the South (where union membership doubled from 1938 to 1948, reaching over one million workers, as a result of wartime industry), created a cohort of legislators who were more aggressive in pushing for federal intervention on policies related to unions, even when they impacted race relations.[27] Republicans were also trying to capitalize on divisions within the Democratic Party. In 1940, Republicans wrote a strong civil rights plank in their party platform, and several African American newspapers announced their support for Wendell Willkie. There were thus more elected officials in the Democratic Party who were willing to challenge Roosevelt's bargain with the South and to take on their colleagues.

The result was that it became gradually harder to stop civil rights legislation from passing in the House, where only a bare majority was needed. Meanwhile, President Roosevelt began to use executive power as a tool to achieve civil rights progress in spite of a recalcitrant Congress. Through executive power, he could circumvent the legislative branch rather than have to negotiate with it. Roosevelt pursued civil rights primarily for political ends. The president had to balance pressure from Southern Democratic opposition to civil rights and increased pressure from African Americans, who had gained more clout in key Electoral College states as a result of the black migration. He also needed to avoid social conflict from disrupting wartime production. A huge spike in racial unrest, which started as early as 1941 and usually revolved around African American soldiers being mistreated near military bases, caused great concern for the president and his staff.[28] At the same time, the African American community had vastly improved its political sophistication in organizing and applying pressure on elected officials. Even as public support for civil rights expanded and more government officials became increasingly sympathetic to the cause of improved race relations for political or ideological reasons, the conservative coalition dug in even deeper.

Unfortunately for proponents of civil rights, World War II did not bring progress on the legislative front. Southerners were angered by what they perceived as Roosevelt's growing interest in tackling racial issues. In a letter written on August 7, 1942, the Commissioner of Public Safety of Birmingham, Alabama, Eugene "Bull" Connor, warned the president that "the federal agencies have adopted policies to break down and destroy segregation [and] . . . destroy the progress made by law abiding white people." Southerners such as Connor feared that agencies like the National Youth Administration were offering federal protections to African Americans.[29] One legislator warned that "the South isn't joking anymore. . . . Back them into the corner a little further and see what they do."[30]

Between Pearl Harbor and the bombing of Hiroshima, the number of Democrats in the House and Senate declined in each election. The Democratic majority in the House fell from 261 in 1938 to 242 in 1944. In the Senate, the Democratic majority fell from 69 to 56 during the same period. With fewer Democrats in Congress, senior Southerners became even more powerful, especially with their control of committees and their alliance with Republicans. In 1942 and 1943, the conservative coalition used its leverage to attack the president's wartime programs, even as they proclaimed their allegiance to the overall war effort. Congressional conservatives, for instance, targeted the Office of Price Administration, conducting investigations into improper activities that pressured the administration into selecting conservative administrators.[31] The House Rules Committee launched a series of hearings—without the support of Democratic leaders—about unionization.[32] Tightened labor markets during the war enabled unions to make headway in Southern markets, thereby triggering Southern Democrats to take a more cautious view of New Deal labor policies.[33]

The coalition weakened the mildest of civil rights measures. There were many Southerners who were genuinely scared that African Americans constituted a sufficient percentage of the voting population that they had become the focus of Democratic electoral strategy. Senator James Byrnes told his colleagues, "The Negro has not only come into the Democratic Party, but the Negro has come into control of the Democratic Party."[34] Senator Russell, the head of the notorious Southern Caucus, warned that there was no "greater menace" to the country than racial equality.[35] The influx of African Americans into defense productions, which were heavily based in the South, threatened defenders of segregation. "There is no such thing as a little desegregation," said Russell, who feared that any change would lead to more. "They are determined to get into the white schools and into the white restaurants and into the swimming pools."[36]

The major battle centered on the Fair Employment Practices Committee (FEPC), which Roosevelt created through an executive order in 1941. This was one of the cases in which the president attempted to stave off grassroots pressure for progress on civil rights—despite Southern control of Congress— through executive power, by the use of executive orders, court appointments, or relying on the Department of Justice to tackle these challenges. After A. Philip Randolph, the head of the Brotherhood of Sleeping Car Porters, had threatened to lead a march on Washington, Roosevelt established the FEPC in exchange for a cancellation. While the FEPC was a modest effort to deal with the problems of racism in employment, the commission constituted the single biggest achievement on race relations since Reconstruction. Many Southerners hated the FEPC and what it represented. They perceived this as an example of how the president was using wartime executive power, thereby working around the Senate to push through a radical social agenda.[37] One Texas newspaper editorialized in a piece about Speaker Sam Rayburn: "You probably do not know that the FEPC is 60 percent negro controlled, or . . . that in many cases throughout the nation, Negro executives are working white girls as secretaries."[38]

Congressional conservatives mobilized in Congress to make certain that the FEPC received only meager funds and that the commission was not allowed to gain much administrative power. When some members of the administration tried to turn the FEPC into a permanent agency after the war ended, Southerners killed the idea. Targeting the commission, Russell proposed an amendment that would prohibit more than a year of spending on agencies without the authorization of Congress. Congress passed the amendment, and FEPC funding ended in 1946. Black activists would make the restoration of the agency a top priority after the war, and President Harry Truman also fought to restore the agency, but Southerners used the filibuster to block his efforts. Senator Eastland warned that the FEPC supporters were hoping to "tear down the partitions between white and black rest rooms and create social equality" between the races.[39] The effort to obtain cloture (the sufficient number of Senate votes needed to bring a filibuster to an end) would fail by a vote of 48 to 36.

Another important wartime battle over civil rights revolved around an effort by liberal Democrats in 1942 to repeal the poll tax. Under Majority Leader

Alben Barkley (D-KY), the Democratic leadership agreed to support legislation to end this tax, which had once been the main mechanism used to disfranchise African Americas. By 1940, this was primarily a symbolic fight since most states had abandoned the practice.[40] To keep the legislation from being killed in committee, Barkley relied on a technical rule that allowed the Senate to directly take up a proposal. In response, Russell worked with fellow Southerners to convince enough senators to stay away from the chamber so that there could not be a quorum. Barkley instructed the Sergeant-at-Arms to bring them back to the chamber forcefully. They used other technical rules as well to delay and block passage. In the end, the bill was defeated.

The November elections brought bad news for supporters of the poll tax legislation and other civil rights measures. Conservatives made dramatic gains. Democratic control in the House fell from 256 seats to 223 seats, and in the Senate their majority fell from 65 to 57 Democrats. According to one analysis, "Not since the 1938 midterms had the Democrats lost so much ground, the Republicans scored so impressively."[41] A few weeks after the election, Democrats shelved the poll tax legislation after Southern Democrats filibustered for the first time since the 1938 anti-lynching bill.[42] "If these few people have the power to thwart the will of the people," Senator Claude Pepper lamented, "they have the power to lose here on the floor of the Senate the war for which our men are fighting and dying all over the world."[43]

Emboldened by the 1942 election, the conservative coalition flexed its muscle. "Government by bureaucrats must be broken, and broken now," said Georgia's Eugene Cox, who sat on the Rules Committee.[44] The coalition eliminated a number of programs, including the Works Progress Administration (WPA), the Civilian Conservation Corps (CCC), and the National Youth Agency (NYA). To be sure, the coalition accepted much of the New Deal agenda, including Social Security, farm price supports, the minimum wage, and banking regulation.[45] Nonetheless, in 1943, the coalition demonstrated that it had significant power to block efforts by liberal Democrats to extend the power of government into new areas of American life and to cut selected programs.

For all of the anger that it caused among Southern Democrats, the Roosevelt administration remained tepid about tackling civil rights. They were cognizant of the bargain from the 1930s, and the costs that had been incurred from breaking it. One aide warned Roosevelt that some civil rights proposals would "translate impotent rumblings against the New Deal into an actual revolt at the polls." Eleanor Roosevelt, one of the most progressive voices in the White House, told an African American who was frustrated with Roosevelt's pace on civil rights that "if he were to be elected President . . . on that day, he would have to take into consideration the people who are the heads of important committees in Congress . . . people on whom he must depend to pass vital legislation for the nation as a whole."[46]

The coalition's ability to subvert legislation related to civil rights culminated with a debate in 1944 over legislation that would have the federal government distribute a ballot to soldiers overseas. Under the existing system, soldiers needed to obtain ballots from state governments, which controlled the entire process. The existing system was so messy that most soldiers were never able to vote. In 1942, Congress imposed the first limits on state authority over these ballots by passing legislation that allowed the federal government to override qualifications that states established. The law also instructed states to craft a federal ballot and required the War and Navy Departments to send cards to everyone in the armed forces telling them how they could request a federal ballot from state officials. Congress included a highly controversial provision that prohibited the collection of poll taxes from soldiers. Most Southern Democrats had allowed this measure to go through, realizing that there would be widespread opposition to taxing Americans who were fighting abroad.[47]

In this case, the war had thus provided a temporary window to allow for a stronger federal role in voting, one of the most sensitive areas of race relations. But the gains were still extremely limited, a token measure to avoid the charge that Southerners had blocked progress for allowing soldiers to vote. The resulting process for soldiers to obtain ballots, however, was extremely cumbersome and rarely resulted in the delivery of the ballot.[48] In 1942, fewer than 30,000 soldiers overseas out of 5 million men actually voted.

The proposal in 1944, sponsored by Senator Theodore Greene of Rhode Island and Senator Scott Lucas of Illinois, aimed to improve the system for soldiers to obtain absentee ballots from their states. "It has been clear for some time," Roosevelt told Congress, "that practical difficulties and the element of time make it virtually impossible for soldiers and sailors and marines spread all over the world to comply with the different voting laws of forty-eight States . . ." The president called proposals that would authorize the states to fix their own systems, rather than empowering the federal government to do so, a "fraud on the soldiers and sailors and marines now training and fighting for us and for our sacred rights."[49]

Under the proposal, the federal government would gain the responsibility for sending out the ballots. The bill would create a Federal War Ballot Commission that would send and receive federal ballots from service members, marines, and other individuals working for the government who were stationed abroad. The commission would be run by two Republicans and two Democrats. The White House wanted more soldiers to vote in the 1944 election. National Democrats were convinced that part of the reason for the poor results in 1942 was that that many Roosevelt supporters had been drafted. In December 1943, a Gallup Poll suggested that the soldier vote would benefit Roosevelt by 61 percent and could determine the next election.[50] Conservatives agreed that soldiers should be given the right to vote, but they insisted that the states, rather than the federal government, needed to administer and control the plan.

Protecting voting practices from federal regulation had been absolutely central to white Southerners since the Civil War. Southern opponents saw the soldier's bill as an opening wedge to federal control of the Southern electoral system, while Republican opponents saw it as an unnecessary extension of federal power. Senators Eastland, John McLellan, and Kenneth McKellar—three top opponents of civil rights—proposed an alternative to the White House legislation that granted states the right to control implementation. Massachusetts Democrat John McCormack complained, "It's all right to vote to send soldiers to die for their country, but it's all wrong to let them vote for the officials of their country." In response, Mississippi congressman John Rankin suggested that communists were behind the legislation. He denounced the radio broadcaster Walter Winchell, who endorsed the administration bill on his shows, as "the little kike. . . ."[51]

The atmosphere in Congress was extremely tense. The Supreme Court *Smith v. Allwright* decision of 1944, which deemed the white primary unconstitutional in 1944, provided a major legal blow to the Southern system of political discrimination against African Americans. The decision resulted in an increase in the number of African Americans who were registered, and meant that the debates over the soldier's vote became that much more controversial. The conservative coalition won the debate by forcing Congress in conference committee to allow states to have the final decision about whether to send out these ballots and to allow states to retain control over authorizing the federal ballots as acceptable.[52] Southerners also warded off an effort to attach an amendment to the legislation that would have eliminated the poll tax. Senator Green, who sponsored the White House version, said, "If I were President . . . I would veto this bill."[53] *Washington Post* reporter Marquis Childs commented that "the ghost of the Negro voter . . . hovered over Congressman Rankin's chair, making low moaning noises at appropriate intervals. No one ever really talked about whether the simplified Federal ballot would make it possible for Negroes to vote. But that was one of the chief reasons why the conference discussion was strung out to such interminable length."[54] The president refused to sign the final bill, although he agreed to abide by the congressional decision.

One Southerner wrote his daughter that "all white people in Alabama are buying pistols and other ammunition in preparation for the race war which is coming. . . ."[55] When Senator Guffey denounced Southern legislators for their actions on this legislation in 1944, Senator Bailey responded to the attacks by telling his colleagues that "there is a reason why the South has voted Democratic . . . the time will come . . . when the southern people will demand that there shall be no meddling with their affairs."[56]

The fight over the soldiers vote had inflamed regional tensions in the legislative branch. When World War II ended in 1945, the conservative coalition was thus stronger politically than when the war began, and its members had shown their ability to block legislation that was directly or indirectly related to civil rights. Although the outcome of the war constituted a great victory for President Roosevelt and his successor Harry Truman, Democrats supportive of civil rights had been decisively rebuffed on several occasions in Congress throughout the first half of the 1940s. In the months running up to the first election after the war, liberals had suffered a number of defeats. A series of battles over the extension of wartime programs triggered high levels of sectional stress.[57] Conservative Democrats had even pressured Truman into firing Secretary of Commerce Henry Wallace, one of the most progressive voices in the administration.

Moreover, Republican conservatives reclaimed control of the House and Senate in 1946, further strengthening the power of the coalition. Republicans claimed 51 seats in the Senate, compared to 38 before the election, and 246 seats in the House, in contrast to 190 before the election. Some of the new legislators elected in 1946 came from the right wing of their party, including Richard Nixon of California, William Knowland of California, and John Bricker of Ohio. Although the GOP took control of Congress for the first time since 1928, they assured senior Southern Democrats that they would continue to play a crucial role on their committees and that their policy interests would be protected. The rightward shift of Congress during the war appeared to have been confirmed.

The Promise of the Future: The Election of 1948

Although the short-term effect of World War II on Capitol Hill was to set back progress on civil rights for almost a decade, there was a hidden, positive long-term effect. A group of Americans who had been deeply affected by the racial arguments that emerged during the war entered Congress in 1948. Committed to expanding the New Deal agenda into the area of civil rights, these legislators would also be prepared to do procedural battle with the conservative coalition.

Tension between younger legislators and senior Southern committee chairmen mounted in 1947 when the Senate pressured Senator Bilbo into stepping down. Bilbo represented the most virulent form of southern racism and anti-Semitism. His downfall began in June 1946 when Bilbo told an audience that "I call on every red-blooded white man to use any means to keep the niggers away from the polls[;] if you don't understand what that means you are just plain dumb." While such language from legislators had previously been acceptable, attitudes had changed after the fall of Nazi Germany. Mainstream magazines, including the *Saturday Evening Post,* started to condemn Bilbo, joining progressive magazines like *The New Republic.* Senate investigations were launched into different aspects of his career, ranging from his interaction with defense contractors to accusations that he had endorsed violence to stifle African American voting in 1946—investigations at which black Mississippi veterans stepped forward to testify, despite threats of reprisal.[58] In 1947, the Republican majority refused to seat him. Senate Democrats worked out a compromise that avoided action, temporarily allowing him to focus on securing treatment of his throat cancer, from which he died in August.[59]

But the end of Bilbo's career did not mark the end of the power of the senior Southern Democrats. During the 1948 Democratic Convention, the young Senate candidate Hubert Humphrey took the podium at the Democratic Convention in Philadelphia. Standing before the television cameras that were covering the convention for the first time, Humphrey proclaimed: "To those who say that this bill of rights program is an infringement of states rights I say this—the time has arrived for the Democratic party to get out of the shadow of states-rights and walk forthrightly into the bright sunshine of human rights."[60] When President Truman announced his support for this plank, the delegations from Mississippi and Alabama stormed out of the convention to form the States Rights Democratic Party. The so-called Dixiecrat candidate for president was the person who directed the revolt, South Carolina governor Strom Thurmond.

Although Truman's victory over New York governor Thomas Dewey is the most famous result of the 1948 election, Northern voters also elected a group of Democrats to Congress who were determined to pass civil rights legislation. In 1948, Democrats took control of both chambers. Democrats enjoyed substantial gains: 9 seats in the Senate, raising their total to 54, and a net gain of 75 House seats, leaving their total at 263. This constituted a huge freshmen class, injecting new blood into both chambers (118 freshmen in the House, with 104 new Democrats; 18 freshmen in the Senate, with 14 new Democrats). Together with the interest groups that supported them, these Democrats were convinced that institutional reforms were essential to achieving their policy objectives. Pundits called these postwar liberals "bomb-throwers" because of their strong-armed tactics.

Based on a keen awareness of the inner workings of legislative institutions, these Democrats were prepared to target the procedural weapons of congressional conservatives. Members of the liberal coalition wanted to create a legislative process that Southern conservatives could not use to block their policy agenda and to foster a style of politics that was more partisan and majoritarian. The liberal coalition equated the internal reform of Congress with a more democratic government. In 1949, the House passed the 21-day rule, which allowed committee chairs to force consideration of a bill on the floor if it had been held up by the House Rules Committee for 21 days.

As a minority within their own party, Democrats such as Hubert Humphrey (MN), Eugene McCarthy (MN), Paul Douglas (IL), Herbert Lehman (NY), and Richard Bolling (MO) worked with liberal interest groups to exert pressure on the leadership. According to their understanding of government, conservative power rested on institutional protections rather than electoral support.

They underestimated the deep strands of conservatism that existed among many citizens, including ethnic blue-collar workers in the North.[61]

The legislators elected in 1948 were not starry-eyed elite intellectuals who were interested in pursuing clean government. Rather, they were political players who were very comfortable in the trenches of politics and who believed that they could only be victorious by undermining the main tool of their opponents: institutional structures. These liberals were committed to taking control of the legislative process. Richard Bolling said: "Ideals are like the stars—you use them to guide you, but you never reach them. Learn the methods that get you there."[62] Most of them believed that centralized parties offered the best hope for a strong federal government and for a political system that did not alienate citizens or privilege interest groups.[63] If they needed any reminders that Southerners remained powerful in Senate, they were given sufficient evidence in 1949. Southerners altered the rule for ending filibusters so that two-thirds of the entire chamber were needed, as opposed to two-thirds of senators present and voting. The NAACP listed filibuster reform as equally important as fighting lynching and segregation.[64]

The liberal legislators elected in 1948 started to attack the committee system by working with interest groups such as the American Federation for Labor and Congress of Industrial Organizations (AFL-CIO), National Association for the Advancement of Colored People (NAACP), American Jewish Congress (AJC), American Civil Liberties Union (ACLU), Leadership Conference on Civil Rights (LCCR), and Americans for Democratic Action (ADA). This coalition of legislators and interest groups directed the drive for civil rights from inside the nation's capital before there was strong presidential support or a mass movement.[65] These organizations were the legislative team in a broader Northern front of activists in the 1950s who were trying to change the hearts and minds of Americans on the question of race.[66] While civil rights was a principal concern, this generation of liberals would champion a whole host of policies that angered many Southern committee chairs, including liberalized unemployment compensation benefits, federal health care for the elderly, urban renewal, macroeconomic intervention, and liberalized immigration policies.

During his first years in office, Minnesota senator Hubert Humphrey (elected in 1948) brazenly defied congressional norms and procedure. Days after starting in office, Humphrey went to the Senate dining room with an African American aide. When an African American waiter informed Humphrey that there was only service for whites, the senator protested in front of his colleagues and insisted that he and his aide eat together.[67] Humphrey attacked senior legislators on television, radio, and in print.[68] Humphrey moderated his position toward the leadership since he believed that Lyndon Johnson (who became Minority Leader in 1952 and Majority Leader in 1955) was more cooperative with liberals than any leader before him. Johnson once warned Humphrey that if he was not more pragmatic, "you'll suffer the fate of those crazies, those bomb-thrower types. . . . You'll be ignored, and get nothing accomplished you want."[69] Johnson believed that Humphrey could help him obtain the support of liberals and shed his sectional label,[70] while Humphrey felt that Johnson might endear him to Southerners. The Minnesotan remained the principal bridge between the liberal coalition and the Senate leadership.

The liberals of 1948 gained strength over the next decade as they were joined by more legislators who shared their concerns. It would take time, though, because Southerners retained control of the institution and used procedure to block civil rights measures. The next important congressional election for liberals came in 1958. Just as Southerners had traditionally formed personal connections with incoming Democrats, younger liberals elected in 1948 assisted candidates running for office and introduced them to the ways and means of Congress once they were in office. Minnesota Democrat Eugene McCarthy's "McCarthy's Mavericks," for instance, provided campaigns with money, polling, and research, as did organizations such as ADA. The 1958 election was a landslide for Democrats, whose advantage in the Senate climbed to 64–34 and 282–153 in the House: Democrats gained 39 House seats and 12 in the Senate. Most new Senate Democrats were elected from outside the South, and the number of junior senators was higher than at any time in the 1950s.[71]

The Democrats elected between 1948 and 1958 were deeply influenced by the racial liberalism that came out of World War II. This proved to be instrumental to weakening the procedural power of the conservative coalition and ultimately led to the passing of the Civil Rights Act of 1964 and the Voting Rights Act of 1965. Indeed, Hubert Humphrey served as President Johnson's chief ally in 1964 in obtaining legislation.

Although the effect was not direct, nor immediate, the war did help to produce a generational change in Congress that benefited civil rights. To trace the contributions of the war, however, it is necessary to focus on long-term generational change rather than the immediate political situation. The combination of institutional stickiness and regional division slowed policymakers' responses to new demands in racial politics. It became clear that institutions moved slowly and that entrenched interests were not easily moved, even by dramatic events such as America's global fight against fascism.

Notes

1. Ira Katznelson, Kim Geiger, and Daniel Kryder, "Limiting Liberalism: The Southern Veto in Congress, 1933–1940," *Political Science Quarterly,* Vol. 108 (Summer 1993): 283–302.

2. Timothy Thurber, "The Second Reconstruction," in *The American Congress: The Building of Democracy,* ed. Julian E. Zelizer (Boston, 2004), 531.

3. Julian E. Zelizer, *On Capitol Hill: The Struggle for Reform and Its Consequences, 1948–2000* (New York, 2004), 14–32.

4. Barbara Hinckley, *The Seniority System in Congress* (Bloomington, 1971); Nelson Polsby, Miriam Gallaher, and Barry Spencer Rundquist, "The Growth of the Seniority System in the U.S. House of Representatives," *American Political Science Review*, Vol. 63 (September 1969): 787–807.

5. Ira Katznelson, *When Affirmative Action Was White: An Untold History of Racial Inequality in Twentieth Century* (New York, 2005), 39.

6. James T. Patterson, *Congressional Conservatism and the New Deal: The Growth of the Conservative Coalition in Congress, 1933–1939* (Lexington, 1967); Mary Elizabeth Poole, *The Segregated Origins of Social Security: African Americans and the Welfare State* (Chapel Hill, 2006); Howard L. Reiter, "The Building of a Bifactional Structure: The Democrats in the 1940s," *Political Science Quarterly,* Vol. 116 (Spring 2001): 112.

7. Anthony J. Badger, *FDR: The First Hundred Days* (New York, 2008), 161–162; Gareth Davies and Martha Derthick, "Race and Social Welfare Policy: The Social Security Act of 1935," *Political Science Quarterly,* Vol. 112 (Summer 1997): 217–235; Robert C. Lieberman, *Shifting the Color Line: Race and the American Welfare State* (Cambridge, Mass., 1998); Jill Quadagno, *The Color of Welfare: How Racism Undermined the War on Poverty* (New York, 1994); Katznelson, *When Affirmative Action Was White*; Poole, *The Segregated Origins of Social Security,* 60–96.

8. Cited in William E. Leuchtenburg, *Supreme Court Reborn: The Constitutional Revolution in the Age of Roosevelt* (New York, 1995), 158–159.

9. Diaries of Harold Ickes, March 2, 1938, September 15, 1938, Franklin Roosevelt Library, 2634–2635.

10. George C. Rable, "The South and the Politics of Antilynching Legislation, 1920–1940," *Journal of Southern History,* Vol. LI (May 1985): 203. For a comprehensive look at the strategy and personalities of the Southern Democrats involved in these battles, see Keith M. Finley, *Delaying the Dream: Southern Senators and the Fight Against Civil Rights, 1938–1965* (Baton Rouge, 2008).

11. Jean Edward Smith, *FDR* (New York, 2007), 399–400.

12. Rable, "The South and the Politics of Antilynching Legislation, 1920–1940," 209.

13. "Black's White," *Time,* January 24, 1938.

14. Rable, "The South," 217.

15. "Black's White."

16. Rable, "The South," 214.

17. David M. Kennedy, *Freedom from Fear: The American People in Depression and War, 1929–1945* (New York, 1999), 343.

18. Rable, "The South and the Politics of Antilynching Legislation, 1920–1940," 211–212.

19. L. C. Speers, "Rift among Democrats Gives New Hope to G.O.P." *New York Times,* May 9, 1937.

20. Harold Ickes to Maury Maverick, 1938, PSF, Box 129, Subject File: Congress 1932–1940.

21. Jamie L. Carson, "Electoral and Partisan Forces in the Roosevelt Era: The U.S. Congressional Elections of 1938," *Congress & the Presidency,* Vol. 28 (Autumn 2001): 162, 168–180.

22. William E. Leuchtenburg, *Franklin D. Roosevelt and the New Deal, 1932–1940* (New York, 1963), 272.

23. Patterson, "A Conservative Coalition Forms in Congress, 1933–1939," 769–772.

24. George E. Reedy, *The U.S. Senate: Paralysis or a Search for Consensus?* (New York, 1986), 49.

25. Patterson, "A Conservative Coalition Forms in Congress, 1933–1939," 758–760.

26. Patterson, "The Failure of Part Realignment in the South, 1937–1939," 603.

27. Katznelson, *When Affirmative Action Was White,* 67–71.

28. Kryder, *Divided Arsenal,* 66–87; 168–242.

29. John Morton Blum, *V Was for Victory: Politics and American Culture During World War II* (New York, 1976), 193–194.

30. Allen Drury, *A Senate Journal 1943–1945* (New York, 1963), 4.

31. Alonzo Hamby, "Congress and World War II," in *The American Congress,* 474–490.

32. Eric Schickler, *Disjointed Pluralism: Institutional Innovation and the Development of the U.S. Congress* (Princeton, 2001), 167.

33. Sean Farhang and Ira Katznelson, "The Southern Imposition: Congress and Labor in the New Deal and Fair Deal," *Studies in American Political Development,* Vol. 19 (Spring 2005): 7.

34. Kevin J. McMahon, *Reconsidering Roosevelt on Race: How the Presidency Paved the Road to* Brown (Chicago, 2004), 101, 116.

35. Lewis L. Gould, *The Most Exclusive Club: A History of the Modern United States Senate* (New York, 2005), 166.

36. Robert A. Caro, *Master of the Senate: The Years of Lyndon Johnson* (New York, 2002), 192.

37. Robert Mann, *The Walls of Jericho: Lyndon Johnson, Hubert Humphrey, Richard Russell and the Struggle for Civil Rights* (New York, 1996), 40.

38. D. B. Hardeman and Donald C. Bacon, *Rayburn: A Biography* (New York, 1987), 298.

39. "FEPC Bill Assailed as Attempt to Force Social Race Equality," *Washington Post,* February 6, 1946.

40. V. O. Key, *Southern Politics in State and Nation* (New York, 1949).

41. "Midterm Verdict," *New York Times,* November 8, 1942.

42. Gould, *The Most Exclusive Club,* 165.

43. Robert De Vore, "Cloture Defeat Spells Doom of Poll-Tax Foes," *Washington Post,* November 24, 1942.

44. Alvin M. Josephy, Jr., *On the Hill: A History of the American Congress* (New York, 1979), 336.

45. Kennedy, *Freedom from Fear,* 783

46. Ibid., 775.

47. Keyysar, *The Right to Vote,* 247.

48. Alonzo Hamby, "World War II: Conservatism and Constituency Politics," 488.

49. Franklin D. Roosevelt, "Message to Congress on Voting by Members of the Armed Forces," January 25, 1944, *The American Presidency Project,* http://www.presidency.ucsb.edu/ws/.

50. Boyd A. Martin, "The Service Vote in the Elections of 1944," *The American Political Science Review,* Vol. 39 (August 1945): 720.

51. Kennedy, *Freedom from Fear,* 788.

52. Gould, *The Most Exclusive Club,* 166–167.

53. Robert C. Albright, "Vote Bill Gets States Rights Straightjacket," *Washington Post,* March 8, 1944.

54. Marquis Childs, "Soldier Vote Bill," *Washington Post,* March 9, 1944.

55. Keyssar, *The Right to Vote*, 246.

56. Gould, *The Most Exclusive Club,* 167.

57. Richard Bensel, *Sectionalism and American Political Development* (Madison, 1984), 184.

58. John Dittmer, *Local People: The Struggle for Civil Rights in Mississippi* (Urbana, 1995), 1–15.

59. Robert L. Fleegler, "Theodore G. Bilbo and the Decline of Public Racism, 1938–1947," *Journal of Mississippi History,* Vol. 68 (Spring 2006): 1–27.

60. Hubert Humphrey, "Hubert Humphrey Speaks Out on Human Rights," July 14, 1948, Hubert Humphrey Papers (Minnesota), Box 150.A.8.1, File: July 14, 1948.

61. See, for example, Thomas J. Sugrue, *The Origins of the Urban Crisis* (Princeton, 1996).

62. Interview with Richard Bolling, February 23, 1959, Harry Truman Presidential Library (Missouri).

63. Jennifer A. Delton, *Making Minnesota Liberal: Civil Rights and the Transformation of the Democratic Party* (Minneapolis, 2002), 19–39.

64. Zelizer, *On Capitol Hill,* 44.

65. The only books that have paid attention to them have been works about Lyndon Johnson, rather than the liberal coalition itself. See, for examples, Caro, *Master of the Senate*; Robert Dallek, *Lone Star Rising: Lyndon Johnson and His Times 1908–1960* (New York, 1991).

66. Thomas Sugrue, *Sweet Land of Liberty: The Unfinished Struggle for Civil Rights* (New York, 2009).

67. Mann, *The Walls of Jericho*, 98.

68. Transcript, WTIC Radio, October 10, 1951, HHP, Box 150.D.10.9 (B), File: S.Res. 41 Cloture; Hubert Humphrey to Editors in the South, November 1951, HHP, Box 150.A.10.1(B), File: Letters to Southern Editors 1948–1951.

69. Cited in Caro, 460.

70. George Reedy, to Lyndon Johnson, January 1957, LJS, Files of George Reedy, Box 420, File: Reedy Memos January 1957.

71. David W. Rhode, Norman J. Ornstein, and Robert L. Peabody, "Political Change and Legislative Norms in the U.S. Senate, 1957–1974," in *Studies of Congress*, ed. Glenn R. Parker (Washington, D.C, 1985), 158–161.

3

Segregation and the City

WHITE SUPREMACY IN ALABAMA IN THE
MID-TWENTIETH CENTURY

J. Mills Thornton III

On September 6, 1944, Walton H. Craft, a sixty-five-year-old white resident of Mobile, dispatched a letter of complaint to Alabama's governor, Chauncey Sparks. Craft had come to Mobile in early 1942 to take a job at the city's booming Brookley Air Force Base, and each day he rode a city bus from his home to the field. He had become increasingly concerned about the pattern of racial segregation on the Mobile buses, under which there was no fixed racial dividing line. Whites filled from the front and blacks from the back, and the dividing line was wherever they met. On this particular morning, as often happened, the driver "allowed the Negroes to fill [the] rear and continue up the aisle two thirds of the way . . . hanging over the white women and girls. Frankly, it is not pleasant, not to mention the fact you have paid your fare to be transported to work, only to have some Negro hanging over you or his body touching you from time to time, the 'Negro Odor' some times almost more than a person can stand." That morning Craft had left the bus in disgust before reaching his destination. "I would suggest that a start be made in our own state to correct these practices that have grown to the extent they have, and I am of the opinion there is a State Law which requires the segregation of races, which is *not being followed by the present bus company*. The excuse some drivers give is, 'The orders are to bring a full load.' That may be an instruction; however, it does not give the Bus Company or the driver the right to disregard a State Law that is on the State's Book, as to the separation of the races. I called the Driver's attention to this matter as I left the Bus," but he seemed wholly uninterested.

The obviously deeply agitated Mr. Craft must have been astonished at the reply he received from Governor Sparks, to whom he had so confidently appealed. "If you will investigate the matter you will find, I think, that there is no law requiring the segregation of races in busses . . . Our segregation laws are few, and apply to such matters as schools, asylums, penitentiaries and things directly under the control of the state. Of course," the governor added, "we have what is known as the Jim Crow, or segregation law on railroads. This has been in existence for many years." But he concluded, "You can readily see, therefore, there are few segregation laws to be enforced."[1]

Many accounts of the Jim Crow South share Mr. Craft's misconceptions, unthinkingly depicting segregation in the region as a universal and uniform system. This error has distorted explanations both of segregation's origins and of the course of events by which it eventually was overcome. But Governor Sparks, an attorney who practiced law in the small Black Belt county seat of Eufaula, knew what he was talking about. In fact, in the summer of 1942, Assistant Alabama Attorney General Walter W. Flowers had undertaken a thorough survey of all state statutes and regulations bearing on racial segregation. State law required racial segregation in most institutions directly funded by the state, though not in all of them; the segregation of the state universities and of the state mental hospitals was merely a policy of their administrations, for instance. But beyond the state's own institutions, state statutes required racial segregation only in county jails (where sexual segregation was also required), railroad passenger cars and stations (a regulation that specifically exempted municipal trolley lines), and county poor houses and tuberculosis sanitariums. State law criminalized miscegenation and interracial sexual relations, and forbade white female nurses to nurse black men. The voter qualification provisions of the state constitution, though they did not mention race, had of course been adopted with conscious discriminatory intent, and the law did require that poll tax receipts be recorded separately by race. But that was the extent of state legislation on the subject of segregation.[2] The laws were exactly as Governor Sparks had said—few indeed.

Other facially non-racial provisions of the state constitution also had important implications for the structure of race relations, as did disfranchisement. White hostility to the substantial black influence on the county commissions of the plantation counties during Reconstruction had induced delegates to the Constitutional Convention of 1875 to place thoroughgoing restrictions on county authority, and these restrictions had been largely carried forward into the constitution of 1901. As a result, the activities of county commissions in twentieth-century Alabama were essentially limited to rural road construction and the maintenance of county property. Commissions did not have the power to adopt such social regulations as ordinances requiring racial segregation. If the legislature had not enacted such a requirement by statute—and generally it had not—then segregation existed in rural Alabama only as a result of the private actions of individual property owners. Rural taverns and roadhouses, for instance, certainly had racial identities, but only because their proprietors chose either to serve only a white or black clientele, or to adopt some other arrangement, such as agreeing to sell food to blacks who came to the back door and waited outside for it. Legal enforcement, when it was necessary, was available not as a result of a segregation ordinance, but through prosecutions for trespassing or disorderly conduct.

This observation leads to an important distinction between the worlds of urban and rural Alabamians. Race relations in rural Alabama were characterized not by segregation, but by white supremacy. Segregation, the statutory requirement of racially separate institutions, is only one manifestation of white supremacy, and by no means the most widespread. In Northern states, where legal segregation was very rare in the early twentieth century, racial discrimination was common. Stores, theaters, and restaurants frequently refused to serve blacks, and businesses quite generally refused to hire them. Indeed, the Congress of Racial Equality (CORE) had its origin in an effort by University of Chicago students in 1942 to induce downtown Chicago restaurants to accept black customers. And the hiring of black bus drivers in Philadelphia, as a result of wartime labor shortages, provoked a transit strike there in August 1944, which eventually required the intervention of the U.S. Army. In the North, as in rural Alabama, trespassing and disorderly conduct prosecutions could lend legal force to the discrimination.

But the pattern of white supremacy in rural Alabama was actually of a third sort. The discriminatory practices of rural stores and businesses were not its essential feature. Rather, it rested on the fact that the overwhelming majority of rural black Alabamians, especially in the Black Belt, were tenant farmers or sharecroppers on the property of white landowners. The direct, personal control by white landlords of each individual black tenant family rendered the compulsion of the state merely ancillary, and the discrimination of rural shopkeepers and restaurateurs simply supplemental. Other than in the public schools, white supremacy in rural Alabama did not express itself in the form of separate institutions, nor was it usually embodied in law. Rather, it was nongovernmental and peremptory, dependent not on political but on economic authority. If it became necessary, of course, the county sheriff could be called in, and here again trespass and disorderly conduct, mounting quickly to far more serious charges, could be deployed to reinforce the landlord's dominion. But intervention by the agencies of the state was not often needed. And when it was, courts, especially in the Black Belt, tended to defer to the landlord's authority. If the landlord appeared at a hearing for one of his tenants and assured the judge that he could handle the matter, the formal charges were very often dismissed.

White supremacy thus found many social expressions and took diverse institutional forms. It was only in the South's towns that circumstances compelled white supremacy to express itself in the form of legal requirements of segregation. And even here, as the situations of towns varied, so the structures of segregation that city authorities imposed were correspondingly manifold. The one thing that towns all shared, to a greater or lesser degree, depending on their size, was anonymity. And it is anonymity that most commended legal segregation to white supremacists in the cities. In urban areas, the direct, personal control possible in the countryside was attenuated. The compulsion available to rural landowners to maintain social discipline was in the towns vested in the police; and police officers sought aggressively to use it, freely administering extralegal discipline or arresting troublemakers whenever they thought it necessary. But the social dominance of the police in the cities either rested on force and fear or was mediated through the courts, and thus it lacked the personalized pervasive quality and the economic component that made the rural landowners' power so inescapable. The diverse occupations and varied sources of economic and social consequence characteristic of urban life afforded black town dwellers a level of independence and self-determination, however limited it may seem to us, that was seldom available in rural areas. And so, as the relations of blacks and whites became increasingly impersonal in the urban setting, so white supremacy inevitably came to seem most effectively expressed in the same impersonal terms of statute and ordinance.

In addition, because urban areas had a far greater variety of institutions and services that were subject to being segregated than did the countryside, the permutations of urban segregation were almost as many as the number of towns and the objects of municipal regulations. Commercial considerations dictated substantial differences between cities and small towns and even very detailed ordinances left much to be decided by individual businessmen. For instance, in cities with elevator segregation ordinances, some buildings maintained separate elevators; some permitted blacks only to use the freight elevator; others relegated them to the stairs. But most cities did not have ordinances on elevators; in some of them, particular buildings required segregation nevertheless, and others did not. In some cities, usually smaller ones, theater segregation took the form of seating blacks in the balcony and whites on the main floor. In other, usually larger, cities, there were separate black and white theaters. White hospitals often had separate black wards, frequently in the basement, but larger cities often also had separate, all-black hospitals. And so it was across the entire range of institutions.

Recognizing the great variety and radical localism of segregation as a manifestation of white supremacy goes far toward clarifying the persistent historiographical controversy over its origins. Howard Rabinowitz noted that the initial expressions of segregation in Southern towns stretched far back into Reconstruction immediately after emancipation, and often were adopted on the initiative of blacks themselves, as they pressed municipalities, for instance, to create a park to serve the new black citizens, as a parallel to an existing one for whites. C. Vann Woodward noted that through the 1870s and 1880s, most institutions in most Southern towns still lacked any legal requirement of racial segregation, and that such ordinances became general only in the decade from 1895 to 1905, as municipal politicians, responding to the political events of the period, rushed to emphasize their devotion to white supremacy by emulating segregation ordinances being adopted in neighboring towns across the region.[3] Each of these contentions is correct. They have appeared to be at odds only because scholars have so often confused the absence of segregation ordinances with the absence of white supremacy. Segregation as a manifestation of white supremacy, outside the schools and churches, ordinarily came late to the region, and when it came, it came as a requirement of law, with the exception of the railroad trains, only to the region's towns and cities. Moreover, its particular expressions evolved throughout the twentieth century, as municipal authorities tinkered with their ordinances and as individual business owners and managers altered its patterns in their own establishments. It was never a uniform system, though by about 1910, some form of it was to be found in virtually every institution in every town in the South. But the white supremacist attitudes of which segregation ordinances were a manifestation long preexisted segregation itself and, in fact, persisted almost as vigorously after segregation's elimination; the end of segregation as a specific expression of white supremacy by no means represented the extinction of white supremacist beliefs, nor foreclosed their appearance in other institutional forms.

The diversity in practice and the radical localism of segregation also form the key to understanding another point too seldom emphasized: that politics and policies at the state level during the twentieth century had very little influence upon the actual experience of race relations in the South. A succession of vitriolic racist demagogues—James Vardaman and Theodore Bilbo in Mississippi, Thomas Watson and Eugene Talmadge in Georgia, Thomas Heflin in Alabama, and too many like them elsewhere—manipulated racial animosities and exploited prejudice to attain political power. It is very easy to think of such men as the embodiment of segregation, and to conceive the ebb and flow of their influence as indicating harsher or more hopeful periods in the lives of black Southerners under the regime of Jim Crow. Nor, of course, was the violent rhetoric of such leaders without power to exacerbate tension and provoke violence. But the daily life of black people was shaped by local circumstance, ordinance, and practice. It could, and often did, vary greatly from town to town, even within a single county. Local authorities and employers, not state or national figures, were the true powers in the lives of ordinary black people, in both town and country. Thus, although the transformation wrought by World War II heralded the fall of empires, begat the United Nations, and transformed many aspects of American life, local authorities and practices shaped the daily reality endured by Alabama's blacks. For all the wartime rhetoric of democratic rights, the belligerency of the black media, and the contribution of black GIs, World War II left untouched, in all its diversity, the quotidian experience of white supremacy in Alabama. This point is crucial because it permits us to understand why the mobilization to disestablish segregation came—once it did, in the years following the war—from local demonstrations that arose from particular situations in individual cities and towns.

Alabama's three governors of the era of World War II—Frank M. Dixon, elected in 1938; Chauncey Sparks, elected in 1942; and James E. Folsom, elected in 1946—held views on race relations as divergent as the mainstream white South had to offer at this time. The fact that, with their very different racial attitudes, they followed each other immediately and served within so short a chronological period—a mere dozen years—makes an examination of their racial policies particularly instructive. It not only clarifies the practical limits that the political culture of the early-twentieth-century state imposed upon the range of views that successful politicians of the era might hold, it also reveals how very small was the significance of these differing attitudes for the actual lives of black Alabamians. The three governors came and went without altering the structure of white supremacy in Alabama in any but the most incremental ways.

Frank Dixon attended Phillips Exeter Academy, received his undergraduate degree from Columbia University, and took his law degree from the University of Virginia. A war hero, he lost a leg in air combat over France in World War I. The principal influence on the young man's developing views was his uncle Thomas Dixon, the former Baptist minister and friend of Woodrow Wilson, whose racist novels *The Clansman* and *The Leopard's Spots* were best sellers during Frank's childhood. Dixon spent much of his youth on his uncle's tidewater Virginia estate, and he thoroughly imbibed Thomas Dixon's deeply antagonistic beliefs about both blacks and Reconstruction. Following World War I, Frank Dixon commenced a law practice in Birmingham, firmly associating himself with the city's great corporations and wealthy industrialists. With their financial backing, he ran unsuccessfully for governor in 1934, and then successfully in 1938, defeating Chauncey Sparks.

The archetypal business progressive, Dixon sought efficiency and economy in government, and was a fierce opponent of Franklin Roosevelt's New Deal. His pro-labor, anti-industrialist predecessor Bibb Graves had built a powerful political organization on the dispensation of state patronage, and Dixon was determined to eliminate this source of liberal influence in the state. In the principal achievement of his administration, Dixon succeeded in driving through the legislature the state's first civil service law, the "merit system," as he called it. He also obtained a thorough reorganization of the state bureaucracy.

In race relations, Dixon was an aggressive and inflexible segregationist. He vigorously opposed federal anti-lynching and anti–poll tax legislation, both of which were initiatives of Northern liberals, intended to strengthen the social position of blacks in the South. Within Alabama, he supported, though unsuccessfully, a state constitutional amendment to limit the accumulation of unpaid back poll taxes to two years; but he insisted on the preservation of the poll tax itself. And though he claimed that state authorities could suppress lynching on their own, when the anti-lynching crusader Jessie Daniel Ames asked him to investigate one such incident, he simply denied that any lynching properly so called had occurred, and told her that he feared violence was always likely when the citizenry lost confidence in the willingness of the courts to punish rapists.

When a white woman wrote to complain about overhearing black men on a Birmingham bus ask white girls on dates, he replied that the situation "is one which is being brought on you by the activities of certain elements within the Federal Government. It is extremely serious and we are doing all that we can, but so long as those elements in Washington keep fomenting the disturbance, there is very little that we can do." And indeed, it was the Roosevelt administration that Dixon regarded as the root of the problem. "How far certain elements of the national administration are willing to go to try to force a change in the social structure of the South, I do not know," he wrote a member of Marengo County's governing body. "But I do know that every white man in Alabama has to be on one side in that particular matter: there aren't any two sides."[4]

It is hardly surprising, therefore, that President Roosevelt's executive order of June 1941, forbidding employment discrimination in war industries and establishing the Fair Employment Practices Committee (FEPC) seemed to Dixon to pose the direst threat; and especially so when, a year later, the FEPC came to Birmingham to hold investigatory hearings. Dixon responded to these hearings with an executive order of his own, creating the Alabama War Manpower Committee with the explicit charge to see that war mobilization did not in any way weaken the barriers of racial separation. Chaired by the segregationist Circuit Judge Walter B. Jones of Montgomery and with the equally segregationist Greensboro newspaper editor Hamner Cobbs as its executive director, the committee actively sought to forestall the federal challenge to white supremacy. As Dixon explained to a prominent railroad executive:

> As a result of the continued pressure of a small group of Northern fanatics at present connected with the national administration, the entire social and economic structure of the South is in danger. It is my sincere belief that the danger is real. Conditions make it impossible for the Southern white people to surrender their control without resistance, and the fact that we are engaged in war is being used by unscrupulous fanatics to put over a program of social revolution. I sincerely hope that we can cause them to see the error of their ways.

With the assistance of his legal-advisor, the arch-racist J. Miller Bonner of Camden, Dixon forbade all state agencies from accepting contracts that contained non-discrimination clauses; constantly pressured the War Department to keep a tight rein on black troops; and strongly opposed efforts to expand the training of black soldiers and airmen in the state. In 1948, Dixon would deliver an impassioned keynote address to the Dixiecrat convention that nominated Strom Thurmond for president.[5]

Dixon's challenger and successor Chauncey Sparks worked his way through Mercer University and its law school, and commenced a law practice in his native Eufaula in 1910. He was elected to the state house of representatives in 1919, and became a legislative floor leader for Governor Thomas E. Kilby. In that capacity he played a significant role in the passage of Kilby's important educational program, which more than doubled state expenditures for the public schools, expanded the authority of the state board of education, and placed new emphasis on vocational education programs. Sparks' devotion to the cause of education dates from this time. In 1930, Sparks was elected to the state senate as an opponent of the Ku Klux Klan and its Montgomery Cyclops (the Klan official immediately below a Grand Dragon), outgoing governor Bibb Graves. Over the next eight years, in response to the devastating national depression, he became a principal legislative advocate of retrenchment and an opponent of tax increases. Although he lost the 1938 gubernatorial election, the campaign allowed him to develop a statewide following. Nevertheless, he entered the 1942 race as an underdog behind his old nemesis Graves, who was seeking a third term. When Graves suddenly died shortly before the election, Sparks unexpectedly became the best-known candidate in the field, winning handily.

Sparks's advocacy of governmental parsimony during his time in the state senate led many observers to expect that he would obstruct progressive efforts, but the booming wartime economy and rapidly increasing tax receipts allowed him to return to his earlier enthusiasm for education. He obtained a doubling of support for public schools, which funded an extension of the school year from seven to eight months. He sponsored the establishment of a full-scale medical school in Birmingham for the University of Alabama, the creation of a forestry school at Auburn University, and a doubling of state support for Auburn's agricultural extension programs. But most importantly for our present focus on his racial attitudes, he championed very large increases in the state appropriations for its two black universities, Alabama State College at Montgomery and Alabama A & M at Huntsville, which permitted each of them to obtain Class A accreditation for the first time. And he sponsored an equally significant increase in state assistance to the semi-private Tuskegee Institute and the creation of a school of veterinary medicine there.

Commentators outside Alabama often thought Sparks's racial views essentially identical to those of Dixon; but the differences were quite clear to Alabamians of both races. Sparks was a classic paternalist. Following his election as governor but before his inauguration, Sparks received a letter from J. J. Green, the president of the Birmingham branch of the NAACP, asking him to meet with a black delegation. Though the letter took what for the time was a rather aggressive tone, insisting that the membership of any such delegation be chosen by blacks themselves rather than by Sparks, the governor-elect responded immediately and warmly. The result was his meeting with the Birmingham and Montgomery NAACP leadership on October 9, 1942, which produced proposals for expanding vocational training to qualify black workers for positions in war industries. Such a meeting with Dixon would have been simply inconceivable, and moved Green to acknowledge Sparks's "friendly and enlightened point of view." In early 1945, a black reporter for the *Pitts-burgh Courier*, John H. Young, visited Montgomery to assess the state of race relations there. Though he found the racism that he doubtless expected from many white leaders, his interview in the governor's office was of a very different order. Sparks greeted him cordially, explained in detail his extensive efforts to improve black higher education, spoke enthusiastically of the decline in black farm tenantry, and in response to the Supreme Court's recent decision forbidding white primary rules, welcomed the participation of qualified black voters in the state's Democratic primaries. "He is prejudiced," Young concluded. "At the same time he is no race-baiter or demagogue. I found him a gentleman who respected me." If Young had been the president of the United States, he said, Sparks could not have received him more honorably.[6]

Sparks's commitment to segregation was uncompromising, of course. In his inaugural address in January 1943, he said:

> The Negro and the white can live in peace in Alabama if they recognize and lay down as fundamentals two principles which are inviolable: first, complete racial segregation; second, independent racial development. With these fundamentals there can be builded [*sic*] in the South a relationship which carries with it justice, fair dealing, equal opportunity on the part of each race to acquire rights to which it is entitled, and which the laws will grant to it when achieved.

But the object of segregation was not, as he saw it, subordination. The acceptance of the inviolability of segregation would permit a society "relieved of the boogey and fear of inter-racial marriages, of amalgamation of any kind, of social equality," he told a convention of the black CME church in Birmingham in May 1944; it would thus allow the races to recognize their mutual interests and cooperate to achieve them. "The friendship between the two races in the South has been one of mutual benefit," he said in an address at Tuskegee Institute in April 1943. "I know there have been exploitation of the colored man and a considerable measure of economic cheating that today should be over. And it will be when we place our relationships upon fixed bases and strive for the bigger and better things of life." He continued, "Do you want economic justice? You are entitled to it. It should be guaranteed upon a basis of complete equality. Do you want a fair deal and all the protections of a civilized government? You are entitled to these and they should be guaranteed, and will [be]." He told the CME delegates, "White Supremacy does not mean injustice, exploitation, unfair discrimination; but means the preservation of that influence and that guiding hand which has enabled both the white race and the Negro race to advance thus far."

Sparks emphasized in his thinking the extraordinary material and educational progress among black Alabamians that he had witnessed since entering public life in 1919, and he conceived of white supremacy as the paternal mechanism through which that progress could be brought to ever greater heights. He defined the three pillars of his program for black racial uplift as education, economic improvement, and civil rights. It will seem odd today that a leader fully committed to segregation could understand himself as an advocate of civil rights, but he was explicit about the claim. "The Negro should be given his civil rights, which includes the right to vote, when he is qualified, on the same basis as the white man." He had, he said:

> urged, and will continue to urge, Boards of Registrars to reappraise their situation and to place upon the voting lists those of all races qualified by education, by training, by intelligence and by character to vote. . . . There can be no trouble here. The interests of the two races are identical. We have our homes side by side. We have our separate schools and churches, our communities. We have those things which tie us to a country and instill that loyalty which is essential. Why should we feel that the Negro, any more than the white man, will stray away from those things that are for the best interests of his community, of his State, and of his section?

It is clear that Sparks understood civil rights in exactly the same terms as he understood educational and economic progress, not as something inherent but as something into which people grew.[7]

Sparks, like Dixon, bristled at the interference of Northern reformers and the federal government. He denounced the FEPC as a foolish gesture. "To say that employment must be on a race percentage basis, denies the right to reward ability, fitness, experience and character. . . . We [might] just as well try to make individuals go to a certain church, dress according to a given style and pray thus." He strongly supported the poll tax. When the *Montgomery Advertiser* reported in August 1944 that the War Department had opened recreational facilities at Maxwell Air Force Base to airmen of both races, he dispatched an outraged telegram of protest to President Roosevelt; and indeed his complaint caused the base authorities quietly to suspend black access. This telegram brought a letter of hearty congratulation from former governor Dixon himself. But neither man would ever have thought he saw eye to eye on such questions. In 1948, while Dixon was taking an active role in organizing the Dixiecrat revolt, Sparks denounced it and supported the reelection of Harry Truman. This action damaged Sparks's reputation with many of his Black Belt admirers, and when he sought a second term in 1950, at the conclusion of James Folsom's first term, he was easily defeated by Gordon Persons. Such was the extent of the polarization in racial attitudes that had overtaken the state by the time of Sparks's death in 1968 that, as one historian observes, obituaries were hard-pressed to determine whether he was best described as a conservative liberal or a liberal conservative. But the commentator who called him a Whig was probably closest to the truth.[8]

James E. Folsom was both the son and the son-in-law of powerful polit-ical leaders in his native Coffee County, in Alabama's southeastern Wiregrass region. He dropped out of college after his sophomore year at the University of Alabama, served for a time as a local official of the New Deal's Civil Works Administration, and eventually became an insurance salesman. Following un-successful campaigns for Congress in 1936 and 1938, he moved to Cullman, in the state's hill country; and in the gubernatorial election of 1942, he finished second to Chauncey Sparks, taking a fourth of the vote. This showing posi-tioned him for his successful run for the governorship in 1946, when he defeated Lieutenant Governor Handy Ellis. He would be elected to a second term by an overwhelming margin in 1954.

Folsom was an egalitarian populist, committed to the cause of the state's small farmers and aggressively hostile to the alliance of Black Belt planters and Birmingham industrialists who in great measure controlled the legislature. But he was also an alcoholic who readily gave his confidence to a group of venal associates who exploited his personal weaknesses in order to line their pockets at the public expense. Despite his idealism, therefore, his time in office achieved far less than his admirers had hoped. The principal achievement of his first term was an extensive farm-to-market road-paving program. His conservative opponents defeated his strenuous efforts to hold a new state constitutional con-vention, to reapportion legislative seats to break the power of the Black Belt in the body, to repeal the poll tax, and to liberalize Alabama's highly restrictive voter registration laws.

Folsom's sincere desire for these reforms has often misled scholars about his racial views. They were reforms for which black leaders also very much wished, and that would have significantly strengthened the position of blacks in the state. But Folsom's enthusiasm for them primarily proceeded not from a concern for blacks but from his eagerness to elevate the fortunes of the white small farmer Wiregrass and hill county regions and to diminish the influence of Black Belt planters. Prominent blacks greeted Folsom's inauguration with great hope, and at once presented him with an extensive list of proposals to advance their race. As the months passed, it gradually became apparent to them that their proposals had simply disappeared into Folsom's files. In a letter to a white constituent in February 1949, Folsom stated flatly that he was opposed to the admission of blacks to white schools or universities under any circumstances. His legal adviser Ira B. Thompson informed a correspondent from Chicago, "As you are aware, the South will always insist on segregation as the best means of preventing race disturbances. In reality there is no race problem in the South. The Governor is very strong for each state settling all such problems by enactment of laws by its own legislature, or in other words the great principle set forth in the foundation of this government of states' rights."

In part, Folsom's refusal to embrace the cause of civil rights derived from principle, but in even greater part it derived from an essential indifference.

As a resident of the white sections of Alabama, he simply did not have a sufficiently strong understanding of the plight of blacks in the plantation and urban areas to see the elements of uniqueness in these areas' social and racial problems. He tended to conflate blacks' plight with the disproportionate political influence of the planter-industrialist alliance, and therefore to think it essentially an aspect of the predicament of white small farmers in the hills and the Wiregrass. His approach to the problem of legislative reapportionment is an example of his fixation on this dimension of the state's larger dilemma. He wanted to redistribute seats in the state house of representatives on a population basis, but he wanted to abolish the population basis altogether in the state senate, and instead to give each of the state's sixty-seven counties one state senator. This plan would indeed have eliminated Black Belt control of the legislature but would have done very little to address the specific and pressing social problems of either the cities or the plantation counties. Instead, it would have delivered permanent power to the rural white regions and their small farmer majorities. From Folsom's perspective, this represented the essential transformation necessary to set the state on the road to social justice.

A third factor that limited the extension of Folsom's egalitarianism to civil rights was that his own poor white electoral base was deeply divided on racial questions. The Ku Klux Klan's imperial wizard Dr. Elihu P. Pruitt, an elderly Birmingham physician, wrote Folsom in the summer of 1949, amidst rising racial violence in that city, to emphasize, "Your enemies are my enemies, my friends are your friends." Folsom himself had absolutely no sympathy for the Klan; indeed, he sought unsuccessfully to persuade Attorney General Albert A. Carmichael to sue to have the Klan's corporate charter revoked, and he led successful efforts to induce the legislature in 1949 to adopt an anti-masking law. But he relied on the support of many strong segregationists. For instance, though Folsom campaigned against the disfranchising Boswell Amendment to the state constitution, its author, attorney E. C. "Bud" Boswell of Geneva, was a powerful Folsom ally, and would become Folsom's legal advisor during the second term.

Against this background it is perhaps less surprising to learn that, though the social philosophies of Folsom and Chauncey Sparks differed vastly, the actual racial policies pursued by Folsom built upon those of the Sparks years. He obtained further large increases in appropriations for the state's black colleges, and in 1949 Folsom appointed a commission whose report urged even more aggressive efforts to expand the colleges' programs. Like Sparks, Folsom urged the county boards of voting registrars to display less hostility to applicants to register, placing his pleas primarily on the ground that returning veterans should have the right to participate in the government of their state. Several of Folsom's appointees to the boards were indeed open to the registration of blacks. But these appointments had less to do with a concerted policy than with rewarding Folsom's supporters in the gubernatorial election, for at least as many of the governor's appointees showed no particular willingness to accept black applicants. And even when the governor's own appointee was favorable, he was restrained by the appointees of the other two appointing officials, the state auditor and the commissioner of agriculture, each of whom was independently elected. Folsom summoned the auditor and the commissioner to public hearings at which rejected applicants told of their experiences before the boards; he hoped that this evidence would lead the other two officials to place pressure on their appointees to reform the various boards' practices, but the tactic was not successful. As complaints continued to pour in, the administration essentially threw up its hands. Folsom's executive secretary, O. H. Finney, wrote a black applicant rejected by the Jefferson County board that Folsom "has made every effort to force the Boards of Registrars of this State to register the people of Alabama according to the law. If the boards fail in their duty to the State and the Federal Government, they cannot blame this office." Folsom did repeatedly, if fruitlessly, urge the legislature to propose a constitutional amendment abolishing the poll tax, something Sparks had flatly opposed. But, in fact, Folsom's small farmer populism proved able to bring no more genuine changes to the lives of the state's blacks than had Sparks's plantation county paternalism.[9]

Like characters from Central Casting, Dixon the segregationist urban progressive, Sparks the Black Belt paternalist, and Folsom the egalitarian hill country populist each played his role to type. They represented in successive gubernatorial terms virtually the entire spectrum of racial attitudes that white Alabama politics had to offer. The hopes of Alabama's black citizens rose and fell with the changes in administration. However great were the differences in the racial attitudes of the three governors—and, within the constraints of Alabama's political culture in the era of disfranchisement, they were very great indeed—the gubernatorial succession nevertheless made virtually no truly lasting impact on the daily lives of black Alabamians.

The reason for the continuity is that the structures of white supremacy did not proceed downward from the state government that the governors headed. Changes in gubernatorial administrations or philosophies—or, for that matter, changes in federal administrations or national or global attitudes toward race—therefore had few real implications for blacks in Alabama. The structures of white supremacy, rather, were intensely, radically local, with the forms of legal segregation differing significantly from town to town and from institution to institution, and with white supremacy in the countryside largely a matter of personal power relationships. State government was far removed from the realities of segregation, and state policies, in practical terms, in large measure irrelevant to them. Increases in spending on black education would have an important longer term legacy—as would migration and economic changes resulting from the war, not to mention news of black military efforts and the postwar return of black GIs—but the war could not bring abrupt change to black life in Alabama.

The life of each town actually determined the shape of segregation within it, and when resistance to segregation arose, it almost invariably arose because of considerations and events as local as was the segregation itself. Events at the level of the state or the nation—even a world war—might contribute to a general mood, whether among whites or blacks. But precisely because the mood was general, it cannot account for the rise of resistance in one place rather than another. If we are to distinguish those towns that produced direct action against segregation from those quite comparable ones that did not, we must attend to the localism of segregation, the peculiarities of its forms, and the fabric of the particular political relations that created and sustained it.

These are precisely the dynamics that underlie the exchange of letters between Governor Sparks and Walton H. Craft about racial segregation on the buses of Mobile in 1944. Craft had assumed that Mobile bus segregation was, or should have been, merely an extension of a statewide pattern. The governor informed him that no such pattern existed. But the specific shape of the segregation on the Mobile buses that Craft noted would in fact have profound significance for the future history of the United States, and is worth further explication.

Segregation had first come to Mobile's streetcars at the beginning of November 1902, when the city council adopted an ordinance mandating it that was modeled on one adopted in Montgomery in August 1900. As had happened in Montgomery, the blacks of Mobile responded to the new ordinance with a boycott of the trolley lines, but in Mobile, unlike Montgomery, the ordinance also produced protests from whites. The ordinance required the streetcar conductors to order the reseating of passengers to preserve racial separation, and passengers of both races resented the inconvenience involved in being moved. Only a month after the ordinance had taken effect, the trolley company announced that the complaints had been so numerous that it had instructed its employees no longer to reseat customers. Blacks then resumed riding. The city at first arrested several conductors for dereliction of duty, but the company held firm and eventually the city quietly yielded. In April 1917, after more than fourteen years during which the streetcars had operated in practical defiance of the ordinance's terms, the city commission finally repealed it and substituted one that codified the actual practice. Under the new law, blacks seated from the back and whites from the front, and the dividing line was wherever they met. No passengers were unseated; the racial division was readjusted only by riders leaving the streetcar as they reached their destinations. When the trolleys were replaced by buses in the 1930s, the same arrangement was transferred to them. It was this pattern of segregation that Walton Craft found so unsettling.

Meanwhile, in Montgomery the unseating of passengers remained the norm. In a pattern that Montgomery streetcars adopted from those in Lynchburg, Virginia, in 1907, several front seats were kept reserved for whites, an equal number of rear seats for blacks, and the racial designation of the middle seats was readjusted by the conductor to accord with the changing composition of the ridership as the trolley moved along its route. This arrangement too was transferred to buses in the 1930s. Because it required the frequent re-seating of black riders, and when the bus was full, often forced them to stand, in violation of the actual terms of the city ordinance, it became a particular focus of black resentment in the crowded conditions on the buses during and just after World War II. Beginning with an appearance before the city commission in October, 1952, black leaders began to press the commission and the bus company to adopt the pattern of segregation in use in Mobile. The different arrangement in Mobile seemed especially salient to Montgomery blacks because both cities' bus companies were divisions of the same corporation, National City Lines of Chicago.

Black leaders continued to raise the Mobile plan of bus segregation in a series of meetings with city and transit officials throughout the early 1950s. It headed the list of proposals that black spokesmen presented to candidates for the city commission in the municipal election of March 1955. And during the campaign it became an even more emotional question when a black teen-ager, Claudette Colvin, was arrested and convicted for refusing a bus driver's order to vacate her seat. After the candidate endorsed by blacks for police commissioner was defeated by a strident white supremacist, black leaders began searching for some way to compel city officials to take their various concerns, and especially their concerns about bus seating patterns, more seriously. These events came to a head on the evening of December 1, 1955, when Mrs. Rosa L. Parks, the secretary of the Montgomery branch of the NAACP and a woman fully acquainted with the series of negotiations over the adoption of the Mobile seating plan, was ordered to yield her seat and was arrested for refusing the order. The black leadership at once rallied to her cause and initiated a boycott of the bus lines on the day of her trial, December 5. In negotiations during December 1955 and January 1956, the black organization created to run the boycott, the Montgomery Improvement Association, made the adoption of the Mobile pattern of segregation a prerequisite for ending the boycott. Only when these negotiations reached a stalemate at the end of January did the MIA's executive board finally, and quite reluctantly, authorize their attorney to file suit in federal court to seek to have the city bus segregation ordinance declared unconstitutional.[10]

Thus the differences in the particular patterns of bus segregation that had so angered Walton Craft in 1944 were precisely the same differences that lay at the heart of the Montgomery Bus Boycott in 1955. The fact that the leaders of the bus boycott initially sought simply the adoption of the Mobile pattern of seating segregation, and only very slowly came to embrace an attack on segregation itself, has sometimes caused students of these events to regard them as distinctly conservative. Indeed, the NAACP refused to assist the boycott in its first months, precisely because the Montgomerians were not seeking integration. A version of these attitudes is to be found also in some accounts of the civil rights struggles in the South during the Depression and World War II. Because those black and liberal white activists in the region who were outside the orbit of the Communist Party generally sought reforms to ameliorate the injustices of white supremacy, rather than genuine racial equality, they are often dismissed as little more than timid ratifiers of the status quo. But such analyses ignore the profound effects that the diverse municipal expressions of segregation had upon regional conceptions of social reality.[11]

Since the patterns of segregation in any one town could differ substantially from those in neighboring ones, and might often impose rather less onerous burdens on its black residents, the result was that reformers of both races conceived of the social reality that surrounded them, though suffused with racism, as malleable. Only after segregation came under sustained assault as the civil rights movement developed—and white supremacist true believers roused themselves to defend the racial status quo—were most blacks, and later whites, able to discover the pervasive inflexibility of the system. This discovery was in fact the greatest contribution of the civil rights movement's direct action phase, because it produced a willingness to embrace far more radical solutions than most racial liberals had theretofore contemplated. Earlier, the gradual amelioration of racial discrimination within the confines of separate development had seemed manifestly possible, because reformers could look to the existence of less burdensome arrangements in other cities, and there seemed to be nothing institutional that inhibited their adoption. The solution appeared merely to be the mobilization of sufficient community goodwill. Therefore the absolutist demands of the far left for immediate transformations in race relations seemed foolishly utopian; to the extent that they were ideally desirable, they would be achieved over time through the example of more progressive municipalities acting upon more recalcitrant ones.

In the light of massive resistance and the violence that surrounded too many of the direct action demonstrations, of course, the true rigidity of white supremacy became undeniable. The region did not possess within itself the capacity to save itself, in large part exactly because of the variety and complexity of its racial structures, since any fundamental reform of them would affect an almost infinite assortment of social interests. Only internal pressure sufficient to compel intervention from outside the South on the broadest possible scale could transform all of these structures at once. From that new perspective, indeed, it becomes clear that the hopeful reformers of the Depression and the wartime South were the genuine utopians. But to denigrate their moderation and optimism is to fail to recognize fully how diverse were the structures of segregation in the region's cities, and how apparently malleable they were in both the requirements and the specific application of the various municipal ordinances.

Those who are not attentive to the emphatic localism of segregation and its manifold peculiarities of place, then, will fail to understand both how it came into being in the first place, and also the process by which it was finally disestablished. Each is in fact a story that is entirely told only through a careful consideration of the level of the individual municipality, notwithstanding the sweeping regional, national and global changes of a world war.

Notes

1. Walton H. Craft to Chauncey Sparks, September 6, 1944, Chauncey Sparks to Walton H. Craft, September 7, 1944, Governor's Correspondence, SG 12491, folder 8, Alabama Department of Archives and History.

2. Walter W. Flowers to Thomas S. Lawson, memorandum, June 29, 1942, in Governor's Correspondence, SG 12491, folder 9, ADAH; see also Bernard F. Sykes to William McQueen, memorandum, August 28, 1944; ibid.

3. Howard N. Rabinowitz, *Race Relations in the Urban South, 1865–1890* (New York, 1978); C. Vann Woodward, *The Strange Career of Jim Crow*, 3rd ed., rev. (New York, 1974) and his *Origins of the New South, 1877–1913* (Baton Rouge, 1951). See also Woodward's *Thinking Back: The Perils of Writing History* (Baton Rouge, 1986), 81–99.

4. Frank M. Dixon to Jessie Daniel Ames, June 5, 1942, Dixon to Editors of *Encyclopedia Britannica*, July 9, 1941, both in SG12278, folder 13; Dixon to Kenneth McKellar, March 4, 1940, SG12248, folder 8; Mrs. Estelle Cassimus to Dixon, November 13, 1942, Dixon to Mrs. Cassimus, November 24, 1942, Dixon to E. A. Barley, September 17, 1942, all in SG12277, folder 29, Governors' Correspondence, ADAH.

5. Richard H. Powell to Frank M. Dixon, November 30, 1942, Dixon to Powell, December 1, 1942, Dixon to Lister Hill, May 12, 1942, Dixon to Gen. John P. Smith, March 4, 1942, Dr. R. B. McCann to Dixon, May 11, 1942, Dixon to McCann, May 13, 1942, all in SG12275, folder 5; Dixon to Pete Jarman, November 25, 1942, Dixon to Paul B. Johnson, November 25, 1942, both in SG12277, folder 25; Dixon to R. M. Jefferies, September 11, 1942, Dixon, undated memorandum to file (summer 1942), both in SG12277, folder 26; Minutes, War Manpower Committee meeting, September 3, 1942, Dixon to Horace Hall, August 21, 1942, SG12277, folder 28; Dixon to Donch Hanks, Jr., October 26, 1942, Dixon to Fitzgerald Hall, September 18, 1942 (quotation), SG12277, folder 29; Dixon to Ralph D. Williams, July 22, 1942, Henry T. DeBardeleben to Joe Starnes, July 29, 1942, Wallace D. Malone to Dixon, July 31, 1942, Joe Starnes to Dixon, July 24, 1942, Dixon to Frank Bone, August 24, 1942, all in SG12277, folder 30; Major Thomas H. Vaden to Chief of Labor Relations Branch, Civilian Personnel Division, Services of Supply, September 15, 1942, and attachments, SG12277, folder 31; Dixon to Richard H. Powell, October 13, 1942, Dixon to W. Logan Martin, October 22, 1942, Harry M. Ayers to Dixon, October 17, 1942, and attachments, all in SG 12278, folder 1; Walter B. Jones to Dixon, September 3, 1942 and attachment, Dixon to John Temple Graves, September 1, 1942, SG12278, folder 11, all in Governors' Correspondence, ADAH. On Dixon, see sketch by Glenn A. Feldman in Samuel L. Webb and Margaret E. Armbrester, eds., *Alabama Governors: A Political History of the State* (Tuscaloosa, 2001), 185–189; see also J. Mills Thornton III, *Dividing Lines:*

Municipal Politics and the Struggle for Civil Rights in Montgomery, Birmingham and Selma (Tuscaloosa, 2002), 144, 318–319, 655.

6. J. J. Green to Chauncey Sparks, July 11, 1942, Sparks to Green, July 15, 1942, Green to Sparks, July 21, 1942, Sparks to Carl W. Bear, September 9, 1942, Bear to Green, October 6, 1942, Wilbur H. Hollins to Sparks, December 10, 1942, all in SG 12491, folder 8; *Pittsburgh Courier*, February 3, 1945, clipping in SG 12501, folder 3, Governor's Correspondence, ADAH, all in SG12491, folders 8,9.

7. Chauncey Sparks, inaugural address, SG12527, folder 1, Tuskegee Institute Founder's Day address, SG12527, folder 3, CME convention address, SG12527, folder 8; see also Sparks to D. Ward Nichols, January 25, 1944, W. D. Hargrove to Sparks, May 8, 1944, C. Wesley Gordon to Sparks, May 27, 1944, all in SG12400, folder 14; John Temple Graves to Sparks, May 6, 1944 and May 7, 1944, Sparks to Graves, May 9, 1944, SG12501, folder 5; Sparks to J. Forney Johnston, June 9, 1945, SG12501, folder 3, all in Governors' Correspondence, ADAH.

8. Chauncey Sparks, CME convention address, SG12527, folder 8 (quotation); Statement of Governor Sparks on U.S. Supreme Court's white primary decision, April 3, 1944, SG12490, folder 8; John H. Bankhead to Sparks, August 31, 1944, Robert P. Patterson to Sparks, September 1, 1944, Frank M. Dixon to Sparks, August 31, 1944, N. Duke Kimbrough, Jr., to Sparks, August 27, 1944, Talmadge Winn to Sparks, August 24, 1944, Sam Erle Hobbs to Sparks, wire, August 26, 1944, Ernest D. LeMay to Sparks, September 13, 1944, Sparks to Horace Wilkinson, August 31, 1944, all in SG12491, folders 5,6; Champ Pickens to Sparks, February 15, 1943, R. F. Finkley to Sparks, February 16, 1943, Harry M. Ayers to Sparks, August 31, 1943, all in SG12491, folder 9; James E. Chappell to Sparks, April 8, 1943, Sparks to Chappell, April 10, 1943, SG12501, folder 5; George Bliss Jones to W. R. Ragland, March 7, 1946, SG 12515, folder 5; R. T. Nelson to Sparks, February 27, 1946, A. H. Harris to Sparks, January 31, 1946, Lillian P. Long to Sparks, October 29, 1945, SG12515, folder 6; Sparks to Dr. J. C. Foshee, December 11, 1946, Henry Husing to Sparks, November 29, 1946, and Text of Associated Press interview with Governor Sparks on the adoption of the Boswell Amendment, November 8, 1946, SG12521, folder 31, all in Governors' Correspondence, ADAH; Harvey H. Jackson, sketch of Sparks in Webb and Armbrester, eds., *Alabama Governors*, 190–193.

9. Mrs. Belzora S. Ward to James E. Folsom, January 21, 1947, Robert Durr to Folsom, March 17, 1947, SG 13422, folder 1; Durr to Folsom, September 23, 1947, Folsom to P. L. Brownlow, February 11, 1948, Ira B. Thompson to Gilbert S. Derr, March 25, 1948, SG 13441, folder 5; Thompson to V. G. Appleby, August 4, 1948, Robert Durr to Folsom, August 30, 1948, Folsom to Durr, September 1, 1948, SG 13441, folder 6; W.H. Drinkard to Mrs. W. H. Duke, May 23, 1946, Mrs. Duke to Folsom, October 26, 1948, Mrs. Duke to Folsom, November 12, 1948, Ira. B. Thompson to Mrs. Duke, November 22, 1948, Thompson to Henry Hannan, September 29, 1948, SG 13461, folder 5; Thompson to Sen. John C. Stennis, September 3, 1948, J. J. Green to Folsom, August 15, 1949, E. D. Nixon to Folsom, June 6, 1949, A. C. Maclin to Folsom, June 2, 1949, Bankhead Bates to Folsom, June 8, 1949, O. H. Finney Jr. to E. D. Nixon, June 8, 1949, Clara Hard Rutledge to Folsom, January 4, 1949, SG 13461, folder 6; Press release, January 3, 1949, W. C. Patton to Folsom, January 7, 1949, Minutes of organizational meeting of Negro higher education committee, January 14, 1949, Minutes of committee meeting, March 12, 1949, Rev. J. R. Wingfield to Folsom, January 14, 1949, SG 13450, folder 6; Minutes of meeting of Negro

higher education committee, March 26, 1949, and attached statistics, SG 13450, folder 7; Minutes and Final Report of Negro higher education committee, April 20, 1949, SG 13450, folder 8; Ira B. Thompson to Alberta Sierras, November 30, 1949, Thompson to Mrs. W. H. Duke, January 12, 1950, Folsom to T. A. Langford, June 9, 1950, SG 13473, folder 7; O. H. Finney Jr. to John G. Hosey, May 17, 1949, Hosey to Folsom, May 18, 1949, E. J. "Gunny" Gonzales to Finney, May 28, 1949, Gonzales to Finney, June 7, 1949, Gonzales to Finney, June 18, 1949, Gonzales to Folsom, July 15, 1949, George D. Patterson Jr. to Folsom, July 12, 1949, Ralph R. Britain to Folsom, June 21, 1949, O. H. Finney Jr. to J. Milton Schnell, June 24, 1949, J. Milton Schnell and Mrs. D. C. Randle to Folsom, July 10, 1949, Gonzales to Finney, July 21, 1949, Finney to Gonzales, July 27, 1949, Gonzales to Finney, August 2, 1949, Gonzales to Finney, August 13, 1949, Ira B. Thompson to John G. Hosey, November 18, 1949, Charles S. Lanier to Folsom, November 23, 1949, Gonzales to Thompson, December 1, 1949, Willie Louis Dick to Folsom, December 3, 1949, Finney to Dick, December 6, 1949, J. D. Culp to Thompson, December 5, 1949, Emory O. Jackson to J. Howard McGrath, December 10, 1949, N. C. Fulmer to Haygood Patterson and Dan Thomas, December 10, 1949, Emory O. Jackson to Folsom, December 6, 1949, Thompson to Jackson, December 14, 1949, O. H. Finney to Haygood Patterson and Dan Thomas, December 14, 1949, Sam S. Douglass to Folsom, January 4, 1950, Robert Thrasher to Folsom, December 19, 1949, all in SG 13473, folder 13; Thornton, *Dividing Lines*, 163–164, 167. On Folsom, see George E. Sims, *The Little Man's Big Friend: James E. Folsom in Alabama Politics, 1946–1958* (Tuscaloosa, 1985) and Carl Grafton and Anne Permaloff, *Big Mules and Branchheads: James E. Folsom and Political Power in Alabama* (Athens, 1985).

10. A full account of these events is in Thornton, *Dividing Lines*, 20–96.

11. This misunderstanding limits the usefulness, for instance, of Glenda E. Gilmore, *Defying Dixie: The Radical Roots of Civil Rights, 1919–1950* (New York: Norton, 2008).

4

Movement Building during the World War II Era

THE NAACP'S LEGAL INSURGENCY IN THE SOUTH

Patricia Sullivan

"There is nothing much to report here," NAACP assistant secretary Roy Wilkins wrote on December 1, 1941, in a letter to field organizer Madison Jones. "Thurgood is back from Texas, Louisiana, Florida and way stops. . . . He left with a tooth brush and one shirt thinking he would be gone only two days, but he was gone twenty-eight. Fred and Walter are in Indiana in a combining job speaking for the YWCA forum and reviving the Indianapolis branch. . . . Daisy had two very fine campaigns in Wilmington, Delaware and Chester, Pennsylvania. Ella managed the campaign in Albany (N.Y.) and is in the office until at least after the holidays. . . . We are continuing to pound on the main theme of the Negro in national defense, and there seems to be a little progress here and there."[1]

Wilkins's letter, written on the eve of America's entry into World War II, reveals a defining feature of the thirty-year-old organization. Its nationwide spread and highly mobile staff made it a vital barometer of black life and race relations across America. The NAACP, dependent largely on membership for funding, was a lean enterprise anchored in communities throughout the country. This loose infrastructure was reinforced in the South by the legal campaign launched by Charles Hamilton Houston in the mid-1930s and carried forward under Thurgood Marshall. With the exception of Wilkins, the association's small professional staff—all named in Wilkins's letter—spent most of their time outside the national office in New York, investigating conditions, recruiting members, working with branches to fight racial injustices, and, in the case of Executive Secretary Walter White, lobbying in Washington. Four of the seven were full-time field workers: veteran organizers Daisy Lampkin and Frederick Morrow and newly hired Ella Baker and Madison Jones.

Social dislocation, wartime expansion of federal power, and the enlistment of nearly a million black men and women in the armed forces combined to fuel heightened black resistance to the racial barriers that structured American life. The NAACP was uniquely positioned to engage these far-reaching changes, providing support for collective protest and sustained activism while putting civil rights on the nation's agenda. During the war, the association established a Washington Bureau, strengthening its lobbying position in the nation's capital and bolstering its role as part of the coalition of liberal and labor groups in ascendancy under the Roosevelt administration. At the same time, membership numbers, which hovered at 50,000 in 1940, skyrocketed to 400,000 by the end of the war, securing the NAACP's position as a mass-based organization with a national reach.[2]

The broad reach and diverse range of NAACP activism offers critical insight to the formative trends that emerged during and after the war—in Washington and in communities across the country—at a time when rising black demands pressed the limits of the nation's willingness to confront the racial inequity and division that became even more pronounced under the strains of war. President Roosevelt's executive order banning discrimination in defense industries, enacted in June 1941 under the threat of a mass march on Washington, was a singular if highly significant development. Overall, federal policy reinforced the racial status quo—from segregated blood banks to segregated armed forces. In Congress, white Southerners shored up their power during the war years while battles along the color line in Northern urban areas intensified and frequently erupted into violence, including major race riots in Detroit and New York.[3]

Within this climate, the South emerged as the staging ground in the struggle to challenge the racial barriers and injustices that permeated American society. Just months prior to America's entry into the war, NAACP field reports revealed a rising spirit of resistance in the most racially repressive area of the country, a sentiment to which the NAACP attorneys and organizers gave voice, form, and structure. War mobilization, experiences of black troops in the region, and the rhetoric of the "Four Freedoms" all served to fuel black challenges to the region's rigid caste system. While a host of restrictions reinforced by a climate of terror kept most blacks from voting, the NAACP's legal campaign emerged as the platform for black men and women to articulate and act upon constitutionally guaranteed rights, inspiring heightened efforts to vote. When veterans returned from battling the forces of fascism in Europe, they invigorated the push against the hard shell of Jim Crow. By the late 1940s, an organized movement targeting the roots of America's racial caste system placed the South on the front line in the burgeoning movement for civil rights.

"I am seeing so much and meeting so many people . . . that I could write a book," Madison Jones reported to Walter White. "There is a gold mine if we want to take the time and money to make an investment of concerted action." The thirty-one-year-old New Yorker traveled South for the first time in the fall of 1941 on a multipurpose assignment that took him from Virginia through South Carolina, Georgia, Alabama, Tennessee, and North Carolina. With his portable typewriter, he catalogued his impressions in a series of lengthy letters as he worked to develop youth councils and college chapters, visited branches, and did preliminary work in North Carolina for Ella Baker with an eye toward building up a state conference of branches. Jones became absorbed in the lives of the people he met and the challenges they faced—from rural areas in Alabama and North Carolina, to centers of defense production, like Memphis, Tennessee, and a major military camp at Fort Bragg in Fayetteville, North Carolina. While circumstances varied greatly from place to place, he repeatedly commented on conditions of resistance that were ripe for cultivation.[4]

In every place he visited, Jones found that blacks were making efforts to vote, and in many cases succeeding. He reported on the gains made following a successful suit against a registrar near Wilkesboro, North Carolina, five years earlier. "Every black who has the courage to register votes," and positive results could be seen in paved streets, street lights, and other community improvements. The Talladega, Alabama, branch of the NAACP had launched a citizenship training program, working in conjunction with the churches and clubs. They sponsored classes in black history and had a public speaking committee—all dedicated toward getting "people out to vote." In Macon County, Alabama, the heart of the Black Belt, T. Rupert Brody, a twenty-four-year-old Tuskegee Institute professor, refused to give up after a registrar turned him away and the judge of the probate court "stormed out in a rage at the hearing" when he realized that Brody wanted to vote. After learning that Brody planned to file a suit, the office of the registrar phoned him and requested that he return the next day. "That spirit," Jones reported, "is indicative of the trend down here through the South."[5]

The "spirit" that Jones described had been engaged by NAACP organizers since the early days of the association, starting with Kathryn Magnolia Johnson, the first NAACP fieldworker to travel South, through an intense period of organizing and growth during and immediately after World War I. But, until the late 1930s, sustained momentum proved elusive. Fierce white opposition to any perceived challenge to the racial status quo wiped out the inroads made during the World War I era. A massive campaign of terror waged against black civic activists from 1919 through the election year of 1920 and culminating with the Tulsa race riot of 1921 illustrated how little the NAACP could do to secure redress against the state-sanctioned repression of black political activity. Despite massive publicity efforts and an intensive lobbying effort in Washington in 1921–1922, the NAACP failed to muster sufficient support for an anti-lynching bill, providing for federal prosecution of those responsible for the vigilante-style torture and murder of black people. In the early 1920s, lynchings averaged one a month. Many concluded that NAACP-led efforts were not only dangerous, but futile.[6]

The initiation of the NAACP's legal campaign under Charles Hamilton Houston in 1934, just as the reformist activism of the New Deal elevated black civic engagement, created a fresh arena for Southern blacks to stand against the brutal and routine violation of constitutional guarantees with the support of a national organization. Houston, a Harvard-educated lawyer and dean of Howard Law School, imagined a unique role for black lawyers, and he implemented his idea as the first Special Counsel for the NAACP. He described the black lawyer as a "soldier" who would serve as an "adviser of the people" and, with them, take the battle for political and civil rights into the courts. Robert Carter, a young attorney and World War II veteran who would help realize Houston's vision, explained it this way: "We were a small operation trying to use the law to revolutionize race relations by seeking to have the Thirteenth, Fourteenth and Fifteenth amendments given their intended effect."[7]

Fundamental to this effort was a patient and long-term program of field-work dedicated to cultivating the political will and courage of people who had long lived under the heel of racial oppression, and creating opportunities for them to act—as petitioners, voters, and plaintiffs—in short, as citizens. The NAACP legal campaign focused on a broad array of issues—jury service, criminal justice, equal education, access to public accommodations, and voting rights. Working closely with NAACP fieldworkers and local NAACP leadership, Houston and his former student Thurgood Marshall traveled tens of thousands of miles through the region, not just to build the program but to demonstrate to people on the ground that they were not alone in the fight for freedom—a critical element in sustaining participation in the face of danger, violence, and even death.

The exposed and unprotected position of civil rights activists in the South was on full display in the late spring of 1940 when whites in Brownsville, Tennessee, set out to eliminate the leadership of a newly established NAACP branch after they had initiated a voter registration effort. A dozen men, including the sheriff-elect, abducted Elbert Williams, the secretary of the branch, beat him to death, and threw his body in the river. The rest of the branch leadership was driven from town. NAACP officials demanded and secured an investigation of Williams's murder by the FBI; Thurgood Marshall pursued his own investigation, tracking down witnesses who had dispersed as far as Chicago and New York, collecting sworn testimony identifying mob members. Despite what appeared to be a clear-cut case, in January 1942 the Justice Department held that there was insufficient evidence to warrant prosecution of Williams's alleged assailants.[8]

The claim made by Williams and his neighbors on the most fundamental element of citizenship grew more insistent during the war, fueling a dramatic spike in NAACP membership in the South. The resiliency of voting rights efforts broadened the civil rights battlefront in the region at a time when the urgency of defense-related issues, particularly concerning jobs and the treatment of black soldiers in the Armed Services, drove much of the NAACP's agenda. Endless cases of court martial, dishonorable discharges, and the rampant branding of black soldiers as rapists demanded much of Thurgood

Marshall's time and attention. These areas temporarily eclipsed the major push for educational equality that had been launched by Charles Houston and Marshall, although equal teacher salary cases continued to percolate through the Southern branches. But the fight for the vote in the South escalated and created the foundation for building a political movement in the region. The war, Madison Jones reported after a trip to the South in the summer of 1942, "caused the Negro to change almost instantly from a fundamentally defensive attitude to one of offense"—the measure of this change expressed in a major push forward on the voting rights front.[9]

Thurgood Marshall and Ella Baker, the lead fieldworker in the South during the war years, were keenly attentive to the unique wartime challenges and opportunities. A new generation of leaders, many seasoned by the activist politics of the 1930s, had come to the fore—A. P. Tureaud and Daniel Byrd in Louisiana, Harry T. Moore in Florida, Reverend Ralph Mark Gilbert in Georgia, Kelly Alexander and Leila Bell Michael in North Carolina, and James Hinton and Mojeska Simkins in South Carolina—individuals who, in the words of Madison Jones, were not afraid "to stick their necks out." Baker and Marshall became well acquainted with local leaders and kept an eye out for leadership talent. Working separately and in tandem, they created structures and supported campaigns targeted to strengthen and reinforce the efforts of local communities and link them in state- and region-wide campaigns against the Jim Crow system. Underscoring a shared understanding of the fundamental importance of this "ground work," Marshall bluntly observed that "the NAACP can move no faster than the individuals who have been discriminated against."[10]

Ella Baker, a native of North Carolina, joined the NAACP as a fieldworker in 1941, and was elevated to director of branches in 1943—making her the highest-ranking woman on the national staff. Her approach to organizing complemented and reinforced the legal insurgency initiated under Houston and carried forward by Marshall. Her field reports and letters reveal tireless efforts to extend the reach of the NAACP to all segments of the community. She visited pool rooms, boot black parlors, and bars and grills, as well as traditional venues—churches, fraternal organizations, women's clubs, and civic groups—working to build up membership, strengthen branches, and cultivate local leaders. No meeting was too small. Baker wrote of the great satisfaction she felt when "one or more persons" who had been "hard to convince" or had even opposed the NAACP experienced "a change of heart" and signed up. The branches, Baker often commented, were the "life blood" of the association—not so much for the membership revenue produced, but the work that members initiated and supported. She instructed her associates that the "aim of raising money be properly placed in the background of an all-out massive offensive against discrimination, injustice, and undemocratic practices."[11]

At a time when Southern blacks were largely excluded from participation in formal electoral politics, the legal campaign became a major instrument for organizing blacks around a program of civic activism, targeting racial barriers. The fight against the all-white primary emerged as the NAACP's major legal battle during the war years. In June 1940, the month Elbert Williams was murdered, Thurgood Marshall joined forces with a vibrant constellation of NAACP leaders in Texas, including Lulu White of Houston and Maceo Smith of Dallas, to revive the challenge to black exclusion from the Democratic primary in that state, a battle that black Texans had been fighting since the 1920s. On April 3, 1944, the U.S. Supreme Court issued a sweeping decision in the case of *Smith v. Allwright,* which, once and for all, knocked the legal props out from under what had been the South's most effective disfranchisement tool. "The Texas primary case was the beginning of a complete revolution in our thinking on the right of suffrage," proclaimed Virginia activist Luther Porter Jackson.[12]

Just three months after the white primary ruling, Walter White offered a grim assessment of America's unwavering color line in the midst of a war fought against Nazism under the banner of freedom and democracy. In a speech to a mass gathering of 30,000 people in Chicago's Grant Park, he bore down on federal policies that supported the expansion of racial division and inequality, citing examples from the discriminatory practices of the Federal Housing Authority to the segregated Armed Services. The government and its agencies, he charged, persisted in "basing their racial patterns on the lowest common denominator of American thought and action," betraying little faith in "the inherent decency of white Americans." Weary of the power of Southern Democrats to hold their party and the nation hostage with its threats of revolt, White mused that "perhaps democracy can be saved only by letting the rebels secede until the South is ready to obey the constitution and the laws of human decency."[13]

White identified the fault line of Democratic Party politics as he looked toward the battles looming after the war. He angled to link the struggles of black Americans to the worldwide movement against colonialism and the "certainty of white supremacy," determined to focus national and international attention on America's race problem just as the nation emerged as the strongest democratic power in the world. These would be major areas of activity for the NAACP in the years immediately following the war. But the campaign to crack Jim Crow and challenge the nation's segregationist culture would take root in Southern communities, initially organized around the effort to enforce the Supreme Court's white primary ruling and to support growing black efforts to vote.

In what, in retrospect, resembled a rehearsal for the white South's response to the *Brown* ruling a decade later, South Carolina was joined by Alabama, Georgia, and Florida in an effort to maintain a whites-only primary, defying the Court's mandate. In other states, registrars experimented with different forms of disfranchisement—arbitrary rules, shortened hours, outright refusal to allow blacks to vote. Working with local NAACP leaders and a handful of black attorneys scattered throughout the South, Marshall orchestrated a major offensive to secure the enforcement of the Court's ruling. He instructed all branches in states where the white primary had been practiced to help get black men and women to the polls on primary day and instructed them on how to proceed in collecting sworn affidavits if turned away. Marshall inundated the Justice Department with evidence of voter violations at the ballot box. Meanwhile, he worked with NAACP officials in South Carolina and other obstructionist states to compel them to obey the Court's ruling, and brought two cases from Louisiana and Alabama that succeeded in streamlining the procedure for suing registrars who violated black voting rights. Marshall prepared for the long haul, predicting that the NAACP would be involved in legal action against "officers in various localities to ensure Negroes in the South the right to vote" for some years to come.[14]

Marshall and Baker worked collaboratively to harness the energy coming out of the war. Along with peak membership, returning veterans infused Southern black activism with a steely determination to vote and exercise the rights of citizenship. "I know I paid the price," said one veteran in Louisiana. "If I could go there and make a sacrifice with my life . . . I was willing to do it here, if it meant death."[15] While Marshall concentrated on the legal front, Baker supported action-oriented branches which, in her words, should serve as "centers of sustained and dynamic leadership." She organized structures and programs designed to support local leaders, strengthen their connections within their individual states and regions, and integrate them more fully into the national program. At the end of the war, she initiated a series of regional leadership training conferences that brought branch leaders in adjoining states together with national staff members, including Thurgood Marshall and Leslie Perry, administrator of the Washington Bureau. Rosa Parks and E. D. Nixon, leaders in the Montgomery, Alabama, branch, were among the participants. In the aftermath of the white primary ruling, Baker was in regular contact with branch leaders to remind them of deadlines for paying poll taxes and to emphasize the importance of "backing up the legal victories . . . with vigorous registration and voting campaigns." She urged them to coordinate their voter registration efforts with labor and progressive groups dedicated to building an inclusive democracy in the South and countering the inflated power of conservative Southern Democrats.[16]

The end of World War II marked ground zero in the civil battles that would rage in the South for the next two decades. In 1946, the first election season in which the impact of the white primary ruling could be fully realized, signs of political change were everywhere as a variety of groups joined in the effort to help register black voters—including regional groups such as the Southern Conference for Human Welfare (SCHW) and the Southern Negro Youth Congress. CIO Political Action Committee organizer Henry Lee Moon found "a politically inspired people . . . who were registered and making the fight to get more registered." Community groups were "setting up schools to instruct new voters in the intricacies of registration, marking the ballot, and manipulating the voting machine."[17] Reporting as a field organizer for the SCHW, South Carolina activist Osceola McKaine found that people had come to a new understanding that "the use and nonuse of the ballot can determine whether they have a job or become jobless, whether they shall have adequate schools and school bus transportation for their children or whether the present handicaps to their educational and personality development shall continue or become intensified."[18] With the ballot, claimed NAACP Florida leader Harry Moore, "we shall be well on our way to solving some of the most serious problems that have faced us during the past fifty years."[19]

A wave of violence and terror in 1946 announced that Southern whites were determined to repress black political aspirations and enforce the caste system, as they had after World War I. At the start of the year, in Columbia, Tennessee, a fistfight between a black man and a white man, both veterans of World War II, sparked a chain of events that led to a massive police raid on the black section of town, backed by state patrolmen and National Guardsmen. They shot up homes and destroyed most of the business establishments in "true storm trooper fashion," in the words of Thurgood Marshall. Scores of blacks were arrested and two died in police custody. Several other incidents exposed the lawlessness that reigned in most parts of the South. In Aiken, South Carolina, a sheriff assaulted and blinded Isaac Woodard, who was still in his army uniform, after Woodard had a verbal dispute with a bus driver. Two black couples were abducted by a mob in broad daylight and executed in Monroe, Georgia, where a climate of terror had been stoked by Governor Eugene Talmadge in his bid for reelection during a tight, three-way primary race.[20]

Appeals to white supremacy dominated the 1946 primary election season, reaching their most extreme expression in statewide campaigns in Georgia and Mississippi. In Georgia a federal district court overturned the state's efforts to bar blacks from voting in the primary, and black voter registration in the state increased by more than sixfold to 135,000. Talmadge described the 1946 primary election as the last chance to "save Georgia for the white man." He pledged to restore the all-white primary and welcomed the endorsement of the Ku Klux Klan—ultimately clinching a win with the aid of supporters throughout the state who terrorized blacks in rural communities and engaged in widespread purging of blacks from the voting rolls. In Mississippi, Senator Theodore Bilbo instructed "every red-blooded Anglo-Saxon in Mississippi" to do whatever was necessary to keep blacks from voting. Mississippi branches flooded the national office with sworn statements by blacks who were barred from voting by a variety of methods—from outright refusals by election officials to abductions, beatings, and threats at gunpoint. "We Negroes are without any protection at all," reported V. R. Collier, president of the NAACP branch in Gulfport, whose tenacity proved no match for determined local officials.

Only half of the 5,000 registered black voters cast ballots on primary day; an estimated 350,000 blacks were of voting age in Mississippi.[21]

Mob terror and state-sponsored violence against black citizens across the South combined with other civil rights battles coming out of the war and tested the ability of the NAACP, as an organization, to hold ground and move forward. The fragility of the enterprise and the internal weaknesses of the association were exposed in developments involving Ella Baker and Thurgood Marshall. Weary of working against the grain of an organizational culture dominated by the authority and personality of Walter White, Baker resigned in the summer of 1946. White, who had established a firm base of operation in Washington, saw the legislative arena as the primary front in the battle for civil rights, and, in the resource-strapped organization, viewed work in the field as most valuable for producing membership fees to support the fight in these larger arenas. He discounted Baker's leadership skills and opinions and failed to provide the branch department with the support it desperately needed. Baker found too much of her "energy was dedicated to fighting a sense of futility and frustration." In leaving, she made a distinction between the leadership that now dominated the national office and the organization she had done so much to shape in five short years. "In every possible way," she wrote, "I shall keep faith with the basic principles of the NAACP and with the faith vested in it by the people."[22]

Thurgood Marshall worked himself to the brink of physical collapse. During the summer of 1946, while running a high fever, he toughed it out through three days of preliminary hearings in the cases resulting from the Columbia, Tennessee, police invasion before finally being hospitalized for pneumonia. He spent an extended period in Harlem Hospital and, under the strict orders of his physician, did not begin traveling again until later in the fall, just as the Columbia cases were winding down. With his health restored, he immediately returned to Tennessee for the trials of the remaining two defendants and came perilously close to the fate that claimed Elbert Williams. The night after the verdicts were issued, Marshall and two fellow lawyers and a news reporter headed back toward Nashville. A mob of men, including several law enforcement officials, stopped their car three times and finally arrested Marshall on the trumped-up charge of drunk driving. His associates ignored orders not to follow the caravan of cars carrying Marshall toward the Duck River, causing his abductors to change course and head to a nearby town. They finally released the attorney after a late night hearing before a local judge.[23]

Barely a month after Marshall's near lynching, a scene in the federal courthouse in Jackson, Mississippi, offered striking evidence of the change that was taking place, even in the deepest reaches of the South. Black Mississippians had filed complaints with the U.S. Senate, documenting the terror and fraud that accompanied Senator Bilbo's primary election, and in response a special Senate committee held an investigative hearing in Jackson early in

December. The five-person committee, chaired by Louisiana senator Allen Ellender, did not subpoena witnesses, but relied on volunteers to come forward. As a consequence, Charles Houston noted, many thought "Mississippi victims might be afraid to testify." But Houston, who represented the NAACP at the hearing, reported on the morning that the hearings opened, two hundred men, mostly veterans, "packed the courthouse volunteering to testify . . . regardless of possible reprisals against their property, businesses, and families." "Not since Reconstruction days," observed the *Chicago Defender,* had there been so "challenging a manifestation of racial solidarity" in the Deep South.[24]

The hearing was most important for what it revealed, rather than the ultimate ruling of Senator Ellender's committee exonerating Bilbo. "For the first time in over fifty years, the stinking record of terror and intimidation was exposed in a public, statewide hearing," reported Houston. Over the course of four days, sixty-eight black men gave testimony describing armed men standing outside of polling places, reporting on beatings and assaults, and telling of ballot boxes stuffed with newspapers. Many named their assailants. There were frequent references to the "new law," the 1944 Supreme Court ruling on the white primary, which secured their right to vote in the Democratic primary elections. The men spoke with "forcefully moving language," observed a *New York Times* reporter, and collectively made "a picture of a steadily awakening political consciousness."[25]

A catalog of Southern outrages during 1946—the blinding of veteran Isaac Woodard, the vigilante execution of two black couples in Monroe, Georgia, the riot in Columbia, Tennessee, and the political fraud and terror on display during the primary election season that summer—gave Walter White a little more leverage in what had been a largely futile effort to attract the attention of President Harry Truman. Since assuming the presidency in the spring of 1945, following the death of Franklin Roosevelt, Truman seemed, at best, indifferent to the nation's racial crisis and solicitous of his party's powerful Southern wing. In September, Truman promised White that he would establish a committee to investigate the problem of mob violence and racial terror in the South. The president found the incentive to act at the end of 1946, following a Republican landslide at the polls in the mid-term elections, which revealed a major defection of black voters from the Democratic Party in crucial Northern urban areas. Early in December, he quietly issued an executive order establishing a committee on civil rights. The statement acknowledged that the federal government was obliged to act affirmatively when state or local authorities failed to protect the "individual liberties and equal protection under the law" guaranteed by the Constitution, and instructed the committee with recommending legislative remedies that would provide the federal government with "more adequate and effective means and procedures for the protection of the civil rights of the people of the United States."[26]

Nearly a year later, the President's Committee on Civil Rights issued *To Secure These Rights,* a major report that exceeded the president's mandate. The report offered a sweeping overview of America's color line at mid-century and documented its impact on all phases of life. The report identified racial segregation as a national problem and provided a blueprint for federal action, serving as a touchstone for civil rights advocates over the next two decades. The report's life within the realm of presidential leadership and national politics, however, was dictated largely by political realities of the 1948 presidential campaign. Harry Truman's civil rights initiatives during the campaign season suggest a careful and ultimately brilliant balancing act that yielded several important civil rights advances, most notably an executive order desegregating the Armed Forces. In the face of challenges by disaffected Southern Democrats to his right and progressives on his left, Truman clinched an upset victory in the hotly contested presidential race, with the help of the black vote in key Northern states. The Truman administration's lackluster leadership on civil rights after the election in 1948, however, and the cautious approach of liberal Democrats marked a retreat from the robust agenda set out by *To Secure These Rights.*

In the wake of Truman's victory, prospects for moving civil rights forward on the legislative front quickly dimmed. No sanctions were meted out to Southern Democrats who had bolted the party. Several "Dixiecrats" assumed powerful committee positions, including Senator James Eastland of Mississippi, who became head of the Judiciary Committee's Subcommittee on Civil Rights. Unbowed, the party's Southern wing succeeded in strengthening the filibuster early in the new Congress, doubling the number of votes needed to cut off the paralyzing debate that doomed any civil rights legislative initiatives. Although Strom Thurmond's States Rights Party garnered barely 2 percent of the popular vote in the 1948 election, observed the *New York Times,* "in the matter of federal action on civil rights, we will still be ruled from Birmingham."[27]

Southern dominance of the legislative process tested the will, vision, and leadership of Democrats who had aligned themselves with the staples of the civil rights agenda—anti-lynching, anti–poll tax bills, and legislation for a permanent fair employment practices act. In the aftermath of the war, with the boom in federally assisted urban redevelopment and public housing, the NAACP's long-time fight to attach no-discrimination amendments to federally funded programs took on heightened urgency. The NAACP supported an amendment requiring no discrimination in any programs assisted under the Housing Act of 1949 in an effort to help insure that federal funds did not reinforce widespread patterns of residential segregation, which amplified the housing crisis faced by a growing black urban population, while also determining access to schools and other public resources and facilities. In the struggle that unfolded around the legislation, the NAACP was pitted against erstwhile liberal allies such as Senators Hubert Humphrey and Paul Douglass, who ardently opposed the anti-discrimination provision on the grounds that it would invite Southern opposition and defeat the housing bill. More than a pragmatic political calculation, noted NAACP publicist Henry Lee Moon, the response of liberal Democrats to the proposed no-discrimination amendment suggested an all-too-easy accommodation to America's racial status quo and disregard for the consequences of more entrenched racial segregation in the North.[28]

Despite the pivotal role of Northern black voters in the Democrats' 1948 victory, "the heart of Congress," wrote Roy Wilkins, "remained as cold as ever to the cause of civil rights." Wilkins led in organizing liberal and labor groups around a major lobbying effort on Capitol Hill to mobilize support for civil rights legislation, leading to the establishment of the Leadership Conference on Civil Rights (LCCR), an interracial coalition chaired by Wilkins. But Southerners stood poised to defeat any civil rights initiatives, while concerns about communism, corporatism, and consumerism eclipsed racial injustice as the major focus of mainstream liberal debates regarding democracy and the future.[29]

By the late 1940s, the cold war had elevated the fight against communism to the major challenge facing American democracy, undermining the confident and eclectic democratic activism that had broadened the civil rights battlefront during the New Deal era. The national leadership of the NAACP retreated to a defensive posture in an effort to maintain hard-won access to the highest levels of government, which was critical to a strategy aimed at making the federal government a partner in the struggle for civil rights. Walter White muted his early criticism of cold war policy and his linkage of black civil rights struggles to anti-colonial movements and publicly embraced the cold war's rhetoric of freedom.

Routinely tagged by Southern whites as "subversive," the NAACP attempted to establish its anti-communist credentials by distancing itself from groups on the Left active in the fight against racial oppression and by establishing procedures to investigate charges of communist infiltration in its branches. At the end of 1948, the NAACP board ousted the uncompromising W.E.B. Du Bois, a fierce critic of U.S. foreign policy and government complicity with racial caste and injustice, who also clashed with White's approach. *Pittsburgh Courier* columnist and attorney Margaret McKenzie noted the inherent contradictions of a civil rights group engaged in "acts of exclusion on political grounds," while conceding that circumstances made it "inevitable." But, she asked, at what cost?[30]

In the constrained and unforgiving political climate of the early cold war years, the NAACP managed to secure its place in Washington as guardian of a more narrowly focused civil rights agenda. Yet it made no legislative advances until the late 1950s. In the decade following World War II, as Ella Baker, Charles Houston, and others active in the field had predicted, the impetus for change would take place far beyond the halls of Congress and established political circles, in communities and courtrooms around the South.[31]

On August 10, 1948, Thurgood Marshall traveled to South Carolina to watch as black men and women waited to vote in the Democratic primary for the first time. Just days earlier, NAACP attorneys succeeded in putting the final nail in the coffin of the white primary when Judge Waites Waring struck down the last-ditch efforts of South Carolina's Democratic Party to bar blacks from what was then the most important electoral arena. Marshall began the day in Charleston, where blacks had lined up before the polls opened at 8 A.M., and reached Columbia when the polls closed that evening. At a packed mass meeting at Allen College that night, the local NAACP branch presented him with a small token of appreciation: "a Hamilton wrist watch, a portable radio, and two boxes of white shirts." Most gratifying, though, were the numbers of voters who turned out across South Carolina—an estimated 35,000, a tenfold increase over the number of blacks registered prior to the 1944 ruling.[32]

That same year, the third-party presidential candidate Henry Wallace campaigned on an activist civil rights platform. Palmer Weber, native Virginian and a member of the NAACP's national board, and Louis Burnham, director of the Southern Negro Youth Congress, organized Wallace's Southern campaign around political changes stirred by the New Deal and the war. Black and white candidates ran on Wallace's Progressive Party ticket in nearly every Southern state, supporters staged mass interracial meetings, and local organizers supported voter registration drives. Harry Truman avoided campaigning in the South during 1948. During his historic tour through the region that summer, Wallace refused to address segregated audiences, drawing large crowds of supporters as well as loud protests. The significance of the Wallace effort in the South would not be tallied at the ballot box, Charles Houston noted, but measured in the growing "resistance to segregation" that it showcased. While the form of the resistance would "vary from place to place," he observed that "the spiritual climate has been formed."[33]

Segregation emerged as the major target of NAACP activity after the war. Although gains on the voting rights front were impressive and hard won, repression of black voting was widespread across the South—further evidence of the unchecked power and determination of Southern whites to enforce the color line in all areas of public life, including the ballot box. An expanded NAACP legal team initiated a challenge to the restrictive covenants that promoted housing segregation in the North while also preparing for a frontal attack on the segregation system in the South. In 1946, the NAACP won a Supreme Court ruling striking down state-mandated segregation in interstate travel. But the expansion of the legal campaign for equal education was the platform for striking at the heart of the caste system.

As has been widely documented, the legal team pursued a multi-track effort in the fight for equal education, targeting the color bar to graduate and professional education while chipping away at the inequalities in primary and secondary education, including teachers' salaries, school facilities, and bus transportation. After the war, Marshall was ready to mount an all-out attack on segregated schooling; exposure to school conditions across the South had made it crystal clear that nothing short of that could secure equal education for black children. But the attorneys, seasoned by extensive travel in the region, realized that for many black communities, the prospect of waging a battle for integrated schools was, at best, a leap into the unknown—fraught with even greater danger than the collective act of turning out to cast a ballot. When Marshall announced plans in 1947 "to fight to the last ditch to remove all segregation" to an audience in South Carolina, the response was typical of other places: "absolutely no applause, but rather a look of apprehension on the faces of most" of the people present. Nevertheless, Marshall remained confident that "intensive field work from branch to branch and person to person" would engage the branches in this fight, and steel their determination "to fight the matter out."[34]

The first of the five cases that would comprise *Brown v. Board of Education* emerged in South Carolina, in rural Clarendon County. It began in 1947 with a petition for a school bus for black students, which then broadened out to a demand for equalization of school facilities. After the 1950 Supreme Court victory in the *Sweatt v. Painter* case, desegregating the University of Texas Law School, the NAACP formally announced plans to attack school segregation across the board. The plaintiffs in *Briggs v. Elliot,* the Clarendon County case, agreed to sue for an end to school segregation. By then, many had already lost jobs and suffered other reprisals for their efforts to secure better educational facilities. "Our determination was hardened at this point," recalled Reverend Joseph DeLaine, leading organizer of the school fight; they were ready "to go for broke."[35]

On May 28, 1951, the federal district court heard arguments in the *Briggs* case. The scene outside of the federal courthouse in Charleston that day was a potent expression of the transformation in black expectations that had grown up around the NAACP's legal campaign. Black men and women had begun arriving at sunrise, taking their place in line outside the courthouse. By the time the lawyers arrived, later that morning, the line stretched from the second-story courtroom down the hall and stairway, through the lobby, down the front steps, and along the sidewalk. The courtroom seated 150; more than 500 people waited, and more came. James Gibson, a farmer who rode over from Clarendon County, was among the hundreds waiting outside. "I never got tired of waiting that day," he said. During the course of the trial, news found its way to him and others gathered along the hallway and on the street. "Whenever the NAACP lawyer made a point," one observer recalled, "someone got up and whispered it to the line and it would travel right down the corridor and down the steps to the throng outside."[36]

The three-judge court voted 2–1 to uphold segregation, and the lawyers prepared to appeal. But even then, those who had long pushed up against the heavy weight of segregation realized that the meaning of the trial reached beyond any court ruling. Shortly afterward, Marshall declared: "The Negroes from Clarendon County and from all over the South jammed the courthouse standing shoulder to shoulder, hot and uncomfortable, for a single purpose—to demonstrate to all the world that the Negroes in the South are determined to eliminate segregation from American life."[37]

Three years after the trial in Charleston, the U.S. Supreme Court ruled on the *Briggs* case and four other school cases in *Brown v. Board of Education,* voting unanimously to overturn school segregation. The ruling effectively struck down the "separate but equal" ruling in *Plessy v. Ferguson*, a decisive turning point in the struggle for civil rights. It was met by a storm of opposition and resistance in the South, given air by a second Court ruling allowing for "all deliberate speed" in the implementation of school desegregation. Republican president Dwight Eisenhower never publicly endorsed *Brown,* and liberal Democrats stretched to placate their Southern wing, advocating a "wait and see" approach that accommodated white resistance. Meanwhile, *Brown* elevated the struggle for full citizenship rights in communities across the South, reinforcing the movement that had taken hold during the war years and providing a legal foundation for the broadening challenge to the South's caste system. The fundamental elements were in place for the revolution that would transform race relations in the South and secure the far-reaching civil rights legislation of the mid-1960s.

The legal insurgency that took hold in the South during the war years married the intellectual capital of a small cadre of black attorneys with a program of fieldwork and organizing dedicated to striking at the roots of America's racial caste system. Working through an infrastructure of NAACP branches, bold civil rights lawyers and a core of talented organizers, most notably Ella Baker, were strategically positioned to give direction and definition to the heightened aspirations and militancy generated by the pressures and demands of wartime. As black Americans internalized the democratic rhetoric of the war, the NAACP's burgeoning legal campaign became a "crystallizing force of Negro citizenship," a movement grounded in basic constitutional guarantees, which actively countered the racial ideas and practices that dominated most facets of American life. While black activists fought for freedom and citizenship on many fronts, it was ultimately the campaign orchestrated around the NAACP's legal challenges that gained momentum and traction during the era of World War II, building toward a frontal attack on the props of state-mandated segregation.

With *Brown* providing a firm legal basis, the way was open for the final campaign against Jim Crow. Key moments included the Montgomery bus boycott in 1955–1956 and the emergence of Martin Luther King, Jr.; the integration of Little Rock's Central High School by nine students with the protection of federal troops in 1957; and, in 1960, the sit-ins, which sparked a wave of direct action protests targeting segregated lunch counters and led to the founding of the Student Nonviolent Coordinating Committee, with the aid of Ella Baker. As the number of women and men openly challenging racial barriers steadily grew, their protests were captured in photographs and by television cameras— creating the story of the movement that lives in popular memory.

Notes

1. Roy Wilkins to Madison Jones, December 1, 1941, Papers of the National Association for the Advancement of Colored People, Manuscript Division, Library of Congress, Part II, Group A, Box 588.

2 .Branch memberships—1946; NAACP Papers, II: B99

3. John H. Bracey and August Meier, "Allies or Adversaries: The NAACP, A. Phillip Randolph and the 1941 March on Washington," *Georgia Historical Quarterly*, Vol. 125 (Spring 1991), 3–7; See Robert A. Hill, ed. *FBI's RACON: Racial Conditions in the United States During World War II* (Boston, 1995).

4. Madison Jones to Walter White, Madison Jones to Roy Wilkins, November 25, 1941, November 27, 1941, NAACP Papers, II: A588

5. Madison Jones to Roy Wilkins, November 14, 1941, November 19, 1941, December 10, 1941, NAACP Papers II: A588.

6. Sullivan, *Lift Every Voice: The NAACP and the Making of the Civil Rights Movement* (New York, 2009), 50–57, 61–102, 105–110. Also see Steven A. Reich, "Soldiers of Democracy: Black Texans and the Fight for Citizenship, 1917–1921," *Journal of American History* (March 1996), 1478–1594.

7. Ibid., 157; Robert L. Carter, *A Matter of Law*, 176.

8. Sullivan, *Lift Every Voice*, 237–241.

9. Madison Jones to Walter White, July 21, 1942, NAACP Papers, II: A77.

10. A number of statewide studies provide in-depth accounts of the work of the individuals cited here. See Adam Fairclough, *Race and Democracy: The Civil Rights Struggle in Louisiana, 1915–1972* (Athens, Ga., 1995); Caroline Emmons, "The Flame of Resistance: The NAACP in Florida, 1910–1960," (Ph.D. dissertation, Florida State University, 1988); Stephen Tuck, *Beyond Atlanta: The Struggle for Racial Equality in Georgia, 1940–1980* (Athens, Ga., 2001); Raymond Gavins, "The NAACP in North Carolina During the Age of Segregation," in Armstead L. Robinson and Patricia Sullivan, *New Directions in Civil Rights Studies* (Charlottesville, 1991); Peter F. Lau, *Democracy Rising: South Carolina and the Struggle for Black Equality* (Lexington, Ky., 2006); Thurgood Marshall, "Legal Attack to Secure Civil Rights," NAACP annual meeting, Chicago, 1944, NAACP Papers (microfilm), Pt I, reel 17; Madison Jones to Walter White, December 2, 1941, NAACP Papers, II: A588.

11. Sullivan, *Lift Every Voice*, 262–265.

12. On Texas primary case, Luther P. Jackson, "The Negro Vote," n.d., Luther Porter Jackson Papers, Johnson Memorial Library, Virginia State University, box 74.

13. Walter White, address at closing meeting of Wartime Conference, Chicago, July 16, 1944, NAACP Papers (microfilm), Pt 1, reel 11; Chicago *Defender,* July 22, 1944, 1.

14. Sullivan, *Lift Every Voice*, 296–297, 307, 315.

15. William Bailey quoted in Fairclough, *Race and Democracy,* 105.

16. Sullivan, *Lift Every Voice,* 295, 305–306, 315–316.

17. Henry Lee Moon, *The Balance of Power: The Negro Vote* (New York, 1948), 178–179.

18. Osceola McKaine, "The Third Revolution," Luther Porter Jackson Papers, box 80.

19. Emmons, "Flame of Resistance."

20. Gail Williams O'Brien, *The Color of Law: Race, Violence and Justice in the Postwar South* (Chapel Hill, 1999), 7–33; Thurgood Marshall, acceptance speech as Spingarn medalist, NAACP conference, Cincinnati, OH, June 28, 1944, NAACP Papers, II-A, box 31; Sullivan, *Lift Every Voice,* 319–320.

21. Tuck, *Beyond Atlanta,* 62–69; Patricia Sullivan, *Days of Hope: Race and Democracy in the New Deal Era* (Chapel Hill, 1996), 211–213; John Dittmer, *Local People: The Struggle for Civil Rights in Mississippi* (Urbana, 1995), 1–3; "On the 2d of July 1946; Gulfport, MS, . . ." statement by V. R. Collier et al., NAACP Papers (mf), pt 4 reel 9.

22. Ella Baker to Walter White, May 15, 1946, NAACP Papers, II-A, box 573.

23. Sullivan, *Lift Every Voice,* 320–325.

24. Charles H. Houston, "Spotlight on Mississippi," *Baltimore Afro-American,* December 14, 1946, 1; "A New Day for the South," *Chicago Defender,* December 14, 1946, 14;

25. Houston, "Spotlight on Mississippi"; *New York Times,* December 8, 1946, December 10, 1946; Dittmer, *Local People,* 3–9.

26. President's Committee on Civil Rights, *To Secure These Rights: Report of the President's Committee on Civil Rights* (New York, 1947), vii–ix.

27. William C. Berman, *The Politics of Civil Rights in the Truman Administration* (Columbus, 1970), 138–163.

28. Henry Lee Moon, "The Politics of Inertia," *New Leader,* February 4, 1950, 5; Sullivan, *Lift Every Voice,* 376.

29. Roy Wilkins, *Standing Fast,* 203; Walter Jackson, "White Liberal Intellectuals, Civil Rights, and Gradualism, 1954–60," in Brian Ward and Tony Badger, eds., *The Making of Martin Luther King, Jr.* (New York, 1996), 97.

30. Sullivan, *Lift Every Voice,* 367–370, 374–375; Kenneth Janken, *White: The Biography of Walter White, Mr. NAACP* (New York, 2004), 310–313; Manfred Berg, *The Ticket to Freedom: The NAACP and the Struggle for Black Political Integration* (Gainesville, 2005), 131–139; Fairclough, *Race and Democracy,* 140–147.

31. Denton Watson, *Lion in the Lobby: Clarence Mitchell Jr.'s Struggle for the Passage of Civil Rights Laws* (New York, 1990), 336–394; John Doar, "The Work of the Civil Rights Division in Enforcing Voting Rights under the Civil Rights Acts of 1957 and 1960," *Florida State University Law Review* (Fall 1997), 1–2.

32. Baltimore *Afro-American,* August 21, 1948.

33. Sullivan, *Days of Hope,* 249–273; Charles H. Houston, *Baltimore Afro American,* September 11, 1948.

34. Thurgood Marshall to Roy Wilkins, February 24, 1947; Thurgood Marshall to Gloster Current, memorandum, July 8, 1947, NAACP Papers, II-B, box 99.

35. Carter, *A Matter of Law,* 97–98; Rev. Joseph DeLaine, interviewed by Richard Kluger, *Brown v. Board of Education* Collection, Beinecke Rare Book and Manuscript Library, Yale University.

36. Sullivan, *Lift Every Voice,* 404–405.

37. Thurgood Marshall, address at the forty-second annual convention of the NAACP, Municipal Auditorium, Atlanta, GA, June 28, 1951, NAACP Papers, II-A, box 45.

5

Hillburn, Hattiesburg, and Hitler

WARTIME ACTIVISTS THINK GLOBALLY AND ACT LOCALLY

Thomas Sugrue

September 8, 1943, was the first day of school in the small village of Hillburn, nestled at the foot of the Ramapo Mountains in Rockland County, New York. The Brook School, a ramshackle wood-frame building that served as Hillburn's Negro school, was silent. All three cramped rooms where a hundred black children were supposed to gather to get their elementary school education were empty. The school's outdoor privies, boarded up since they had been replaced by indoor plumbing earlier that year, stood watch over the untrammeled grass in the schoolyard. Across a busy highway from the Brook School, the small American Legion hall that the schoolchildren used as a surrogate gymnasium stood dark and still. Only six children attempted to attend classes that morning. The other ninety-four had joined a "general strike."[1]

A half mile away, in the center of town, the school day was also off to an unusual start at the proud Main School, a sturdy brick and limestone building built in the 1920s with state-of-the-art classrooms, a library, a clinic, a music room, a gymnasium, and a large playground, all for the village's white children. The very physical plant of the two schools embodied ideas of racial difference. Main was a stately masonry building; Brook was a sagging wood frame structure. Local black parents derisively called Brook "the dump." As white children shuffled into their new classrooms, attorney Thurgood Marshall escorted five-year-old Allen Morgan, Jr., a black student from the Brook School, and his parents into the principal's office and demanded that the young man be enrolled. The outcome was a surprise to no one: Marshall and his young client were rebuffed. Marshall drafted an official letter of complaint to the school board, the first step in a possible lawsuit. Later that morning, a delegation of parents marched up the hill overlooking the town to the palatial home of school board president J. Edgar Davidson and demanded that the district allow black students to attend classes in the all-white Main School.[2]

The events of September 8 were just the beginning of what would be a six-week struggle in Hillburn—one that would bring together activists from the small town together with black radicals and leftists in Rockland County and in New York City. The struggle of fewer than one hundred black students and their parents against Jim Crow would take on national significance—inspiring protestors in Harlem, in an archipelago of towns within a hundred miles of New York, and at the Highlander Folk School in Tennessee.

Hillburn was one of hundreds of wartime battlegrounds over the future of race, rights, and equality in wartime America. Around the country, local activists—like those in Hillburn—mobilized around American war aims and fashioned protests that were performed on a local stage, but always with an eye toward the national and international. Northern activists took on every major manifestation of Jim Crow. In cities as diverse as New York, Saint Louis, and San Francisco, local civil rights activists protested segregated housing and launched legal challenges to racially restrictive covenants. In Detroit, the local chapter of the NAACP and the United Automobile Workers pushed the city to provide affordable housing for black war industry workers and marched against hate strikes in defense plants. At Fort Dix, New Jersey, and Fort Selfridge, Michigan, soldiers struggled to break down Jim Crow in bars and restaurants on- and off-base. In Los Angeles and Chicago, labor activists used the temporary wartime Fair Employment Practices Committee to open jobs for blacks in whites-only industries. In Chicago, Cleveland, Detroit, and Cincinnati, interracial teams of activists pried open the doors of Jim Crow restaurants and movie theaters. In New York City, schoolchildren and laundry workers protested the existence of racially segregated blood banks. The list of wartime protests is nearly endless.[3]

It is well established in the scholarly literature that the war fueled black demands for a "Double V"—victory against fascism abroad and Jim Crow at home. It is also well established that the economic opportunities unleashed by the war generated intense racial conflict on the streets, trolleys, and shop floors of nearly every major city in the North. And it is well established that the experience of military service and the indignities of military-sanctioned segregation galvanized black protest against segregation both North and South. But most historians who have written about wartime protest start with a simple, compelling assumption—an assumption profoundly shaped by post– World War II political science, survey research, and social theory—namely that wartime protest succeeded because it created a moral crisis: it highlighted the gap between what Gunnar Myrdal, author of the enormously influential *An American Dilemma* (1944), called the "American creed" of egalitarianism and the irrational and immoral practice of segregation. Wartime activists were acutely aware of the "hypocrisy" argument—and deployed it with great effectiveness. But blacks' vernacular wartime understanding of racial equality was broader and deeper. It rested on a deep strain of black anti-colonialism, which dated well before World War II and viewed the African American freedom struggle as one chapter in a global battle against white supremacy. Black activists offered a subversive critique of the United States as analogous to Hitler's Germany and Mussolini's Italy. And they offered a popular notion of democracy that was broader than an evocation of the "American creed" of liberty and equality. White Americans could not simply be goaded into accepting blacks as equals: they would have to be forced to do so through systematic political pressure.[4]

To understand the Hillburn struggle—and to shed light on the meaning of the remarkable wartime black insurgency—requires an analysis of how wartime activists framed their local struggles. At the heart of the Hillburn protest—and so many similar Northern battles against segregation, discrimination, and racial inequality—were two keywords: democracy and Hitlerism. By the middle of World War II, pro-democratic, anti-fascist language had become so commonplace in American political discourse that its widespread use nearly drained them of meaning. Both keywords could be—and were—used by a wide range of political actors simplistically: democracy as a synonym for the American form of government and an antonym for the totalitarian regimes that the United States was battling overseas; fascism as an easy term of derision to throw at political opponents at home or abroad. Many civil rights activists used the language of democracy and anti-fascism instrumentally and uncritically—just as their successors in the cold war would use the language of anti-communism to build political credibility for their cause in a climate of political hostility. But for African Americans and their white allies during World War II, both terms had a deeper significance and a longer history—one that can only be seen by looking at the networks of activism and ideology that tied together African Americans during the war.

For most white Americans—except for those on the political left—the language of anti-fascism was a product of World War II. For African Americans, however, anti-fascist language was rooted in the intertwined struggles for racial and economic justice during the 1930s. Many of the earliest black critics of fascism came from the political left. Popular Front activists—including leaders in the National Negro Congress and the NAACP—pointed out that Hitler imposed American-style Jim Crow laws on its Jewish minority. Hitler's invigoration of theories of racial supremacy gave further credibility to charges that America's white supremacists were homegrown fascists. Advocates of black civil rights in the 1930s powerfully linked second-class black citizenship to the Nazis' vision of Aryan supremacy. Also hovering as a shadow over black America in the mid-1930s was Mussolini's 1935 invasion of Ethiopia. The fascist domination of Ethiopia—the conquest of an African people by a European authoritarian power—outraged many black commentators. For many black intellectuals, Ethiopia became a metaphor for the racial oppression of black Americans, and they made Ethiopian liberation a cause. In 1936, A. Philip Randolph advocated a boycott of Italy and the National Negro Congress issued a forceful denunciation of Il Duce.[5]

A group of black dissident intellectuals proffering anti-fascist and anti-imperialist rhetoric in the mid-1930s were not themselves the agents of an intellectual or ideological shift. Ideas—especially political ideas—do not simply spread by word of mouth: they move outward and broadly through networks. The rise of Hitler and his overtly racist ideologies received widespread coverage in the black press, almost from the first moment that Hitler assumed power. During the mid-twentieth century, the black press became the primary vehicle for connecting disparate local activists and citizens together in shaping the black freedom struggle, particularly in the North; 155 black newspapers nationwide collectively formed what one observer called a "crusading press which serves the special needs of a militantly struggling people." The black press was led by two giants—the *Pittsburgh Courier* and *Baltimore Afro-American*—which both published editions in many Northern cities in addition to their hometowns, and were closely followed by the *Chicago Defender* and the *New York Amsterdam News*. What was most important about the black press as a tool for publicity and organization was its wide circulation. During World War II, the readership of black newspapers increased by an estimated 40 percent. And 60 percent of black newspapers circulated across state lines. The result was a virtual web of information about black life, about politics, and about grassroots protests and organization. No place was isolated, not even little Hillburn.[6]

Sociologist E. Franklin Frazier described the black press as "an organ of protest" that "reflects the growing race consciousness of the Negro." While the politics of black journalists ranged widely, from Republican to socialist, black newspaper editors saw their role in crusading terms. The goal of the *Afro-American*, recounted its longtime editor, John Murphy, was to "really unify the black people." Their front page stories seldom—if ever—made it into the white-owned dailies: efforts to break down segregation at white-owned restaurants, hotels, and movie theaters, attacks on a black family moving into a white neighborhood, struggles to abolish workplace discrimination, and acts of police brutality. To be sure, press coverage of the outrages of segregation and the battles against it was often spotty. Most black papers were weeklies and seldom had the staff to cover a story in great detail or to follow it over time. But the sum of many small articles—especially during the war—was clear. Segregation was widespread, but blacks were on the move. Just as important, through editorials, guest columns, and everyday news coverage, black papers turned elite anti-fascism into a popular vernacular in black America by the end of the 1930s. At a time when few white news outlets were covering Hitler's atrocities against the Jews and hardly any paid attention to the racialist underpinnings of Nazi policy, black writers and journalists drew extensive comparisons between Nazi race purity laws and Jim Crow legislation, and their respective victims. The crusading press conveyed to its readers the sense that the struggle against Jim Crow was part and parcel with the struggle against fascism.[7]

Vernacular anti-fascism took on even greater significance during the war—in part because it entered the political mainstream—but also because the black press continued to use it to frame the struggle against segregation and Jim Crow. "History and tradition combine to form a bulwark for native fascism that is no less dangerous than that of Hitler," argued NAACP activist Gloster Current in 1943. When a group of white clergymen organized to prevent blacks from moving into their North Philadelphia neighborhood, the *Philadelphia Tribune* denounced the efforts as "precisely the technique which Goebbels . . . has employed so effectively in crushing Germany under the heel of brutal Nazism." Thurgood Marshall criticized the "Gestapo in Detroit," the city police who engaged in "criminal aggression" against blacks during the Detroit riot of 1943. "Jim Crow Uber Alles" screamed the headline of another 1943 *Crisis* article. And NAACP officials labeled Inkster, a blue-collar suburb of Detroit with a rapidly growing population of black migrants and defense workers, "Michigan Sudetenland" when the town's whites proposed to secede and form their own government, taking with them all of the public buildings, but leaving blacks with the $750,000 village debt. Black newspaper editorials railed against America's "homegrown fascists," and ordinary blacks, writing to elected officials or to local newspapers, echoed the anti-Nazi theme when they referred to racial injustices at home. Those who did not stand up to Jim Crow were "appeasers," just as pusillanimous as the European leaders who stood cravenly by as Hitler vanquished Czechoslovakia.[8]

Many black wartime workers viewed their labor as part of the struggle for liberation. Anti-fascism gave meaning to black contributions to the defense effort. Part of that battle was winning white recognition that blacks were indispensable citizens. "We brown women of America need victory so much, so desperately," wrote Leotha Capshaw, a black worker, in the Urban League's *Opportunity* magazine. "We must prove it to white Americans as well—that our country can't get along without the labor and sacrifice of her brown daughters." Defeating Hitler would also deal a blow to the ideology of white supremacy on the American home front. Hortense Johnson, who worked as an inspector in a munitions factory in New Jersey, found purpose in the skills that her job required—and above all in its contribution to the struggle against Hitler "and the Talmadges and Dieses who will run the country if Hitler wins."[9]

Existing simultaneously with anti-fascism was a widespread rhetoric of democracy—one that was shared widely by blacks and whites, but given a different valence by ordinary African Americans. "Democracy" was a vague term in American political discourse in the early twentieth century, frequently evoked but seldom defined. In the official war rhetoric of the United States, "democracy" was one of those taken-for-granted words, one that was synonymous with America and its allies. But for African Americans, democracy was not a reality—it was an aspiration. It was not synonymous with the United States; it was something that America has systematically withheld from its

citizens. Rhoza Walker, a regular contributor of poetry to the *Crisis*, powerfully captured the war's unfulfilled democratic promise.

> I believe in democracy, so much,
> That I want everybody in America,
> To have some of it.
> Negroes,
> Denounced and deprived of Democracy,
> Insulted and inveigled in Industry,
> Shunned and shamed in Society
> Murdered and mangled,
> On the very land for which they must fight!
> They shall have some of it.[10]

The gap between the wartime rhetoric of democracy and the day-to-day
reality of Jim Crow became a persistent theme in black politics. "It is an
established fact," wrote Louis Martin, a black journalist who would go on
to a prominent career in national Democratic Party politics, "that the Negro
is frankly skeptical of our sincerity in our announced war aims which are
summed up in the Atlantic Charter, the Four Freedoms of President Roosevelt,
and the recent speeches of Henry Wallace and Sumner Welles, all proclaiming
that we are fighting for the liberation of all peoples." One year after America
entered the war, the Bureau of Public Sentiment, the polling operation of the
black-owned *Pittsburgh Courier*, found that 82.2 percent of black respondents
replied "no" to the question: "Have you been convinced that the statements
which our national leaders have made about freedom and equality for all peoples include the American Negro?" A survey of black residents of Chicago
and Detroit in the spring of 1943 found that 78 percent were dissatisfied that
they did not "get as much chance as they should to help win the war." Federal
government officials also fretted about the problem of "Negro morale." Office
of War Information surveys revealed that blacks supported the war effort, but
were deeply disaffected at the persistence of racial inequality on the war and
home fronts. Martin catalogued the "resentment and despair" that blacks felt
about wartime race relations. Blacks "want to feel that this is their war and that
their contribution to the war will also be a contribution to their own liberation.
The mounting bigotry of white America reflected in farm, field, and factory as
well as in the armed forces of the nation clouds this hope and obscures their
vision."[11]

Black activists throughout the war developed a particularly broad and
inclusive notion of democracy. To some extent, black activists highlighted
the discrepancy between America's democratic "creed" and its undemocratic
practices. The contrast was obvious—and it gave moral force to arguments
for racial equality. But most black intellectuals, activists, journalists, and their
comrades harbored no illusions about the existence of an egalitarian national

creed. American democracy, wrote social scientist Charles S. Johnson, is a "theoretical way of life." "No one can seriously call our way of life a mature democracy as long as there are millions condemned to poverty in a land of plenty . . . so long as there are persecuted races . . . so long as the lawmakers of the nation are still unwilling to say, by deterring legislation, that it is a crime for one group of citizens to torture and murder other citizens." The struggle for racial equality was one to make America democratic for the first time—not perfecting a political system whose only fault was its aberrant racial intolerance and irrational prejudice.[12] "In a sense," wrote Thomas Sancton in the *New Republic*, "it is 1776 for the Negro. Perhaps a more accurate analogy is 1789."[13]

In the aggregate, black activists embraced a vision of democracy that was far broader than the narrow notion of individual rights and liberties enshrined in the founding documents of American democracy. World War II, wrote Louis Martin, must become "truly a war of universal liberation."[14] What did "universal liberation" mean? A growing number of blacks saw the struggle against Jim Crow at home and fascism abroad as two fronts in a global war against racist empires of all varieties. In addition to its extensive use of anti-fascist language, the wartime black press also provided extensive coverage of freedom struggles in South Africa, India, and elsewhere in the British Empire; the largest and best-funded papers even had overseas correspondents in major European cities and in colonial capitals. "It may seem odd to hear India discussed in poolrooms on South State Street in Chicago," wrote Horace Cayton, but blacks took growing pride in the rising tide of revolution. Sociologist L. D. Reddick encapsulated the increasingly global view of democracy and rights that reshaped wartime black politics. "The northern Negro," he wrote, "seems to have developed a definitely international outlook." America did not have a monopoly on democracy: it resided in "the struggle of India for independence and of China for national equality." This international vision, Reddick hoped, would "lead the American nation to a broader and deeper approach to human relations."[15]

The vision of war as a struggle for liberation gave rise to wartime strategies for accomplishing change. It gave black activists a sense of urgency. Above all, it led them to perceive the struggle for black emancipation as a struggle for power. Black activists worked for change through a variety of means—there was no one single formula for accomplishing political change. Through lobbying efforts, they put pressure on the White House and on an increasingly intransigent, conservative Congress. Through litigation—a strategy that the NAACP had deployed for nearly twenty years—they pushed for a legal expansion of civil rights through challenges to discriminatory housing, voting, and labor practices. But a sizable number of Northern activists—in labor and leftist organizations like the National Negro Congress, but also in established civil rights groups like the NAACP and the Urban League—saw racial equality as a contest for power, one that required protest and disruption.

The NAACP, in particular, shifted its political agenda sharply at the end of the Depression and beginning of the war. That the established civil rights group would take a militant turn seemed impossible in the mid-1930s, when W.E.B. Du Bois resigned his membership. That year, Ralph Bunche argued that "the NAACP does not have a mass basis. It never has assumed the proportions of a crusade, nor has it attracted the masses of people to its banner." Bunche's criticism seemed dated just a few years later. Local NAACP branches faced insurgencies throughout the North. A "new crowd" of younger, more militant activists pushed local branches to organize blue-collar workers, to stage visible protests, and to support industrial unionism. During the war, NAACP chapters became even more militant—attaching themselves to the fledgling industrial union movement, sponsoring mass rallies and protests, and putting pressure on segregated housing, workplaces, and schools throughout the country. This grassroots insurgency paid off. NAACP membership doubled between 1935 and 1940 and took off exponentially during the war. Skyrocketing membership—and a wartime paper shortage—caught the NAACP unprepared nearly everywhere. Local branches complained of the lack of envelopes to collect membership dues.[16]

The protests in Hillburn in 1943 took the form and timing that they did because of the economic, political, and ideological impact of World War II. The problem of segregated schools was not new to the town, nor to the North, where through the mid-twentieth century, racially segregated schools were commonplace and where, during World War II, only a little more than a third of whites supported their children attending classes with even a single black classmate. Black educator Doxey Wilkerson wrote in 1940 that education "in the North is characterized by tendencies toward structural separateness."[17] Separation took different forms in different Northern communities. Where state laws permitted it, districts often constructed separate "colored" or "Negro" schools, like Hillburn's Brook School. But, unlike the South, laws in the majority of Northern states, many dating to the nineteenth century, forbade racial exclusion in public schools. In these states, educators regularly honored them in the breach, allowing separate schools to remain intact, or maintaining the fiction of integration, confining black students in separate classrooms and even separate playgrounds. Some public school officials, especially in cities with rapidly growing black populations, devised subterfuges to keep blacks out of white-dominated schools, most frequently gerrymandering school attendance zones as the racial composition of neighborhoods changed. In *An American Dilemma*, Gunnar Myrdal observed that in Northern cities and towns, "school boundaries . . . are usually set at the boundary of the white and Negro neighborhoods." Those boundaries hardened because of the officially discriminatory policies of New Deal and World War II–era federal housing programs (Home Owners Loan Corporation, Federal Housing Administration, and Veterans Administration). As housing segregation hardened—reinforcing school segregation—Northern whites, wrote sociologist Alfred McClung Lee, "often take the position that their school is a 'neighborhood' one and that their district 'happens' to be white." Despite its roots in public policies—whether school district practices, state laws, or federal housing programs—educational segregation in the North was so ubiquitous as to appear to be part of the natural order of things, so commonplace that it was taken for granted.[18]

But World War II disrupted the natural order of things in Hillburn. What changed most was Hillburners' sense of their own political efficacy. To be sure, the town's separate and unequal school had long been a source of resentment— and it had sparked civil rights protest before the war. T. N. Alexander, a postal worker who commuted to New York, first challenged the Hillburn's segregated schools in 1931. Even with NAACP support, he found it very difficult to organize the town's residents around the issue. Alexander's efforts did not bear fruit, In the next dozen years, however, the conditions for civil rights protest changed. Black New Yorkers grew more militant and civil rights organizations—bolstered by their alliance with New Dealers, leftists, and religious activists—began pushing for civil rights legislation, including a 1938 state law that forbade official, racially separate schools in the state. That law provided one crucial political resource for Hillburn's advocates of educational equality. But the law alone did not suffice. It would be another five years before local activists pushed for its enforcement.

The economic and political transformations that the war wrought awoke Hillburn's civil rights activists, providing them with the economic security to challenge the town's white elites, the political opportunity to protest, and a powerful political language to frame their discontent. The economic disruption of the war was crucial—especially in empowering black women to spearhead local protest. Because many of the town's young men—black and white—left to fight overseas, employers sought out women workers. Black women entered local factories, including the brake works—Hillburn's largest employer, owned by the school board president—as defense workers. Wartime economic security gave Hillburn's workers the resources to challenge the town's white ruling elite—and to follow the path that T. N. Alexander had blazed a decade earlier. Hillburn residents were also part of the wartime revival of the NAACP, an organization whose national membership increased nearly tenfold in the early and mid-1940s. In the summer of 1943, local activists, most of them women, revived the town's dormant NAACP branch. Hillburn's revitalized NAACP took on the most obvious local target: Hillburn's schools. That these remained "Jim Crowed," in the North, in the midst of World War II, generated a new-found outrage. The wartime rhetoric of anti-fascism and democracy, along with the widespread examples of popular militancy, empowered Hillburn's boycotting students and their parents. The very language that they used to describe the school boycott—a "general strike"—reflected the degree to which a militant understanding of social change had made its way to their community.[19]

Hillburn's NAACP branch, which coordinated the protests, invited attorney Thurgood Marshall to visit and to begin preparations for litigation against the Ramapo Central School district that included Hillburn. Marshall pledged to "back the local group to the limit in the fight against segregation." Marshall's presence early in the boycott led local whites to charge that their town was the target of outside agitators. Surely Hillburn's "fine colored people," as school board president Davidson called them, if left to their own devices, would not have risen up against the school district. "I'm afraid," he contended, "a few are being led astray by outsiders." Davidson was partially right: Marshall played an invaluable role in helping coordinate the protest. But the school board head's blindness to the wartime black revolt led him to overlook the fact that Hillburn's grievances were wholly homegrown. Local activists—not Marshall—generated the idea of a general strike. Marshall linked Hillburn residents to an empowering past by reminding them of school boycotts that had taken place elsewhere. The fledgling NAACP legal department had supported similar school boycotts in the 1920s and 1930s in places as far flung as Berwyn, Pennsylvania; East Orange, New Jersey; and Springfield, Ohio. In Hillburn—as with so many protests in the North—the local and the national blurred. Local activists quickly learned that their local struggles were part of a nationwide battle; national leaders like Thurgood Marshall relied on local rebellions to develop a strategy for litigation. Local agitation and outside intervention were two wholly intertwined processes.[20]

The two-front attack on Hillburn's Jim Crow schools lasted for the remainder of September and well into October. More than half of the district's black students remained out of school. "Nobody's going back," proclaimed local NAACP head Marion van Dunk. For those students who remained out of classes, local activists started what they dubbed a "Freedom School" in a local church. Two local parents volunteered to run classes until the NAACP paid for the hiring of a professional teacher. School district officials, still recalcitrant, took legal action against the boycotting black parents for violating the state's mandatory education law. The threat of persecution did not deter the parents. "We'll go to jail if we have to," stated one parent. "We aren't scared and we won't quit," asserted another. When a local judge levied $10 fines (with suspended jail sentences) to the parents of 46 boycotters, they "trooped across the highway which has been arbitrarily set up by the school board as the school dividing line between 'white' and 'colored' and presented their patient, mystified tots to Hillburn Main School." Once again, they were turned away. Angry parents "roared": "You'll be sorry!" "We won't go back." The NAACP reported that "children shall not return again to the [Brook] school which, unlike that old time religion, is no longer good enough for them."[21]

The town's whites were upset at the black uprising, which caught them off guard. They had no inkling that Hillburn's "quiet and industrious Negroes" (in Davidson's words) were so angry. When a delegation of parents marched to the Davidson estate to present their grievances, Davidson's overwrought wife complained: "I've been nice to these people . . . I've fed them when they're sick and given them money when they needed it. Why should they try to enroll their children in the white school? What do they want to do that for?" To the embattled school board president, the protest was but "a celebrity stunt." School board member Jacob Schenck argued that "we have no feeling against the colored people. We proved that by improving their school building [by replacing the outdoor privies with indoor toilets]." Hillburn mayor John Creelman more bluntly expressed his shock at the boycotting parents' high aspirations for their children's education. In his view, "all a Negro wants is a full belly." How could it be that the good Negroes of Hillburn had become such ingrates? Why did they want their children to mix with white children?[22]

The Hillburn protests put a spotlight on Northern segregation and linked it to the struggle against fascism. Hillburn's separate schools were "Grist for Hitler," argued one boycott supporter. The struggle to desegregate their school district was one battle in the ongoing, conjoined struggle against Jim Crow at home and fascism abroad. When a group of parents marched to the all-white Main School, they posed for a photograph—with more than a dose of irony—in front of a wartime propaganda poster that read "Democracy at Home." Hillburn parents, encouraged by the outpouring of support for their boycott, came to see themselves as part of a movement with national and even international significance.[23]

Hillburn became a powerful symbol of Northern Jim Crow, a local controversy that was covered extensively by the black press, by leftist newspapers, and by New York–area dailies and weeklies. Through the *Crisis*, NAACP members—nearly a half a million strong—got news of the battle. The black and radical presses also carried news of the Hillburn boycott to their readers far and wide.[24] National NAACP activists denounced the school board for its "astonishingly 'southern' viewpoint." The American Labor Party and the American Civil Liberties Union joined in their support of the boycott, denouncing the "Mississippi Jim Crowism" of Hillburn's school board.[25] A blue-ribbon committee of leftist and liberal Rockland County residents, including playwright Maxwell Anderson, actress Helen Hayes, and composer Kurt Weill, signed a petition in support of the striking students and used their celebrity to further publicize the Hillburn protests.

Through the black press and through the efforts of civil rights activists, the Hillburn boycott became national news. In early October, over 20,000 posters appeared on telephone poles, storefronts, and in bars, grocery stores, and churches throughout Harlem advertising a "mass rally" on behalf of Hillburn's boycotting parents. "Jim Crow Blocks School House Door in New York State," read one. "Hillburn and Hattiesburg!" read another. When an NAACP sound truck rolled through the streets of Harlem announcing the event, crowds of pedestrians broke into spontaneous applause. The Harlem efforts culminated on October 10, when Thurgood Marshall, Adam Clayton Powell (the minister of Harlem's influential Abyssinian Baptist Church), and a group of striking parents addressed several thousand supporters at Harlem's Golden Gate Theater. The event generated such a buzz that Harlem NAACP activists, including Ella Baker, decided to hold similar mass meetings on issues like the poll tax and Jim Crow in the military, all with hopes of making the Manhattan branch of the NAACP "an organization for the masses of the people."[26]

Word of Hillburn's protests traveled quickly through radical and civil rights groups. In late October 1943, the left-leaning *People's Voice* published Harlem poet Countee Cullen's "Hillburn—The Fair," an angry little poem about the town's whites. Folksingers at the Highlander Folk School—the leading training ground for civil rights and labor activists throughout the 1940s and 1950s—set Cullen's verses to music.

> OH—God have pity on such a city
> OH—Where parent teaches child to hate
> God have pity on such a city where parent teaches child
>   To hate
> OH—God looks down on such a town
> OH—where prejudice the great rules drunkenly and evilly
>   What should be Liberty's Estate.[27]

By mid-October, the protests and the threat of litigation bore fruit. In response to the NAACP's complaint, the state commissioner of education overruled the district's policy of segregation, shut down the Brook School, and ordered the enrollment of black students at Main. It was—like many wartime civil rights victories—hardly complete. White parents withdrew their children from the Main School en masse, enrolling them in local parochial schools. Over the course of the next two years, NAACP activists tried and failed to form a biracial committee to bring black and white parents together, to attract white students back to the Main School, and to keep the school district from closing the now all-black Hillburn public school. The boycotting parents had won the immediate battle, but found themselves still on the defensive in a larger, still unresolved struggle against Jim Crow education. Both Hillburn parents and national NAACP officials had learned—the hard way—that the fight to break down school segregation would not be quick and easy.

The story of Northern resistance to Northern school desegregation after *Brown*, and later to busing, should not have come as a surprise. At the grass roots, Hillburn kept alive a long tradition of school boycotts. Although organized protests against schools were scattered geographically, both North and South, and spread out over a long period of time (between the late 1890s and the 1960s), such dramatic actions resonated in local memories and inspired protestors elsewhere. In fact, the well-publicized events in Hillburn sparked the imagination of civil rights activists throughout the Northeast. Dozens of telegrams and letters of support and donations to the boycotting parents flooded into the NAACP office, most of them from leftists, black church leaders, and parent-teacher associations in black schools in places like Brooklyn, Montclair, New Jersey, and Gary—all places that had been or would be rocked by school protests of their own. Trenton, New Jersey, activists—who led a 1944 boycott of their city's segregated Lincoln School—took direct inspiration from the Hillburn protest. The NAACP, working through its local branches, also disseminated information about school boycotts—using the pages of the *Crisis* to link local activists to a longer history of protest which they might not have otherwise known about. The fact that the NAACP was a national organization that connected together hundreds of local chapters—and that it had institutional memory—was crucial in the spread of boycotts. The NAACP had adopted a strategy in its litigation work that allowed it to think nationally and even internationally, while abetting local protests.[28]

The story of Hillburn is not just of local interest. It was but one of hundreds of examples of the way that the struggle against fascism and for democracy had remade the political terrain of black America during the war. The war against fascism had unleashed black demands for inclusion in America's economic and political institutions. And it had given civil rights activists a powerful new language to express their grievances and their aspirations. Black activists would continue to express their discontents in the wartime language of anti-fascism (indeed, it would appear in letters to elected officials from ordinary blacks well into the 1950s). And, to an extent unthinkable among whites, black activists continued to frame their freedom struggle in international terms. As countries as diverse as India, Nigeria, and the Congo struggled for independence after World War II, black activists would continue to think globally. And finally, Hillburn's protestors—and those whom they inspired throughout the North—would accelerate a grassroots movement for quality education, one that would eventually reshape Northern and Southern politics.

Notes

1. *Ramapo Independent*, September 9, 1943; *PM*, September 9, 1943: *New York Herald Tribune*, September 30, 1943.

2. *Ramapo Independent*, September 9, 1943; *New York Times*, September 10, 1943; "Jim Crow Enrolls for New Term in Hillburn Schools," n.d., NAACP, Group II-B, Box 144.

3. See Thomas J. Sugrue, *Sweet Land of Liberty: The Forgotten Struggle for Civil Rights in the North* (New York, 2008), esp. chapters 2–5 for these and other examples. An excellent overview of the impact of World War II–era black protest and rioting is Daniel Kryder, *Divided Arsenal: Race and the American State During World War II* (New York, 2000).

4. Gunnar Myrdal, *An American Dilemma* (New York, 1944); on WWII, see among: Philip Klinkner with Rogers Smith, *The Unsteady March: The Rise and Decline of Racial*

Equality in America (Chicago, 1999), chapter 6; Neil A. Wynn, *The Afro-American and the Second World War* (New York, 1975; rev. ed.,, 1993); Richard M. Dalfiume, "The 'Forgotten Years' of the Negro Revolution," *Journal of American History,* Vol. 55 (1968): 90–106.

5. See chapter 8 by Jane Dailey and chapter 9 by Penny von Eschen in this volume. See also William R. Scott, *The Sons of Sheba's Race: African-Americans and the Italo-Ethiopian War, 1935–41* (Bloomington, 1993); Mark Naison, *Communists in Harlem During the Great Depression* (Urbana: University of Illinois Press, 1983), 173–177; Lunabelle Wedlock, "Comparisons by Negro Publications of the Plight of the Jews in Germany with That of the Negro in America," [1942] in Maurianne Adams and John Bracey, eds., *Strangers and Neighbors: Blacks and Jews in the United States* (Amherst, 1999), 427–443.

6. Ralph N. Davis, "The Negro Newspapers and the War," *Sociology and Social Research* (May–June 1943), 373–380; Thomas Sancton, "The Negro Press," *The New Republic*, April 26, 1943, 557–560; E. Franklin Frazier, *The Negro in the United States* (New York, 1949), 512–516.

7. Doxey A. Wilkerson, "The Negro Press," *Journal of Negro Education,* Vol. 16 (1947): 511–531; Myrdal, *AD*, Vol 2, 933; Frazier, *Negro in the United States*, 515; Lewis H. Fenderson, "The Negro Press as a Social Instrument," *Journal of Negro Education,* Vol. 20 (1951): 181–188; Interviews with John H. Murphy, III, June 26, 1971; Cecil B. Newman, August 26, 1971; and Al Sweeney, June 22, 1972, in Black Journalists Project, Oral History Research Office, Columbia University, New York.

8. Gloster Current, "Let's Get Ten Thousand," *Crisis*, September 1942, 293; *Daily Worker*, March 7, 1941; Thurgood Marshall, "The Gestapo in Detroit," *Crisis*, August 1943, 232–233, 246–247, quote 233; "Jim Crow Uber Alles," *Crisis*, October 1943, 309; "Michigan Sudentenland," *Crisis*, December 1943, 372.

9. Hortense Johnson and Leotha Hackshaw, "What My Job Means to Me," *Opportunity*, April 1943.

10. Rhoza Walker, "I Believe in Democracy So Much," *Crisis*, September 1942, 280.

11. Louis E. Martin, "To Be or Not to Be a Liberal," *Crisis*, September 1942, 285–286; Albert Parker, "Negroes in the Postwar World" (Pioneer Publishers Pamphlet, 1942), reprinted in C.L.R. James et al., *Fighting Racism in World War II* (New York, 1980), 300; *Pittsburgh Courier*, December 19, 1942; Alfred McClung Lee and Norman D. Humphrey, *Race Riot* (New York, 1943), 7–8.

12. Charles S. Johnson, "The Negro and the Present Crisis," *Journal of Negro Education,* Vol. 10 (1941): 590.

13. Thomas Sancton, "Something's Happened to the Negro," *The New Republic*, February 8, 1943, 176.

14. Martin, "To Be," 286.

15. Horace R. Cayton, "Fighting for White Folks," *The Nation*, September 26, 1942; L. D. Reddick, "What the Northern Negro Thinks about Democracy," *Journal of Educational Sociology,* Vol. 17 (1944): 304–306; Rayford Logan, "Negro Youth and the Influence of the Press, Radio, and Cinema," *Journal of Negro Education,* Vol. 9 (1940): 428; on black internationalist intellectuals, see Penny von Eschen, *Race Against Empire* (Ithaca, 1997).

16. Frazier, *Negro in the United States*, 507; Manfred Berg, *"The Ticket to Freedom": The NAACP and the Struggle for Black Political Integration* (Gainesville, 2005), 109–101.

17. Doxey Wilkerson, "The Status of Negro Education," 226; cited in David Tyack, *The One Best System: A History of American Urban Education* (Cambridge, Mass., 1974), 229;

Charles S. Johnson, *Patterns of Negro Segregation* (New York, 1943), 12–22; Noma Jensen, "Are Negroes Integrated into our Northern School Systems?" June 20, 1946, in NAACP, II–A, 244: Paul B. Sheatsley, "White Attitudes Toward the Negro," *Daedelus* (Winter 1966), 222.

18. Myrdal, *American Dilemma*, 630; National Association of Intergroup Relations Officials, Commission on School Integration, *Public School Segregation and Integration in the North: Analysis and Proposals* (Washington, D.C., 1963), Meyer Weinberg, *Race and Place: A Legal History of the Neighborhood School* (Washington, D.C., 1967); United States Civil Rights Commission, *Civil Rights USA: Public Schools: Cities in the North and West* (Washington, D.C., 1962); Alfred McClung Lee, "The Impact of Segregated Housing on Public Schools," in William W. Brickman and Stanley Lehrer, eds., *The Countdown on Segregated Education* (New York, 1960), 78; generally see Sugrue, *Sweet Land of Liberty*, chapter 5, and Matthew D. Lassiter, "De Jure/De Facto Segregation: The Long Shadow of a National Myth," in Lassiter and Joseph Crespino, eds., *The Myth of Southern Exceptionalism* (New York, 2010), 25–48.

19. William T. Andrews, Report on Visit to Hillburn, February 2, 1931, NAACP Papers, Group II–L, Box 36. On women's mobilization during World War II, see among others, Karen Anderson, *Wartime Women: Sex Roles, Family Relations, and the Status of Women During World War II* (Westport, Conn., 1981): generally, see Doug McAdam, John McCarthy, and Mayer Zald, eds.,. *Comparative Perspectives on Social Movements: Political Opportunities, Mobilizing Structures, and Cultural Framings* (New York, 1996), introduction.

20. On earlier school boycotts, see August Meier and Elliott Rudwick, *Along the Color Line: Explorations in the Black Experience* (Urbana, 1976), 290–306, and Meier and Rudwick, "Early Boycotts of Segregated Schools: The East Orange New Jersey Experience," *History of Education Quarterly,* Vol. 4 (1967): 22–35; Davison Douglas, *Jim Crow Moves North: The Battle over Northern School Desegregation, 1865–1954* (Cambridge, 2005).

21. Segregation of Pupils Story Stirs Residents of Hillburn," NAACP Papers, Group II–B, Box 144; *New York Herald Tribune*, September 30, 1943; *New York World Telegram*, October 1, 1943; NAACP Press Release, October 1, 1943, in NAACP Papers, Group II–B, Box 144; "Hillburn Negroes Firm: Set up School in Church," in ibid.; *The Journal-News* (Westchester County, N.Y.), May 12, 2002; ""Stand Firm in Fight on Brook School" [*Cleveland Post*] clipping, October 9, 1943, in August Meier Papers, Schomburg, Box 92, folder 10.

22. "Town's Negroes Strike Against Jim Crow School, *PM*, September 9, 1943; "Upstate Town Hit by Racial Row," *New York Daily News*, September 13, 1943; "Showdown Is Due of Jim Crow School," *PM*, n.d., in NAACP Papers, Group II–B, Box 144;

23. *PM*, September 17, 1943.

24. In addition to articles above, see *Philadelphia Tribune*, October 9, 1943, *NAACP Annual Report, 1943* (New York, 1944), 9–10.

25. NAACP Press Release, September 10, 1943 in NAACP, Group II–B, Box 144.

26. Posters: "Hillburn and Hattiesburg" and "Jim Crow Blocks Schoolhouse Door"; NAACP Press Release, September 25, 1943; Memorandum for the Files, Re: Mass Meeting Held at Golden Gate Ballroom, all in NAACP, Group II–A, Box 227; *People's Voice*, October 9, 1943; *Amsterdam News*, October 9, 1943.

27. "Hillburn—The Fair," Poetry by Countee Cullen, Music by Waldemar Hille, Highlander Folk School. Copy in NAACP Papers, Group II–B, Box 144.

28. See letters and telegrams re: Hillburn in NAACP Papers, Group II–B, Box 144; Press Release from Milton Konvitz, Re: Briefs Filed in Trenton Case, January 26, 1944, in NAACP Papers, Group II–B, Box 143; *Ex Rel Hedgepeth v. Board of Education of the City of Trenton*; *New York Times,* February 1, 1944; and "New Jersey School Admits Bias," December 7, 1945 in Vertical File, Moorland-Spingarn Research Collection, Howard University, Folder: Education, New Jersey; for an alternative view on black protest as wholly local and uncoordinated, see Meier and Rudwick, *Along the Color Line*, 378–382.

6

"You can sing and punch . . . but you can't be a soldier or a man"

AFRICAN AMERICAN STRUGGLES FOR A NEW PLACE IN POPULAR CULTURE

Stephen Tuck

In his contribution to his own edited collection of essays by black leaders, *What the Negro Wants* (1944), the distinguished black historian Rayford Logan insisted "The Negro Wants First-Class Citizenship." He did not expect black Americans to gain equal rights quickly, because "the will of the majority is opposed to granting them now." But he believed that there were steps that could be taken to win equality in the longer term. Logan called for changes in the law, the inclusion of black workers in unions, and an end to colonialism. Then he added, "A young woman informed me in all seriousness that her whole attitude changed when she saw a colored girl in a class at Columbia University wearing better clothes than she did."[1]

For Logan, changing the black image in the white mind was crucial because "thirteen millions, largely unarmed, have no chance to win equality by force from an adamant, powerfully armed one hundred twenty millions."[2] White assumptions of black American inferiority and, by extension, the presumption that black Americans should occupy a subordinate place in society, underpinned racial discrimination—by individuals, by employers, and by the government. The justification for the infamous *Plessy* decision of 1896, for example, which upheld the principle of racial segregation, held that "if the two races are to meet upon terms of social equality, it must be the result of natural affinities, a mutual appreciation of each other's merits." But "if one race be inferior to the other socially, the constitution of the United States cannot put them upon the same plane."

Thus for many black leaders, like Logan, the question of the black image was not a sideshow to the main story of wartime protest. It was integral to the main story, taking its place alongside campaigns for black inclusion in the war effort and for black rewards because of their contribution to the war effort. Changing the black image was fundamental if African Americans wanted to progress to the "same plane" of rights and resources as white Americans in a majority white society. As the NAACP's *Crisis* magazine put it on the eve of war, "We need, in short, to inoculate the American public with the vaccine of critical judgement."[3] The war era—where black Americans could prove their worth as patriots against a racist enemy—seemed the perfect opportunity to reach for the syringe.

On May 11, 1942, the U.S. Navy press office released a statement: Admiral Chester Nimitz was set to award the prestigious Navy Cross to black mess-man Dorie Miller onboard ship, somewhere in the Pacific. The Cross honored Miller for "his distinguished devotion to duty" and "extraordinary courage" in manning a machine gun at Pearl Harbor."[4] Seemingly, Miller, in the chaos and cauldron of war, had risen above his station—he had stepped out of his subordinate place. An unknown black laborer on a ship had become a celebrated black defender of the nation. It was precisely the sort of transformation that gave Logan hope. In years to come, Dorie Miller's heroism would become part of American popular memory.

Yet a closer look at Miller's tale reveals a rather more complicated and ambiguous story. Black journalists had to campaign for six months before Naval officials would acknowledge the news of the black messman's heroics. Even then, the Navy refused to identify Miller for a further three months, and rebuffed black leaders' calls for Miller to return to shore and receive the award from the president in person. Nor did Miller's award set a precedent. In December 1942 black journalists pressed in vain for confirmation of a long-standing rumor that black messman Charles French had dragged a raft holding wounded white sailors two miles across the Pacific.[5] Above all, Miller's award had no obvious effect on the Navy's racial policies. African American sailors were not allowed above the rank of messman until near the end of the war, and even then they remained segregated.

Logan's hopes and Miller's experience sum up much of the story of the struggle over the black image in wartime. In the first place, there was a struggle. Activists for—and against—black equality poured time and thought and energy into the question of the black image, believing wider questions of black Americans' place in society, and thus their citizenship, were at stake. Civil rights leaders, black officials in the War Department, and black publicists sought to portray black men (and it was mostly about men) as worthy soldiers, high achievers, and everyday guys. They achieved some notable successes. Miller's breakthrough was more than matched by the rise of black musicians and sports stars in popular culture, and there were a smattering of path-breaking magazine articles, radio programs, and movies portraying positive black role models. Citing such examples, historians of race and popular culture often point to the war as a decisive moment of change—the moment when civil rights leaders focused on popular culture as never before, and the moment when the black image began to improve.[6]

As Miller's tale suggests, however, the overall outcome was rather more ambiguous. The war did not mark the start of the campaign for a better image—
black leaders had long sought to improve the black image in popular culture.
Moreover, the random gains during the war did not herald a more general
improvement. Examples of positive black images in mainstream popular culture were actually few and far between. The more common black images were
those of subservient black men and women, and by far the most common
images in popular culture remained those of white heroism. The one area
in which black Americans did break through into popular culture, as entertainers, reinforced the image of black men as amusement servants, thereby
reaffirming white superiority.

Yet if the war did not mark a watershed in mainstream culture's treatment of the black image, it did produce important changes in the way in
which black Americans addressed the issue. During the war years, prominent
civil rights leaders learned new tactics about manipulating popular culture to
their advantage and, for the first time, they had some power to pressure the
government—from within, as well as from outside—to tackle the question of
black stereotyping. It was not enough power to force major changes in the short
term. Indeed, which images were acceptable and which were not reveal much
about the dynamics of white supremacy during the war era. But in the longer
term, the lessons of the war years prepared the way for the revolution in the
black image that was to come during the cold war and the civil rights movement.

From a Brute to a Fool: The Pre-war Campaign for a Positive Image

At the start of the century, U.S. popular culture caricatured African Americans
as subhuman: from "zip coons" or bug-eyed bandana-wearing "mammies,"
to dangerous brutes and justifiably lynched rapists.[7] Indeed, some aspects of
America's expanding culture—such as the market in collectible figurines and
the "coon song" dance craze—were built on such stereotypes. The first epic
movie in the history of cinema, D. W. Griffith's *Birth of a Nation* (1915), had
an explicit, white supremacist agenda. Set in the Civil War era, the movie celebrated the triumph of the Ku Klux Klan. The main black character, Gus, a soldier (played by a white actor in dark face), tries to rape a young white woman,
but she leaps from a cliff. The movie's white hero—the girl's brother—cradles
her during her (ludicrously) prolonged death. Burning with righteous rage, he
then determines to purge the South of Gus and other black beasts, and helps
launch the noble Ku Klux Klan. Griffith was a master moviemaker. *Birth of a
Nation* broke new ground in cinematography and popularity. Therein lay its
power.

Little wonder, then, that black leaders targeted racial stereotypes throughout the segregation era. In the late nineteenth century, Frederick Douglass

would point to the picture of boxer Peter Jackson, the "Black Prince," in his study and say, "Peter is doing a great deal with his fists to solve the Negro question."[8] Through his program of industrial education, Booker T. Washington hoped to show that the race was heading—to quote the title of his autobiography—*Up from Slavery*.[9] Washington's great rival on most other matters, W.E.B. Du Bois, agreed on the importance of a positive black image. On his twenty-fifth birthday, Du Bois vowed "to make a name in science, to make a name in literature and thus to raise my race."[10] One of the NAACP's formative campaigns was against *Birth of a Nation*. In the 1920s, civil rights leaders celebrated the Harlem Renaissance of black literature. Praising the "art approach to the Negro problem," the novelist, songwriter, and NAACP executive director James Weldon Johnson thought "nothing will do more to raise [the Negro's] status than a demonstration of intellectual parity by the Negro."[11] The young Walter White—executive director of the NAACP during World War II—wrote *The Fire in the Flint* (1924), a tragic novel of an implausibly upright and heroic young black doctor.

On the ground, too, African Americans asserted positive images. Some joined campaigns against negative stereotypes. During the early 1930s, the *Pittsburgh Courier* collected 275,000 signatures to protest *Amos 'n' Andy*—the first radio comedy serial sensation, which followed the incompetent efforts of two black men (played by white actors) to cope with urban life. Most black Americans coped with the cultural color line by creating a separate popular culture. In movies and the radio, all-black companies barely survived.[12] But in sports (with all-black leagues), magazines, and especially music, black popular culture thrived.[13] In the context of white supremacy, such cultural resilience was inevitably subversive. Dressing up, playing, dancing, and listening allowed African Americans to reject their subordinate place, and to reclaim their individual and group identities as something other than workers and second-class citizens.[14]

Black Americans made some advances in terms of their popular image, especially by the time of the New Deal. In Hollywood, Hattie McDaniel's Oscar-winning performance in *Gone with the Wind* (1939) lent at least some dignity to the role of a servant. The same year, *Life* magazine featured a story of African American debutantes.[15] A few black athletes and musicians began to establish themselves in mainstream popular culture. In each of the four years running up to 1939, at least one black athlete ranked in the top ten of America's annual sportswriters' poll (and twice topped the poll).[16] On the radio, the Office of Education sponsored the 1938 CBS series *Americans All, Immigrants All*, which included an episode about the contribution of black Americans. *Americans All* became the first government-sponsored broadcast to win the Women's National Radio Committee Gold Microphone Award.[17] Eleanor Roosevelt and Secretary of the Interior Harold Ickes supported the NAACP's successful campaign to allow Marian Anderson to sing at the Lincoln Memorial.

Moreover, African American culture had crossover appeal, thereby challenging both the distinctiveness and superiority of white supremacy. During the 1920s, a rash of all-black musicals won acclaim on Broadway. Jazz and the jitterbug were popular with both black and white—and sometimes interracial groups of—dancers.[18] The key to Harlem's vogue during its so-called Renaissance was the interest of white patrons. Black baseball teams played, and often beat, leading white teams. More generally, black culture influenced the form of "mainstream" popular culture, nowhere more than in music. Duke Ellington coined the "swing era" (though he preferred the term "Negro music") with *It Don't Mean a Thing (if It Ain't Got That Swing)*.[19] White basketball and baseball teams copied the jump and base-running tactics of their black counterparts.

Yet overall, pre-war black campaigns for a better image—or against negative images—had little impact. Mayor "Big Bill" Thompson in Chicago, responsive to African American voters, banned *Birth of a Nation*. But, in general, African Americans had little leverage to oppose derogatory caricatures and even less to replace them. Rather, Southern censors held power over Hollywood studios and radio networks. Lloyd Binford in Memphis cut black actor Eddie Anderson's character from *Brewster's Millions* (1935) because there was "a too familiar way about him."[20] Censors even cut Louis Armstrong's fledgling music radio show.[21] Harlem's vogue, such that it was, was brief. *Amos 'n' Andy* remained a hit with white (and many black) listeners. *Americans All* was the exception that proved the rule, and was soon thwarted by Congress.[22] In contrast, the popular 1930s radio documentary of U.S. history, *Cavalcade of America*, did not include a single black leader.[23] In the eighteen months (and nearly one hundred issues) preceding World War II, neither *Life* nor *Ladies Home Journal* carried a single advertisement that portrayed black men or women as anything other than servants.[24] The crossover influence of African American culture had its limits, too. On the radio and records, mostly white bands played "Negro swing."

Even the improvements during the New Deal were incremental at best. The stereotype of the black brute may have lost some traction by the outbreak of World War II—but the brute was replaced by a fool. The sociologist Guy Johnson reckoned that a catalog of "What Every White Man Thinks He Knows about Negroes" would include the following themes: "The Negro is lazy . . . cannot manage complicated machinery . . . is dirty, smelly . . . fond of loud colors . . . a naturalized clown . . . inordinate sexual passion. . . . His mind works like a child's mind."[25] In the world of popular collectibles, for example, black figurines were happy and stupid in equal measure. Some toys required children to beat the figure over the head.[26] Thus, for all the activism of the early twentieth century, the image of the black man remained firmly in its subordinate place on the eve of war—a place that in turn set the parameters for discussions of the black man's rights. Johnson's "Every White Man" concluded,

"He is incapable of self-government, and therefore must have the supervision and guidance of the white man." To make matters worse, "every white man" was to be found deep within the New Deal government—so too was "every white woman." The renowned liberal journalist Lorena Hickok, friend of Eleanor Roosevelt, toured the country to be the ears and eyes of the Works Progress Administrator, Harry Hopkins. Hickok wrote that black Southerners "act like creatures barely removed from the Ape. . . . Northerner that I am, raised in the sentimental traditions that all men are created equal—I'm not so sure these Southerners aren't right."[27]

Lobbying the Government to Act: The Great Expectations of Wartime

With the onset of war, black leaders continued to campaign for an improved image. The National Urban League liaised with major radio networks. The NAACP's Walter White was especially drawn to the power of movies. He told fellow activists that "the matter of treatment of the Negro in the motion pictures is of such importance that it takes rank over some other phases of our work." Consequently, he courted Hollywood assiduously, visiting three times during 1942 and 1943. He urged the Screenwriters Guild to treat black Americans as normal people. Just as Hollywood inserted servicemen into crowd scenes, so too it should include black men and women. In an impassioned plea, White declared "the importance of these media by which ideas are formed and propagated is more crucial than the making of guns and planes."[28]

The war gave African American leaders grounds for optimism—an optimism they shared with white liberal thinkers. In his seminal survey, the Swedish sociologist Gunnar Myrdal believed that America's race dilemma could—and ultimately would—be resolved through changed white attitudes. Intellectual culture had already disavowed race hierarchies. Surveying recent findings on "race inferiority" in the journal *Scientific Monthly* in 1943, Wilton M. Krogman concluded, "In words of one syllable *there is no such thing*."[29] Now the war promised to popularize scientific orthodoxy. Most obviously, Hitler gave racism a bad name—and gave African Americans a weapon to tarnish the image of white supremacists. New York representative Adam Clayton Powell, Jr., for example, often quipped, "We recognized [Hitler] immediately, because he is like minor Hitlers here."[30] In contrast, Roosevelt's "Four Freedoms" raised the hope of social equality. Liberals in the media, from *Time/Life* publisher Henry Luce to cartoonist Dr. Seuss, criticized white supremacy.[31] Hollywood moguls promised White that they would act on his suggestions. Meanwhile, Roosevelt created an Office of War Information (OWI)—the propaganda arm of the war effort—that was staffed by New Deal liberals.

The optimism of the war evoked memories of the Harlem Renaissance of the 1920s, and to some extent, the New Deal. What was new was the confidence of black leaders that they had real power, at last, to shape the black image. Sensitive to the black vote, and in need of black loyalty, Roosevelt famously gave in to the threat of a March on Washington. Within the War Department, Roosevelt created a post of a black civilian aide to the Secretary of War, while officials at the OWI kept a nervous eye on black morale. Meanwhile, the fevered patriotism of war allowed black leaders to wrap positive black stereotypes in the flag. The fact that the recruitment of black soldiers coincided with the rise of truly mass media seemed particularly opportune.

In practice, however, the government was reluctant to act. On race matters, the OWI's aim was to lessen social tensions rather than tackle white supremacy. In any case, the War Department's innate conservatism offset any liberal outlook in the OWI. Secretary of War Henry Stimson opposed "deliberate use of the war emergency to . . . force new policies," and senior officers assumed that black soldiers made poor fighters.[32] OWI officials were also aware that Southern congressmen held their purse strings.[33] Black journalists complained that the government co-opted moderate black leaders merely to marginalize "the newsmen and national figures who really mould Negro public opinion."[34] They also castigated Roosevelt for gesture politics. Claude Barnett, director of the Associated Negro Press, believed that only African Americans were subjected to the "paternalistic pap which OWI is spewing." Barnett pointed out that only four black men held any responsibility in OWI.[35] One of these, black lawyer Theodore Berry, soon resigned in frustration. So too did the civilian aide to the Secretary of War, the forthright black lawyer William Hastie. His successor, Truman Gibson, lasted to 1945, but by then "I had had enough . . . of the incredible balancing act I was performing."[36]

Nonetheless, during the war, African Americans did have some new leverage over the government's propaganda effort. The potential of African Americans to destabilize the war effort alarmed the War Department. In a government poll of black New Yorkers in 1942, less than a third of respondents said that they would be worse off if Japan won the war.[37] Wavering sentiment was one thing, unrest another. On the evening of June 21, 1943, central Detroit erupted in violence, leaving twenty-three dead. War Department officials worried more that the riot resulted in the loss of more than 1,250,000 man-hours.[38] Or as the *Chicago Sun* put it, "Hitler won a battle in Detroit today."[39] Detroit turned the spotlight on widespread racial unrest. In 1943 alone, there were over 200 major disturbances across the country. Black soldiers were at the heart of the violence, rioting on bases and battling with local police. In July, OWI bureaucrats worried that "the condition becomes more critical with each passing day,"[40] and that Axis powers were using the radio to foment trouble.[41]

Walter White drove the point home. "Some of them," he reported, "have become so embittered that they call their white fellow-American soldiers 'the enemy.'"[42] Citing this low morale, black leaders such as White and black officials within the War Department pushed for radical measures. Much of their rhetoric focused on jobs and army discrimination. But they also called for a more positive portrayal of African Americans in popular culture. Berry suggested two key principles: (a) "convincing the Negro that he is part of the general war effort and (b) educating mass white opinion that negative racial attitudes retard progress."[43] Clearly, "(b)" was the opening that black leaders had been waiting for.

In this unique nexus of war, government responsiveness and the growth of mass media, African Americans were able to make some unprecedented gains. On the radio, NBC broadcast the landmark series *Freedom's People* during late 1941–1942. The show documented the contribution of African Americans to all aspects of American life. Such a series would have been unthinkable before the war, and indeed NBC prevaricated for fear of Southern censors. But under pressure from the government, NBC went ahead. Militant spokesmen, such as A. Philip Randolph and the famous actor and outspoken anti-colonialist Paul Robeson, made dignified speeches. Franklin Roosevelt even made a guest appearance.[44]

The single greatest prize, though, would be the positive portrayal of black soldiers, and the most remarkable wartime message on race, the movie *The Negro Soldier* (1944), suggested that the prize was in reach. Both the production and the distribution of the film illuminated the way in which black Americans—both inside and outside the government—sought to take advantage of the war. At the suggestion of black officials in the War Department, the OWI commissioned *The Negro Soldier* in the hope that real life "Negro soldiers" would develop "an enthusiasm for their part in the war."[45] *The Negro Soldier* was part of acclaimed director Frank Capra's *Why We Fight* series of propaganda movies.[46]

Capra's remit was strictly limited. The movie could not mention racial problems. The OWI planned to show it to black recruits only. Yet *The Negro Soldier* became politically charged. Acclaimed by civil rights activists, it portrayed black men extremely positively—equally impressive in uniform and at leisure. By the end of 1945, the movie was being shown to both black and white new recruits, and a shortened version had been screened in some 5,000 commercial theaters. Thus the propaganda aimed at "Negro soldiers" was instead used as propaganda by black Americans against white supremacy.

On the face of it, the forty-three-minute movie fulfilled its conservative remit. The *New York Times* thought "it definitely sugarcoats an issue which is broader than the Negro's part in the war."[47] Set in a black church, the movie focused on the contribution of black Americans to U.S. democracy. A preacher, in measured tones, traced the heroism of black soldiers from the Boston Massacre to the First World War. In turn, the preacher warns the congregation of the Axis powers' racism, contrasting it to the freedom—particularly of religion—available to black Americans. With no obvious irony, the congregation learns that the Nazis have enslaved millions of people. The hanging corpses in Russia look uncannily similar to images of Southern lynch victims. The movie then followed the progress of two black recruits in the army. To upbeat music, the soldiers swiftly progress to officer status. As with many war films, *The Negro Soldier* also painted an idyllic view of army life with plenty of baseball, girls, and fun on the assault course. In a rousing finale, the final hymn *My Country 'Tis of Thee* leads into military marching sequences and a musical crescendo (played by the army air forces band).

What was conservative at face value, though, was anything but in context. Capra had passed the project to Carlton Moss, his "Negro consultant," who had been involved in the New Deal's Federal Theater Programs and had mounted a patriotic revue, *A Salute to the Negro Soldier*. Far from being an apologist for the federal government, however, Moss supported the wartime "Double V" campaign for racial change. He also shared the conviction that a positive perception of black Americans would undermine white supremacy.[48] As he told the press in 1944, the film was designed to "ignore what's wrong with the Army and tell what's right with my people."

Moss himself told "what's right" by playing the role of the preacher. His summary of black achievement made clear the debt owed by white America to black sacrifice.[49] In addition, the two young cadets countered the prevailing stereotype of black men as lazy, ignorant, and hypersexed—and in search of white women. These black soldiers were self-disciplined, read (Negro) poetry in their spare time, and courted black girls respectfully. Consequently, the film did anything but "sugarcoat" the race issue. As Moss noted later, "You didn't *need* any dialogue, you didn't *need* any preachment."[50] The NAACP agreed. *The Negro Soldier* "has enormous potentialities for good . . . in educating white Americans to the true place of their fellow citizens in our country."[51]

The alliance between African American officials and activists proved to be the key to the promotion of the movie. Army leaders screened the first cut to 200 black journalists in New York in January 1944. But unbeknownst to the army, Moss and Gibson had primed the journalists to demand that the movie be put on general release. Meanwhile, Capra returned to take credit for the film, which added further pressure for its distribution. In a sense, the army was caught in a trap. The War Department duly made the movie compulsory viewing for all soldiers and agreed to put it on general release.[52]

However, the War Activities Committee, which distributed movies, only made 92 prints (far less than the average of 350 prints).[53] In response, Walter White cashed in the promises of goodwill from his Hollywood contacts, persuading many movie moguls to endorse the film. Harry Cohn, the president of Columbia Pictures, described *The Negro Soldier* as "the greatest war department picture ever made."[54] The NAACP also publicized high-profile support for the racial message of the film.[55] The Hollywood Writers Mobilization felt that *The Negro Soldier* "explodes the lies . . . the Negro soldier is shown as a man . . . no different from the white soldier. We believe that showings of this picture ... would go far to eliminate prejudice and bigotry." Local interracial groups in the West and North joined the campaign. In March 1944, for example, the Los Angeles Mayor's Committee for Home Front Unity agreed to sponsor the picture.[56]

Many African Americans recognized that the film had limitations. Indeed, even one anonymous *white* soldier denounced the film in a letter to the *People's Voice*. "There are those who believe that *The Negro Soldier*, bad as it is, represents at least a beginning of a movement to tell the truth. But no movement to tell the truth can ever be founded on a basic lie."[57] In a memo to a colleague, White agreed that the movie "does not tell the truth" about the plight of black soldiers. But he was content with the irresistible message of black ability. It was certainly better than a rival movie about black Americans, Jack Goldberg's *We've Come a Long Long Way*—against which, with NAACP support, the OWI won an injunction.

Gibson and the NAACP leadership still faced the challenge of ensuring that *The Negro Soldier* was taken up widely. The NAACP sent telegrams to sympathetic journalists with news of a petition of some 200 people "who work in the motion picture industry" calling for the movie to be shown at neighborhood theaters.[58] Using the *Crisis*, the NAACP instructed thousands of readers "to write or telephone leading theater managers in their cities urging them to book this film."[59] Nonetheless, fewer than 2,000 theaters took the film, compared with a typical showing in at least 12,000 theaters for hit movies.[60] Part of the problem, as one NAACP member pointed out, was that the film was too long.[61] When it was re-released as a short, it reached a much wider audience. Some 5,000 theaters took the film, with over 80 percent catering to whites. In Brandt's theaters in Manhattan, *The Negro Soldier* played with *Snow White*.[62]

Civil rights activists desperately hoped that *The Negro Soldier* would mark a turning point both in terms of government propaganda and racial attitudes. It did neither. To be sure, army orientation materials began to include pictures of black soldiers. A 1944 pamphlet, the *Command of Negro Troops,* insisted that "all peoples seem to be endowed by nature about equally with whatever it takes to fight a good war." But the pamphlet also justified segregation. Postwar evaluations showed that white soldiers were happy enough to watch the movie, but it made no difference to their views on the army's racial policies.[63] The war also finished too soon for activists to build on *The Negro Soldier*. Although the NAACP pushed for a sequel focusing on combat units (and Moss went to Europe to film it), the army dropped the idea as soon as the war was over.[64]

Meanwhile, black leaders in and outside the government complained that the regular diet of war newsreels remained segregated. A year into the war, Hastie pointed out that newsreels for white audiences had yet to include a *single* black soldier. At the end of the war, newsreel companies were still pleading fear of Southern censors.[65] White wrote the Bureau of Public Relations to say that although African Americans enjoyed watching their all-black newsreel, "much,

much more important is acquainting the 117,000,000 Americans who are *not* Negroes with the fact that the Negro is doing his full share in the war effort, as far as he is permitted to do so."[66] White was right. OWI polls found that less than half of white Americans thought that African Americans were doing enough to support the war, and 90 percent thought that black and white troops should be trained separately.[67] One short propaganda movie about the Negro soldier could do virtually nothing to counter a lily-white newsreel service.

Similarly, barely any propaganda posters portrayed "colored" servicemen (save for those that showed "evil" Japanese soldiers).[68] On radio, there was no network follow-up to *Freedom's People*, nor a direct counterpart to the *Negro Soldier*. Gibson planned such a broadcast, *America's Negro Soldiers*. Intended as a mix of music, sketches, interviews, and speeches, it ended up purely as an entertainment feature. Under the headline, "The Army's Radio Flop," the *Pittsburgh Courier* reckoned the show "amounted to a praise of a jim crow system."[69] Gibson later agreed, "There's no denying the soft soap" of the show.[70]

The Persistent Whiteness of Popular Culture During the War

Unable to force the government to change, black leaders had little chance of forcing civilian media outlets to promote the black soldier. Hollywood followed radio's lead in using black soldiers merely as a vehicle for entertainment. One of two all-black movies, *Stormy Weather*, started in a 1919 soldier's ball with Lieutenant Jim Europe's famous army swing band playing. The other all-black movie, *Cabin in the Sky*, was a musical with no military connections at all. In print culture, the good black soldier remained conspicuous by his absence. *Life* magazine supported the war with gusto. But in seventy-eight glossy issues during the final year and a half of war, when black soldiers were at last in combat, *Life* published a mere ten pictures of black men in uniform—out of some 14,000 photographs.[71] Most of these ten pictures were very small, and most of the soldiers were clearly service troops. One black soldier carried an accordion. None carried weapons.[72]

If positive images of black soldiers were absent, negative images of cowardly black soldiers abounded. A team of black researchers following the national press in wartime reported a revival of derogatory stories about black soldiers as the war progressed.[73] To Truman Gibson's despair, the *New York Times* reported on the black 92nd Infantry's "more or less panicky retreats" in Italy, which corroborated comments from high sources that "Negro troops can't fight."[74] In Alabama, a leading businessman mourned the death of his son after an accidental collision between two planes, one piloted by a black man. In his grief he condemned the "sudden elevation of the Negro to duties he is not yet qualified to perform."[75]

To the frustration of civil rights leaders, mainstream culture rarely included black adults or families, either. To be sure, *Ladies Home Journal* did feature a middle-class black family—"Meet the Hinksons"—for the first time, in one early wartime issue. But the ensuing eighteen months of wartime issues (and some 2,000 pictures) did not include a *single* other black character. On the radio, soap operas *Our Gal Sunday* and *The Romance of Helen Trent* introduced black characters. But the most famous such character, Rochester, on the hit comedy *The Jack Benny Show*, sent mixed messages. Rochester was integrated into the cast and was intelligent (and, unlike the characters in *Amos 'n' Andy,* was played by a black actor, Ernest Robinson). Nevertheless, he was a domestic servant whose sexual prowess was the foil for Benny's problems in that department. Meanwhile, Truman Gibson failed in his repeated attempts to persuade the most popular radio soap of them all, *As the World Turns*, to introduce a black character.

In some respects, there were no improvements in the image of African Americans in wartime popular culture at all. *Life* published far *fewer* pictures of black Americans at skilled work or leisure in the final eighteen months of the war than across a similar period at the end of the 1930s. In the world of collectible figurines, wartime black figures tended to be old or young. Adults were still not portrayed as anything other than cooks and servants, and there was nothing to suggest the existence of functional black families. The only new developments of wartime in the collectibles market were the rise of the tragic mulatto figure, and the beginnings of sexual female images to replace the "mammy."[76]

It was a similar story in Hollywood. The NAACP sent plaques to studios for good movies, and angry letters for bad ones.[77] But such tactics hardly swayed the studios. Again, there were some exceptions. A handful of wartime movies were based on a crisis that forced one black man into a white crowd. The results were sometimes positive. In *Sahara* (1943), an African soldier called Tamboul (Rex Ingram) leads a U.S. sergeant (Humphrey Bogart) and his lost tank crew to water. The crew then overpowers a superior German force. In Harlem, children cheered the movie. In contrast, in *Lifeboat* (1943), the sole African American, called Joe (a steward from the sinking main ship, played by Canada Lee), was predictably shifty and musical in equal measure. An internal NAACP review reckoned "Absolutely the best that can be said for it is that it represents . . . some slight departure from the harsher techniques of conventional stereotype. Joe Spencer was not called upon to do a belly-laugh jig on the boat's heaving gunwales."[78]

Overall, progress was slight. Although the OWI set up a branch in Hollywood, a Columbia University study in 1945 found that of 100 black appearances in wartime films, 75 perpetuated old stereotypes, 13 were neutral, and only 12 were positive.[79] Indeed, for every *Sahara*, there were plenty of films like Universal's *Captive Wild Woman* (1943), in which a mad scientist transforms a gorilla into an attractive mulatto woman—a stereotype compounded by her reversion to type as soon as the thought of sex crosses her mind. Or for children, Warner Brothers put out a popular cartoon, *Coal Black and de Sebben Dwarves* (1943). Black audiences jeered phony caricatures, but they couldn't change the images offered to white audiences.

There were limits to the crossover influence of black culture, too. When *Life* covered the new Lindy dance craze in 1943—popularized in African American dance halls—all the dancers in the photo story were white.[80] The following year, the *Baltimore Afro-American* published a survey of entertainers performing for troops during the war, finding that only 39 of 2,066 artists were African American.[81] Black servicemen were sometimes banned from big band shows that even welcomed German prisoners of war. On radio, the very few shows that took a positive interest in the place of African Americans tended to be broadcast on local stations in the urban north.

Meanwhile, white propagandists also used the war to shore up the color line. Thomas Dixon (whose novel about the Klan inspired *Birth of a Nation*) updated his prose for a new era. *The Flaming Sword* (1939) saw a combination of black Americans, communists, and assorted baddies try to overthrow the U.S. government. War against Japan reinforced the idea of non-white deviousness and danger—black poet Langston Hughes wondered "How come we did not try them [atoms bombs] out on Germany?"[82] Southern politicians played the patriotism card to uphold the color line, too. Bus signs in Charleston, South Carolina, urged passengers to observe Jim Crow laws—and thus urged black men and women to know their place—since "co-operation . . . will make the war shorter."[83]

Some African Americans with a vested interest in popular culture turned on each other. African American actors complained bitterly that White was doing a lot more harm than good and was putting their livelihoods at risk. In turn, White and many East Coast activists blamed the actors. In a letter to *The People's Voice* in September 1942, one writer complained that "it's up to our Negro film actors to stand their ground, as a few have already, and NOT ACCEPT blackface buffoon parts."[84] Black soldiers in the South Pacific wrote home that they, too, were "ashamed" of such buffoonery.[85] In fact, the main problem was not the tactics, but the simple realities of who held power in American cultural life in wartime. Southern censors and theater owners—empowered by their own calls for wartime unity—simply refused to accept positive African American stereotypes that challenged white supremacy and the status quo. Black commentators blamed the movie moguls for their limited liberalism. The *New York Amsterdam News* took aim at the Jewish "Producers Who Protested Discrimination of Own Group Now the Most Chief Oppressors."[86] Even the more sympathetic studio owners were primarily interested in profit, and thus beholden to white audiences. As Sam Goldwyn famously put it, "If you want to send a message, call Western Union."

The Rise and Ambiguous Benefits of Black Entertainers

While black soldiers and everyday black men and women remained absent from white mainstream culture during the war, black entertainers gained new prominence. That they did so was, in fact, in large measure due to the war. By proving their patriotism, black entertainers were able to become acceptable, even useful. Yet the fact that it was the entertainer, not the soldier or black high achiever, who became the acceptable black face in popular culture is telling. A new prominence for the entertainer was not the same as a new place for the black man or woman. Indeed, black entertainers could trace their lineage back to minstrels and slave group singers of old.

The rise, the patriotism, and the limitations of the popular image of the black man as entertainer can be seen most clearly in the careers of Joe Louis and Duke Ellington. Both men were well-known before the war, but white and black audiences clearly responded to the celebrities in different ways. While the black *Pittsburgh Courier* celebrated one early bout with the headline "Joe Louis vs. Jim Crow," the white *New York Times* merely hailed "Detroit Boxer's Right to the Jaw."[87] Yet, at the same time, an awareness of the "Brown Bomber's" race almost certainly explains the early lack of mainstream affection for Louis. In June 1939, Louis prepared to fight Tony "Two Ton" Galento, an Italian American from New York. Galento was hardly popular. His reputation for fouling and fighting "easy" opponents meant that crowds booed him when he was sparring. Yet in a Gallup poll ahead of the fight, barely half the respondents wanted Louis to win.[88]

Indeed, when the mainstream media acknowledged Louis's race in his early bouts, they often confirmed racial stereotypes. After Louis dethroned James Braddock, one white reporter thought Braddock "was determined, courageous and game." Contrast "Louis, who turned primitive with the savage instinct to kill."[89] More generally, black achievement in jazz and boxing—the versions of music and sports most associated with vice and low culture—conformed to type. Media reports on black support for Louis further confirmed negative stereotypes. The *New York Times* juxtaposed coverage of Louis's 1939 title defense in Detroit with news that an extra 759 policemen were sent in to Harlem, and that in Chicago, "Bonfires were built in the streets and around them Negroes danced."[90]

The coming of war enabled black celebrities to gain credibility as well as recognition. Both Louis and Ellington allied themselves firmly with the war effort. Ellington's Carnegie Hall debut in January 23, 1943—which began with the "Star Spangled Banner"—was for the benefit of Russian war relief.[91] Joe Louis knocked out Hitler's champion Max Schmeling in 1938, famously donated the proceeds of two fights to the navy and army fund, and put on morale-boosting boxing exhibitions for the troops. This patriotism, as they well knew, was out of step with wider African American ambivalence about the war. The *Amsterdam News* lambasted Louis as a "sacrificial goat."[92] But once established as American patriots, both Louis and Ellington became genuine superstars in American popular culture. In 1942, Ellington's orchestra became the first African American orchestra to win *Down Beat's* annual poll for America's favorite swing band (voted on by some 15,000 musicians and readers).[93] His Carnegie Hall debut capped "Duke Ellington" week in the mainstream press, and he followed it with lucrative tours on both coasts, and then annual returns to Carnegie Hall.[94] Louis's fights were the first to take in $1 million since Jack Dempsey.

The rise of black entertainers fell far short of the goals of black leaders to promote African Americans as soldiers and responsible citizens. But it was still important. In the first place, the image of the patriotic accomplished performer was a step forward from that of a brute or a fool. Furthermore, since the OWI thought that this image was safe, it opened up state broadcasts to black entertainers in a way that commercial radio was still unwilling to do. Gibson was delighted when the Armed Forces Service Radio (AFRS) put on *Jubilee*, a prime-time all-black variety show. Black soldiers tended to listen to the show in groups, their pleasure in the designated "Negro music" a subversive action in itself.[95] Similarly, African American public pride in Joe Louis had a defiant quality. The crossover of some African American performers into the mainstream also implicitly challenged the universality of white culture.

Furthermore, both Louis and Ellington intended to challenge white supremacy through their performances. Louis hoped that his image would shame the navy into a fairer policy. Ellington argued that "you gotta be careful with words" but "you can say anything you want on the trombone."[96] His 1941 production, *Jump for Joy,* sought to "eliminate the stereotypical image that had been exploited by Hollywood and Broadway." It even included a scene celebrating the death of Uncle Tom.[97] Meanwhile, his Carnegie Hall debut featured a performance of *Black, Brown and Beige*, a dramatic musical equivalent of *The Negro Soldier.* Starting with slavery, it told of the heroic contribution of black Americans to the development of the United States.

However, the dazzling careers of Louis and Ellington can obscure the stubborn reality of the subordinate black place in American culture and society. The very reason that Ellington tried to bury Uncle Tom was because negative stereotypes were still alive and very much kicking. Though white consumers could buy "Lucky Joe" (Louis) piggy banks, they were far more likely to buy "nigger" salt-and-pepper shakers. The adulation of black performers even prompted Ellington to complain, "The Negro is not merely a singing and dancing wizard."[98] In contrast, in the annual Schomburg poll to select a dozen leading black men and women, African Americans voted for educators and workers as well as entertainers. Whereas, for example, the black press celebrated the story of Captain Hugh Mulzac, the "first Negro captain of a United

States merchant ship," mainstream white newspapers barely noticed.[99] If the black face appeared at all in advertisements in white newspapers—which was rare (except for the servant image)—it was as a musician.

Indeed, the association of African American high achievement with jazz and sports actually underscored the idea of innate racial difference—and black primitiveness and lack of intelligence. In 1941, sports writer Dean Cromwell speculated on the rise of black athletes. "It was not long ago . . . that his ability to sprint and jump was a life-and-death matter to him in the jungle."[100] Moreover, the fact that some individuals could prosper served to indict all other black Americans for failing to do so. White reporter John Kieran pondered the question of Joe Louis's "Color? Only in the tint of his skin. He doesn't drink or smoke. He doesn't turn racing cars upside-down. He doesn't sing or whistle or imitate four Hawaiians. He never has been sued for breach of promise. He puts his money in the bank. These are very sober qualities. All his striking qualities are in his two fists."[101]

The Ambiguous Legacy of Wartime

Why this failure to change the black image in popular culture mattered was that most white Americans outside the rural South had little contact with African Americans in everyday life.[102] Thus their perception of black Americans was drawn from other sources. During the war, popular culture almost always celebrated positive white images. With a very few—though notable—exceptions, the images on offer kept black men very firmly in their place. Indeed, with the rapid rise of new media, white Americans were bombarded, as never before, with images of patriotic white men and women and subservient African Americans.

Little surprise then that, overall, white attitudes toward African Americans seemed to change little during the war. One postwar poll found that 53 percent of whites thought that black Americans were potentially as intelligent as whites, a step up from 42 percent in 1942 in the only previous poll.[103] How accurate these two polls were and what influence popular culture (as opposed to changes in intellectual culture) played in any change are impossible to gauge. In any case, "potential" was not the same as commonsense understanding of the black man's natural place. Influential British journalist Alistair Cooke was struck by "the persistence of lazy clichés among the whites," especially in Northern cities.[104] Black novelist Ralph Ellison agreed, writing in 1949 that *Birth of a Nation* "forged the twin screen image of the Negro as bestial rapist and grinning, eye-rolling clown—stereotypes that are still with us today."[105] Significantly, the postwar poll found that a majority of white Americans still thought black Americans should not have an equal claim to jobs.[106]

Indeed, there is no evidence that the prominence of high-profile black performers made any impact on white supremacist views. A survey of Southern newspapers by the Southern Regional Council in 1949 concluded, "As pictured in many newspapers, the Negro is either an entertaining fool, a dangerous animal, or (on the comparatively rare occasions when a Negro's achievements are applauded) a prodigy of astonishing attainments, considering his race."[107] One woman in Bristol, Virginia, wrote to the Southern moderate John Temple Graves, I "would rather live with the Germans and Japs than for the laws of segregation to be wiped out . . . Joe Louis has a strong arm but what else did he have?"[108]

If anything, the postwar peace made matters worse. With the war over, civil rights leaders lost what little leverage they had over the government (though they would regain it with more force once the cold war warmed up).[109] A despondent black White House correspondent Harry McAlpin, reporting on the award of the Congressional Medal of Honor to twenty-eight white soldiers, was outraged that there were "no Negroes among the heroes."[110]

With the war won, the mainstream media felt no obligation to include positive images of African Americans either. Rather, the postwar era would be marked by conservatism across all aspects of American life. In 1951 the de facto producer of *The Negro Solider*, Carlton Moss, was named by the House Un-American Activities Committee as a communist. Hollywood pulled back from message movies. The production side of the studios remained lily-white, and in-house Southern advisors maintained their hold. Acutely aware that more needed to be done, Walter White raised funds for a permanent NAACP Hollywood Bureau. But the plans fizzled out, and the NAACP turned away from Hollywood. In music, black rhythm and blues remained a segregated phenomenon for a decade after the war. Meanwhile, major magazines continued to portray few positive images of black adults (other than entertainers) into the late 1950s.[111] As for radio, in 1949, leading black actor Canada Lee asserted in a speech, "We are not a people according to radio . . . for, with rare exceptions, it is the cannibal, the lazy gambler, the shiftless-thieving razor-wielding Negro, that has come to represent the totality of Negro life."[112] The fact that there were exceptions at all was a positive development. But the lone crossover stars continued to be self-effacing and loyal rather than militant or edgy.

It is impossible to measure the latent impact of wartime with regard to the black image in popular culture. But what is clear is that the major breakthroughs in popular culture did not occur during the war. White youths started buying black music records in bulk in the mid-1950s. Black-oriented radio prospered for the first time after the war. Jackie Robinson's dignified emergence as a black sports star in America's favorite pastime—rather than boxing—began in 1948. Truman Gibson reckoned that boxing did not really impact mass American culture until television's boxing nights of the mid-1950s.

Intriguingly, though, the war years did leave a clear legacy for the civil rights movement. Civil rights leaders' high wartime expectations for changing popular culture, and the promise of an alliance (however tentative) with the government and mass media, lingered. Thus, for a generation after the war, many civil rights leaders clung to the hope that assimilation into mainstream culture would reap practical benefits. Their hopes for popular culture mirrored their political hopes for—and postwar loyalty to—liberal Democrats. They learned their tactics well. It was not by chance that a dignified woman, Rosa Parks, and not a pregnant teenage girl, became the catalyst for the Montgomery bus boycott. In some ways, such black leaders would be proved right, when television pictures of white mobs attacking clean-cut, prayerful, young activists shocked viewers across the nation. But others drew markedly different lessons from wartime, lessons born of frustration and disillusionment. Carlton Moss, creator of *The Negro Soldier*, became an early member of the Negro Theater Movement during the late 1950s. His aim, prefiguring a later generation of Black Power activists: "to concentrate on our own culture and stop trying to imitate or get the approval of white people."[113]

Notes

1. Rayford W. Logan, "The Negro Wants First-Class Citizenship" in Rayford W. Logan, ed., *What the Negro Wants* (Chapel Hill, 1944): 1–30, 15, 29.

2. Ibid., p.15.

3. Box A279, Series II, Folder: Films: Portrayal of Negroes in Film, 1940–June 1942, NAACP papers, LC.

4. Press Release: Navy Dept, May 11, 1942, RG208, E76, Box 237, File: Negro Activities, National Archives, College Park, Maryland (hereafter, NA).

5. Theodore R. Poston to Nicholas Roosevelt, December 18, 1942, RG208, E76, Box 237, File: Negro Activities, NA.

6. In his fine overview of civil rights protest from the civil war the present, for example, Jeff Norrell suggests that the changing image of African Americans during 1938–1948 made the civil rights movement possible; see Robert J. Norrell, *The House I Live In: Race in the American Century* (New York, 2005). Also see Thomas Cripps, *Making Movies Black: The Hollywood Message Movie from World War II to the Civil Rights Era* (New York, 1993), 28; Barbara Dianne Savage, *Broadcasting Freedom: Radio, War, and the Politics of Race, 1938–1948* (Chapel Hill, 1999); Lauren Rebecca Sklaroff, "Variety for the Servicemen: The Jubilee Show and the Paradox of Racializing Radio During World War II," *American Quarterly*, Vol. 56 (December 2004): 945–973, 949; Chris Mead, *Champion: Joe Louis: Black Champion in White America* (New York: Scribner, 1986).

7. See, for example, Grace Elizabeth Hale, *Making Whiteness: The Culture of Segregation in the South, 1890–1940* (New York, 1998); Alessandra Lorini, *Rituals of Race: American Public Culture and the Search for Racial Democracy* (Charlottesville, 1999); Kenneth W. Goings, *Mammy and Uncle Mose: Black Collectibles and American Stereotyping* (Bloomington, Ind., 1994), 1–25; Cripps, *Making Movies Black*.

8. James Weldon Johnson, *Along This Way: The Autobiography of James Weldon Johnson* (New York, 1933), 208. Jackson never won the world crown because the white champion

refused to fight black opponents. But he did fight leading white boxer James Corbett to a draw (after 61 rounds).

9. Robert J. Norrell, "Understanding the Wizard: Another Look at the Age of Booker T. Washington" in W. Fitzhugh Brundage, ed., *Booker T. Washington and Black Progress: Up from Slavery 100 Years Later* (Gainesville, 2003): 58–80.

10. Joel Williamson, *The Crucible of Race: Black-White Relations in the American South since Emancipation* (New York, 1984), 408.

11. A. B. Christa Schwarz, *Gay Voices of the Harlem Renaissance* (Bloomington, 2003), 28; Gilbert Osofsky, *Harlem; the Making of a Ghetto: Negro New York, 1890–1930* (New York, 1966), 182.

12. Thomas Cripps, *Slow Fade to Black: The Negro in American Film, 1900–1942* (New York, 1977), 86, 8.

13. Gena Tabery-Caponi, "Jump for Joy: Jump Blues, Dance, and Basketball in 1930s African America" in John Bloom and Michael Nevin Willard, eds., *Sports Matters: Race, Recreation, and Culture* (New York, 2002): 39–74, 64; Montye Fuse and Keith Miller, "Jazzing the Basepaths: Jackie Robinson and African American Aesthetics," in John Bloom and Michael Nevin Willard, eds., *Sports Matters: Race, Recreation, and Culture* (New York, 2002): 119–140. So, too, did intellectual and consumer culture. See, for example, J. Moses Wilson, "The Lost World of the Negro, 1895–1919: Black Literary and Intellectual Life before the "Renaissance," *Black American Literature Forum* Vol. 21 (Spring-Summer 1987): 61–84.

14. See, for example, Robin D. G. Kelley, *Race Rebels: Culture, Politics, and the Black Working Class* (New York, 1996); Tera W. Hunter, *To 'Joy My Freedom: Southern Black Women's Lives and Labors after the Civil War* (Cambridge, Mass., 1997).

15. *Life,* March 1939.

16. Annual reports of polls in *New York Times.*

17. Some 10 million clubwomen had a right to nominate for the award. "Americanism Wins in Radio Poll," *New York Times,* April 23, 1939, 134.

18. Anthony F. Macias, "Bringing Music to the People: Race, Urban Culture, and Municipal Politics in Postwar Los Angeles," *American Quarterly*, Vol. 56 (September 2004): 693–717.

19. Howard Taubman, "The 'Duke' Invades Carnegie Hall," *New York Times*, January 17, 1943, SM10.

20. Cripps, *Making Movies Black*, 178.

21. Sklaroff, "Variety for the Servicemen," 948–949.

22. Savage, *Broadcasting Freedom.*

23. See Erik Barnouw, *Media Marathon: A Twentieth-Century Memoir* (Durham, 1996), 74–77.

24. *Ladies Home Journal*, July 1938–December 1939.

25. Guy B. Johnson, "The Stereotype of the American Negro" in Otto Klineberg, ed., *Characteristics of the American Negro* (New York, 1944): 1–22, 1–22, 3.

26. Goings, *Mammy and Uncle Mose,* 48.

27. Lorena A. Hickok, *One Third of a Nation: Lorena Hickok Reports on the Great Depression*, ed. Richard Lowitt and Maurine Hoffman Beasley (Urbana, 1981), 151–152.

28. Speech by Walter White, 1, Writers Congress, LA, October 1, 1943, Series II, Box A, 277, Folder: Film: Hollywood Writers Mobilization Writers' Congress 1943, NA. See also Johnson, "Characteristics," 3–22.

29. Wilton M. Krogman, "What We Do Not Know about Race," *Scientific Monthly*, Vol. 57 (August 1943): 97–104, 103.

30. R. Koppes Clayton and Gregory D. Black, "Blacks, Loyalty, and Motion-Picture Propaganda in World War Two," *Journal of American History*, Vol. 73 (September 1986): 383–406, 385.

31. Dr. Seuss, *Dr. Seuss Goes to War: The World War II Editorial Cartoons of Theodor Seuss Geisel*, ed. Richard H. Minear (New York, 1999); Robert Edwin Herzstein, *Henry R. Luce: A Political Portrait of the Man Who Created the American Century* (New York, 1994), 89.

32. Daniel Kryder, *Divided Arsenal: Race and the American State During World War Two* (Cambridge, 2000), 31.

33. Indeed, Congress did vote to cut the OWI budget on account of stirring up racial discord. Elmer Davis, "The Office of War Information, 13 June 1942–15 September 1945, Report to the President," 43, RG 208, Entry 6H, Box 3, Records of the Office of War Information: Records of the Historian, Draft Historical Reports, 1941–48, NA.

34. RG 208, Office of War Information, Office of Facts and Figures 1941–2, Entry 7, Box 10, NA.

35. *Detroit Tribune*, 28 November 1942.

36. Truman K. Gibson and Steve Huntley, *Knocking Down Barriers: My Fight for Black America* (Evanston, Ill., 2005), 222.

37. Survey S–1, In the field 4–15–42 to 5–11–42, RG 208, Entry 3D, Box 6. Folder "Negro Morale, 1942." 18 percent reckoned they would be better off, and an unlikely 23 percent said they didn't know (officials guessed that these respondents also supported Japan, but didn't dare admit to a treasonable offence).

38. Report by Research Branch, Special Service Division, ASF, On "Attitudes of the Negro Soldier," July 31, 1943, File: Attitudes of Negro soldiers, RG107, E91, Box 181, NA.

39. *Chicago Sun,* June 22, 1943.

40. "Race Riots: Sub-Committee Report to the Production Information Committee," Chair Charles Levitt, 7/5/43, File: Riots, RG208, E87, Box 582, NA; "Most Negro soldiers have secreted ammunition." prob. Report by Research Branch, Special Service Division, ASF, On "Attitudes of the Negro Soldier," July 31, 1943, File: Attitudes of Negro soldiers, RG107, E91, Box 181, NA.

41. Radio Tokyo, January 16, "When He Speaks of Humanity, Does President Roosevelt Refer Only to His Own White Skin?" Folder: Negro, RG 208, Office of War Information, Office of Facts and Figures 1941–2, Entry 7, Box 10, NA.

42. Observations and recommendations of Walter White on Racial Relations in the ETO, Folder NAACP, RG107, E91, Box 221, NA.

43. Report Theodore M. Berry, Blue Print of Program for Strengthening Negro Morale in War Effort, March 4, 1942, Folder "Race Relations 1942–3," NA.

44. Savage, *Broadcasting Freedom*.

45. "4 Theatres Show Negro War Film," *New York Times*, April 22, 1944, p.8.

46. Joseph McBride, *Frank Capra: The Catastrophe of Success* (London, 1992), 467.

47. "4 Theatres."

48. See, for example, Carlton Moss, "The Negro in American Films," *Freedomways*, Vol. 3 (Spring 1963): 134–142 and Carlton Moss, "The Great White Hope," *Freedomways*, Vol. 9 (Spring 1969): 127–138.

49. This point was made explicit by NAACP press releases, e.g., Press Release, March 27, 1944, Group II, Box A278, File: Films: *The Negro Soldier*, 1943–45, NA.

50. McBride, *Frank Capra*, 492–493.

51. NAACP Press Release, 27ᵗʰ April, 1944. NAACP 1940–55, General Office File, Films: The Negro Soldier, 1944–45, NAACP Microfilm.

52. Truman Gibson, Office Secretary of War, DC, to Roy Wilkins, January 14, 1944, NAACP 1940–55, General Office File, Films: *The Negro Soldier*, 1944–45. NAACP Microfilm.

53. Letter Truman Gibson, Civilian Aide to the Secretary of War, 31ˢᵗ March 1944, General Office File, Films: *The Negro Soldier*, 1944–45, NAACP Microfilm.

54. 1944, Press Release, sent as telegram, NAACP 1940–55, General Office File, Films: *The Negro Soldier*, 1944–45, NAACP Microfilm. See also *PM*, Friday, April 28, 1944.

55. See, for example, Press Release, sent as telegram, NAACP 1940–55, General Office File, Films: *The Negro Soldier*, 1944–45, NAACP Microfilm.

56. Robert Rossen to Frank Capra, 30ᵗʰ March 1944, NAACP 1940–55, General Office File, Films: *The Negro Soldier*, 1944–45, NAACP Microfilm; Dr. E. C. Farnham to Marshall, 29ᵗʰ April, 1944, NAACP 1940–55, General Office File, Films: *The Negro Soldier*, 1944–45, NAACP Microfilm; *PM* Sunday April 30, 1944.

57. *People's Voice*, 29th April 1944.

58. Copy of Telegram to Walter Winchell, 1944 (no day or month recorded), NAACP 1940–55, General Office File, Films: *The Negro Soldier*, 1944–45, NAACP Microfilm.

59. *Friends Intelligencer*, Vol. 101, Fourth Month 8, 1944, No. 15, (Quaker Weekly): 226; Press Release, March 16, 1944, NAACP 1940–55, General Office File, Films: *The Negro Soldier*, 1944–45, NAACP microfilm.

60. Cripps, *Making Movies Black*, 113.

61. Carolyn Davenport, to Walter White, 3ʳᵈ May 1944, NAACP 1940–55, General Office File, Films: *The Negro Soldier*, 1944–45, NAACP microfilm.

62. *PM*, Friday, April 28, 1944.

63. The army's official publication, *Army Talk*, condemned racial discrimination at times. Sherie Mershon and Steven L. Schlossman, *Foxholes and Color Lines: Desegregating the U.S. Armed Forces* (Baltimore, Md., 1998), 115–117.

64. Assistant Secretary NAACP to Major General Alexander D. Surles, 22ⁿᵈ August, 1945, NAACP 1940–55, General Office File, Films: *The Negro Soldier*, 1944–45, NAACP Microfilm; Memo from Moss to Gibson, 20 March 1944, US Army Signal Corps Photographic Center, Western Division, Special Coverage Section, Folder The Negro Soldier, RG107, E91, Box 224, NA.

65. *Negro Marches on Inc., v. W A C of the Motion Picture Industry, US District Court for the Southern District of NY*, Deposition of Andrew Weinberger, Counsel for NAACP, May 9ᵗʰ, 1944. NAACP 1940–55, General Office File: Films: The Negro Soldier, 1944–45, NAACP microfilm; Letter Hastie to White re Newsreels, December 8, 1942, Folder "Race Relations 1942–3" Folder—Race Relations, 1942–43, RG 208, Entry 1, Box 8, NA; Memo: Lyman Liggins to Lt. Colonel Gordon Swarthout, n.d., File: Bureau of Public relations, Pictorial Branch, BPR, RG107, E91, Box 184, NA; "Motion for Leave to File Brief Amicus Curiae by NAACP, Negro Marches On, Inc., against War Activities Committee of the Motion Picture Industry, US District Court of Southern District of NY, n.d. (1944)," File: Negro Soldier Injunction, RG107, E91, Box 225, NA.

66. Folder—Race Relations, 1942–43, RG 208, Entry 1, Box 8, NA.

67. *Current Surveys,* "Negro-White Attitudes Toward the Negro's Role in the War", July 7, 1943, OWI Surveys Division, Re Chicago, Detroit, Oklahoma, Raleigh, Birmingham, File: Riots, RG208, E87, Box 582, NA.

68. See George H. Roeder, *The Censored War: American Visual Experience During World War Two* (New Haven: Yale University Press, 1993)

69. Sklaroff, "Variety for the Servicemen," 957.

70. Gibson and Huntley, *Knocking*, 92.

71. The photographs of black soldiers were counted—the total number of photographs estimated.

72. *Life* was actually more inclusive than the *Ladies Home Journal*, which did not carry a single picture of a black soldier. White soldiers, by contrast, were the heroes in many a story. *Life* and *Ladies Home Journal*, July 1944–December 1945.

73. Charles S. Johnson, *A Monthly Summary of Events and Trends in Race Relations*, Vol. 1 (April 1944): 1.

74. Milton Bracker, "Negroes' Courage Upheld in Inquiry," *New York Times*, March 15, 1945, 12. See also Ronald N. Jacobs, *Race, Media, and the Crisis of Civil Society: From Watts to Rodney King* (Cambridge, 2000), 48.

75. Charles S. Johnson, *A Monthly Summary of Events and Trends in Race Relations*, Vol. 2 (December 1944): 121.

76. Goings, *Mammy and Uncle Mose*, 87.

77. Neil Scott to Roy Wilkins, February 10th, 1944, Folder: Films—General 1944, Group II, Box A275, NAACP.

78. Folder: Films: General, 1943, Box A275, Series II, NAACP.

79. Clayton and Black, "Blacks, Loyalty," 404.

80. Tabery-Caponi, "Jump for Joy," 50.

81. Sklaroff, "Variety for the Servicemen," 959.

82. C. K. Doreski, "'Kin in Some Way': The Chicago Defender Reads the Japanese Internment, 1942–1945," in Todd Vogel, ed., *The Black Press: New Literary and Historical Essays* (New Brunswick, N.J., 2001): 161–187, 181.

83. Neil A. Wynn, *The Afro-American and the Second World War* (New York, 1993), 109.

84. *People's Voice,* September 19, 1942.

85. Charles S. Johnson, *A Monthly Summary of Events and Trends in Race Relations*, Vol. 2 (June 1945): 339.

86. *New York Amsterdam Star News*, 1944 (no day or month), General Office File: Films, Newspaper Clippings and Press Releases 1942, NAACP microfilm.

87. *Pittsburgh Courier, New York Times.*

88. "Galento Booed on Coast," *New York Times*, April 27, 1939, 33.

89. James P. Dawson, "Louis Knocks Out Braddock in 8th, Wins World Title," Ibid., June 23, 1937, 1.

90. "Festive Harlems Celebrate Victory," *New York Times*, June 23, 1937, 30.

91. Harvey G. Cohen, "Duke Ellington and Black, Brown, and Beige: The Composer as Historian at Carnegie Hall," American *Quarterly*, Vol. 56 (December 2004): 1003–1034, 1010.

92. Lauren Rebecca Sklaroff, "Constructing G.I. Joe Louis: Cultural Solutions to the 'Negro Problem' During World War II," *Journal of American History*, Vol. 89 (December

2002): 958–983, 971. See also Lewis A. Erenberg, *The Greatest Fight of Our Generation: Louis v. Schmeling* (New York, 2007).

93. "Favorite Band Named," *New York Times*, January 1, 1943, 27.

94. *Look*, January 12, 1943.

95. Sklaroff, "Variety for the Servicemen," 945.

96. Richard Boyer, *New Yorker* (see Duke Ellington, *The Duke Ellington Reader*, ed. Mark Tucker (New York, 1993), 238; Cohen, "Duke Ellington," 1003.)

97. Tabery-Caponi, "Jump for Joy," 61.

98. Taubman, "'Duke' Invades."

99. "Negro to Command Ship," New York *Times*, September 23, 1942, 27.

100. Dean B. Cromwell and Alfred F. Wesson, *Championship Technique in Track and Field: A Book for Athletes, Coaches, and Spectators* (New York, 1941), 6. See also David Kenneth Wiggins, "'Great Speed but Little Stamina': The Historical Debate over Black Athletic Superiority," *Journal of Sport History*, Vol. 16 (Summer 1989): 158–185, 162–164; Patrick B. Miller, "The Anatomy of Scientific Racism: Racialist Responses to Black Athletic Achievement" in Patrick B. Miller and David Kenneth Wiggins, eds., *Sport and the Color Line: Black Athletes and Race Relations in Twentieth-Century America* (New York, 2004), 327–344.

101. John Kieran, "The Big Punch Stirs Pugilism's Hopes," *Times*, September 22, 1935, SM6.

102. David O. Sears and Donald R. Kinder, "Racial Tensions and Voting in Los Angeles," in Werner Z. Hirsch, ed., *Los Angeles: Viability and Prospects for Metropolitan Leadership* (New York: Praeger, 1971), 51–88.

103. Hazel Gaudet Erskine, "The Polls: Race Relations," *Public Opinion Quarterly*, Vol. 26 (Spring 1962): 137–148.

104. Alistair Cooke, *Alistair Cooke's American Journey: Life on the Home Front in the Second World War* (London, 2006), 203.

105. Guthrie P. Ramsey, *Race Music: Black Cultures from Bebop to Hip-Hop* (Berkeley, 2003), 166.

106. Howard Schuman, Lawrence Bobo, and Charlotte Steeh, *Racial Attitudes in America: Trends and Interpretations* (Cambridge, Mass., 1985), 75.

107. Southern Regional Council, *Changing Patterns in the New South: A Unique Record of the Growth of Democracy in the South in the Last Decade* (Atlanta, 1955), 52–53.

108. John Temple Graves, *The Fighting South* (University, Ala., 1985), 143.

109. Mary L. Dudziak, *Cold War Civil Rights: Race and the Image of American Democracy* (Princeton, N.J., 2000).

110. Charles S. Johnson, *A Monthly Summary of Events and Trends in Race Relations*, Vol. 3 (October 1945): 95.

111. Audrey M. Shuey, Nancy King and Barbara Griffith, "Stereotyping of Negroes and Whites: An Analysis of Magazine Pictures," *Public Opinion Quarterly*, Vol. 17 (Summer 1953): 281–287; Ronald Humphrey and Howard Schuman, "The Portrayal of Blacks in Magazine Advertisements: 1950–1982," *Public Opinion Quarterly*, Vol. 48 (Autumn 1984): 551–563; Harold H. Kassarjian, "The Negro and American Advertising, 1946–1965," *Journal of Marketing Research*, Vol. 6 (February 1969): 29–39.

112. Savage, *Broadcasting Freedom*, 275.

113. *Contemporary Black Biography* (Detroit, 1992), Vol. 17, 131.

7

"A War for States' Rights"

THE WHITE SUPREMACIST VISION
OF DOUBLE VICTORY

Jason Morgan Ward

On October 13, 1942, the United States House of Representatives voted by a three-to-one margin to abolish the poll tax. At the time, eight Southern states still required the measure, one of several disfranchisement tactics aimed at African Americans. Civil rights advocates cheered the bill's passage, which moved them a step closer to dynamiting a pillar of Jim Crow. Yet as the battle moved to the Senate, leaders of the leftist National Negro Congress (NNC) gloomily predicted a filibuster by "pro-Hitler" Southern Democrats. If the NNC's politics were radical, its wartime rhetoric was typical. Racism was now enemy ideology, and civil rights advocates of all stripes demanded that the white South choose sides. "Policies of racial discrimination divide us and aid the enemy," declared the National Association for the Advancement of Colored People (NAACP). "The man who discriminates against Negroes is a Fifth Columnist."[1]

W. M. Burt saw things differently. The white Mississippian worked at an ordnance plant that produced powder bags for artillery shells. He spent 10 percent of his income on war bonds, and his only child was a bomber pilot. Burt watched with apprehension as civil rights activists and Northern politicians took aim at the underpinnings of segregated society. "I claim in every way to be a 100% American and as patriotic as any man in the United States," he declared in 1942, "but I want to say that if we win this War against the Germans, Italians, and Japs, and yet have this Poll Tax bill rammed down our throats, we of the South will have won only HALF a victory, and the remaining half will have to be won all over again."[2]

The poll tax fight was one of several episodes in which white Southerners reconciled their racial convictions with the struggle against the Axis. Even as civil rights activists mobilized a wartime "Double V" campaign—victory over fascist aggression abroad and racial discrimination back home—Southern conservatives linked their struggle to save Jim Crow with the war effort. Like their domestic adversaries, they rallied behind appeals to freedom and democracy. They too argued that the global struggle against totalitarianism could not be isolated from battles back home. Yet defenders of segregation articulated their own vision of Double Victory. Championing white supremacy and demanding freedom from outside interference, Southern conservatives deemed civil rights agitation and federal encroachment to be as dangerous as an Axis invasion. The white South, like African Americans, had entered the war fighting on two fronts.

Despite mounting challenges to their racially exclusive brand of democracy, Southern conservatives regarded themselves as the inheritors of sacred American traditions. Deep South elites worried that the wartime civil rights drive would penetrate the last bastion of true Americanism, defined by one Mississippian as "white supremacy, strict interpretation of the Constitution, and freedom in our domestic affairs."[3] Oscar Bledsoe, a powerful Delta planter, openly questioned whether the American war effort would preserve or erode those values. "Are we fighting this war to destroy everything we inherited from our forefathers?" he asked. "This is a conservative war . . . It is not a war for Fascism, Nazism, Communism, Socialism, New Dealism or Democracy." The only "ism" worth fighting for, in the words of Bledsoe's friend and powerful state legislator Walter Sillers, was the "100% Americanism" embodied by "the white democracy of the South."[4]

Confronted with the combined threat of racial unrest and a federal government increasingly sympathetic to civil rights advocates, Southern racial conservatives rallied behind a white supremacist vision of Double Victory. Well before Pearl Harbor, Southern politicians and industrialists warned that the New Deal threatened the segregated status quo. Wartime mobilization and migration only heightened their anxiety. Racial clashes, real and imagined, preoccupied Southern leaders and everyday folks on the home front. Wartime attacks on two blatant disfranchisement tactics—the poll tax and the white primary—focused white resentment and spurred a rebellion against racial change. Faced with unprecedented threats to the segregated status quo, Southern conservatives linked fascism, communism, and racial egalitarianism together under the umbrella of totalitarianism. Even as they fought the Axis abroad, Jim Crow's defenders declared their "white democracy" its antithesis.

In the months following Pearl Harbor, race tension rose with the temperature on the Southern home front. For many anxious whites, black soldiers portended racial trouble. As recruits poured into Southern army bases in early 1942, white apprehension increased at the sight of armed and uniformed blacks. White Southerners charged early and often that black troops were abusing their military privileges, but these grievances frequently revealed a steadfast refusal to grant African American servicemen any semblance of authority. When a convoy of black troops rolled through Lincolnton, Georgia, in the spring of 1942, angry locals reported that the soldiers blew kisses and showered catcalls on white women. A lawyer claimed that one serviceman cursed out a white road crew for refusing to salute him. Town officials forwarded their complaints to Senator Richard Russell, who demanded a War Department investigation of the "outrageous conduct" of the unit. "No stone will be left unturned," he pledged, "to mete [out] proper punishment to those guilty."[5] Military inquiries, however, failed to turn up any evidence of misconduct. The Georgia Motor Police escort that had accompanied the battalion, according to one military investigator, "reported that it was the most orderly convoy of soldiers, either white or colored, with which they had ever come in contact."[6]

White officers in the convoy offered their own explanation for local hostility. As the convoy passed through Lincolnton, they had assigned some of their soldiers to direct civilian traffic. The sight of uniformed blacks halting white motorists proved too much for some residents. "Their displeasure," concluded the investigator, "resulted in unfounded reports of misconduct on the part of these colored soldiers." The town's newspaper primed local whites for such protests with editorials blasting the "insidious work" of the wartime civil rights campaign. "It is not necessary to go to Atlanta, Detroit, or New York, or any other metropolitan city, with their large negro populations, to see the changes taking place," the editor warned. "It can be seen right here in Lincolnton and in hundreds of other rural towns." Arguing that the campaign for "Full Equality" was on the march, the newspaperman stressed the urgent need to keep Southern blacks in their place. "The negro has his rightful place in the American way of life, and he has no friends who are as good to him as the white people of the South," he argued, "but as for accepting [him] on a plane of equality, as is being advocated by some negro leaders—it must and shall not be done."[7]

While some whites resented the black troop presence, others complained that too few blacks were entering the service. Across the region, whites spread rumors that the military was rejecting nine out of ten Southern blacks due to venereal disease. Others warned of the dangers of leaving too many black men on the Southern home front. Fearing that they would "steal, kill, [and] worse, rape white women," a Georgia woman offered to "furnish a long list of names" for the draft board. A father of two girls reported that Georgia and South Carolina blacks were "becoming more and more brazen day by day and gloat over the day when all the [white] male population will be taken away to fight for them." Furthermore, the man complained, his black laundrywoman sent her daughters to boarding school with the money that her three sons earned in Northern defense jobs. Unable to send his own daughters to such a school, he resented the fact that none of the woman's sons served "in the armed service of the country that avails more for them than some white folk of the very best and purest American people."[8]

Resentment frequently manifested itself in acts of intimidation. The Army's Fourth Corps Area, headquartered in Atlanta, received scores of complaints as black recruits flooded into Southern army installations. "Incidents have occurred recently," reported the Fourth Corps Area's commanding officer, "which have led the War Department to believe that the negro in the uniform of the United States Army has not always received the equitable treatment which is due him by virtue of the fact that he is a soldier." Arguing that such mistreatment undermined morale in camps across the South, the general implored Southern leaders to protect black servicemen. At the same time, he pledged "to maintain pleasant relations between its garrisons and the adjacent civilian communities with due regard to the local and state and community laws and customs."[9]

As the top brass balanced appeals for tolerance with deference to Jim Crow, some particularly apprehensive Georgians clashed with military officials. In July 1942, just one week after 20,000 local supporters helped Governor Eugene Talmadge kick off his race-baiting reelection campaign in Moultrie, a feud erupted between the city council and officials at nearby Spence Field. "Negro soldiers congregate and block our streets on Saturday so that white ladies cannot get by," a council member complained. "They are demanding to eat at the same places white people do and drink at the same fountains, and we have every reason to believe that this view is fostered by the officers in charge of the base." Warning that "there is going to be some killing of negroes unless the officers at the Air Base change their views," the councilman declared that city officials would "not permit any negro soldier to commit any breach of peace or show disrespect to white people whether the Army likes it or not." The commanding officer at Spence Field implored local authorities to treat black soldiers with courtesy and respect. In response, city leaders reminded their police force that "a negro soldier is just another negro with a different sort of clothes on."[10]

Moultrie police chief Tom Bell quickly acted on that premise. On a midsummer Saturday night, a white blacksmith complained that black servicemen were carousing outside his shop. Within minutes, Chief Bell had bloodied three soldiers with his blackjack. Although Bell claimed that the servicemen were drunk and disorderly, two white military policemen who had accompanied the chief on his rounds told a different story. They, along with the medic who stitched up the soldiers, denied that the victims were drunk or defiant. In sworn testimony, the white servicemen and the three beaten black soldiers all reported that the chief had threatened to kill them.[11]

City officials alleged that, in the days after the beatings, a white officer at Spence Field "threatened to put machine guns on our street corners and mop up the City Police force if his negro soldiers didn't get the treatment he thought they ought to have." Incensed at the demands and alleged threats of the Northern officers, the mayor called a special hearing at city hall. Police Chief Bell reported that he had simply subdued a few black soldiers for cursing and threatening whites. Charging that uncooperative Northern officers and white military policemen were making his job infinitely more difficult, Bell offered a solution: "Southern boys on the Military Police force." Responding to denials of mistreatment by lawmen and city officials, a colonel from Spence Field interrupted, "It is a well known fact that you don't treat the colored people like the white." The mayor responded flatly, "We don't expect to do so." A hostile city councilman interjected that another officer, Lieutenant Colonel Dan Moler, "said that when you put a uniform on a negro he is not considered a negro anymore." Moler was sitting a few feet away. "That is a bad statement to make," the councilman continued, "You put a Lt. Colonel's uniform on a jackass and it is the same."[12]

The feud in Moultrie revealed that white Southerners frequently resisted attempts to adapt Jim Crow to the exigencies of war, but the confrontation also brought underlying racial anxieties to the surface. "Is it true," the mayor grilled the officers, "that they take our southern negro soldiers up north and teach them the same as the northern soldiers in way of equality?" Officials at Spence Field denied that the military was indoctrinating black soldiers with subversive racial ideas, but Moultrie city leaders persisted with their complaints and investigations. Later claiming that base officials had dismissed two civilian employees for disrespecting black soldiers at Spence Field, the city council concluded that "the teaching of social equality is bringing on all this trouble with the negroes here in Moultrie."[13]

The confrontation in Georgia reflected wider concerns about the wartime influx of African American servicemen. Unsympathetic military officials offended some whites, but defiant black soldiers portended racial disaster. In South Carolina, Governor Richard Manning Jefferies had closely monitored the black troop presence in the state after taking office in early 1942. In tandem with South Carolina senator Burnet Maybank, Jefferies worked behind the scenes to minimize the number of black servicemen entering the state. "I want you to know," Maybank reported in April 1942, "that I protested to the Air Corps in reference to the sending of negro troops to guard the air bases in South Carolina." A few months later, Jefferies apprised Maybank of "widespread rumors" that the military was planning to established "a large Negro army camp" near Columbia. Jefferies confided that South Carolinians feared "that white troops will be displaced at Fort Jackson with Negro troops and that the Fort will become a Negro camp." While the War Department assured Maybank that no such plan existed, he reported that his Washington office had also received "many reports in reference to colored troops and colored officers in the South."[14]

Claiming that "the situation in Alabama and Georgia is even worse than in South Carolina," Maybank suggested a coordinated effort to meet the black troop problem. Georgia senator Richard Russell confirmed Maybank's assessment. Russell claimed that he had received "protests from nearly all of the cities which have camps against having negro soldiers stationed there." After a summer of similar complaints and clashes, Alabama senator John Bankhead implored General George C. Marshall to keep Northern blacks out of the South. "Our people," Bankhead declared, "feel that the government is doing a disservice to the war effort by locating Negro troops in the South . . . at a time when race feeling among the Negroes has been roused."[15]

Fears of emboldened black soldiers meshed with concerns about the military's adherence to Jim Crow. Although the armed forces remained officially segregated throughout World War II, alarmed white Southerners reported frequent violations. To the chagrin of many locals, Southern military installations often permitted or overlooked de facto integration. Responding to reports that black and white servicemen shared cafeteria tables at a Mississippi army base, an alarmed Georgian deemed it "unfair to draft a white boy in the Army and force him to associate with negroes." Such a situation made him concerned for his son. "I am willing for my boy to fight for our country," he declared, "but I don't think he should be humiliated."[16]

Some whites chafed at reports that military officials were putting blacks in positions of authority over whites. "I have been watching the Negro situation in this part of the country," reported one Mississippian, "and trying to figure out just what is causing the negroes to attempt to do the things that they are trying to do." He pointed to "things happening in this Army of ours" as the source of racial unrest, and identified "Yankee officers" as the culprits. Even in southern Mississippi, he complained, military officials allowed casual integration and even assigned black soldiers to guard white convicts on work detail. "I know," the Mississippian wrote to his senator, "that you would not stand for a negro to stand on the roads with a rifle and give your boy orders."[17]

Many racial grievances focused on military medical facilities. At Mississippi's Keesler Field, reported a civilian employee, "right in the Hospital the Damn Negro is Bed by Bed in the same ward with white Soldiers and eat in mess Halls together."[18] In Georgia, alarmed parents and relatives complained of integrated hospital wards at Camp Lawson. An Atlantan with a nephew at the hospital alleged that "negroes have to use same mess and toilet facilities as whites use." Another claimed that black patients were ordering white nurses to make their beds. "I do not believe that the exigencies of war make this necessary," declared another Georgian, "or that patriotism should be used as a cloakroom for embittering the white people of the South and bringing about disunity."[19]

Southern leaders entered wartime civil rights battles armed with such accounts, supplied by anxious whites from the home front to the battlefield. When the defenders of segregation criticized the military or denigrated black soldiers, the national media, government officials, and Southern moderates denounced their attacks as demagoguery run amok. Yet Southern servicemen and civilians supplied their elected officials with enough provocative stories to keep the diatribes coming. "If you need any information to prove that the 'niggers' stationed here during the war lived up to their true characters of being shiftless, contemptible, and arrogant," a white sergeant wrote to Mississippi senator Theodore Bilbo, "I shall be able to furnish you proof." Offering "the factual situation on the majority of the colored troops," another white officer listed acts of insubordination, sabotage, and criminal behavior in his black battalion. Worse, the major reported to Bilbo, black soldiers had developed a militant racial outlook. "These misfits and agitators often write to the President of the United States and his wife citing petty and imagined grievances," the officer complained. "They read and circulate negro newspapers bearing large headlines of white aggression on negroes."[20]

Throughout the war, Southern conservatives slandered black soldiers to undermine demands for racial equality. "In spite of all the ballyhoo that has been put out about Negroes making good soldiers," Mississippi congressman William Colmer assured his constituents, "any Army officer will tell you that they do not."[21] Defamatory attacks embarrassed Southern moderates, yet overt praise for black servicemen posed political risks as well. In a racially charged wartime environment, Southern leaders felt substantial pressure to avoid such gestures. South Carolina congressman Joseph Bryson, attempting to moderate an anti–civil rights speech, complimented black soldiers in an initial draft. "Large numbers of Southern Negro youth have been called to the colors and are acquitting themselves with honor in our armed forces on land, on the seas and in the air," he wrote. "We of the South are proud of them and gladly pay them tribute." Yet, by the time Bryson delivered the speech, he had crossed out those lines with a pencil. Instead of commending black servicemen, Bryson complained that the "liberal family allowances" provided by the Army had made it "almost impossible to obtain domestic or other needed help in the South." He hoped aloud that blacks would "proudly slip back into their normal pursuits" when the war ended.[22]

More than a demagogic ploy to stave off civil rights legislation, the uproar over black soldiers reflected a collision of grassroots concerns with elite resistance strategies. Whether complaining to military officials or criticizing black servicemen, Southern leaders amplified their constituents' wartime anxieties and deployed them to refute the demands of civil rights activists. And while the uproar over black troops bolstered the claim that racial agitation was imported from elsewhere, white Southerners clearly feared internal threats as well. Even as Governor Jefferies monitored black troop activity in South Carolina, he mobilized his state constabulary to investigate homegrown subversives. Responding to rampant rumors that local blacks were buying up firearms and ammunition, Jefferies ordered South Carolina lawmen to gather information quietly from local merchants. While the governor's constable corps uncovered little evidence to suggest that black South Carolinians were hoarding guns and ammunition en masse, many reported even the slightest hint of trouble. One officer in Sumter furnished a list of two dozen blacks who had purchased guns from a pawn shop. After visiting local merchants, the constable informed the governor, "they are willing to co-operate with us 100 percent, in not selling shells or ammunition, or any kind of firearms to negroes."[23]

The statewide investigation also targeted an alleged conspiracy of cooks and maids. Supposedly encouraged by Eleanor Roosevelt, a shadowy network of "Eleanor Clubs" allegedly fomented racial revolution throughout the South by encouraging black domestics to enter white homes through the front door, sit with white families at the dinner table, and skip work without notice. These wartime rumors reflected white Southern contempt for the First Lady as well as widespread fears of black rebellion.[24] Eleanor Club hysteria also revealed how grassroots racial concerns fed hostility toward the increasingly suspect New Dealers and their fellow travelers. "I understand that already they are advising colored servants to demand higher wages and to refuse to do certain kinds of work," a Charleston resident reported. "Perhaps this movement is connected with the plans of the Communists to foment a 'black revolution' in the South. It probably is worth investigating."[25]

Governor Jefferies agreed. At his request, the State Law Enforcement Division scoured South Carolina for any sign of Eleanor Club activity. Most constables uncovered only hearsay, but some provided detailed evidence to substantiate the rumors. A Cheraw constable reported the date, time, and address of an "Eleanor Society" meeting in his town. "At this meeting," he claimed, "they decided that cooks and nurses would not work for less than $6 per week." And even when they did not find evidence of Eleanor Clubs, they discovered substantial white anxiety. "This situation does not seem to be restricted to any particular group but is found in all social groups. . . . The white people appear to be considerably disturbed."[26]

As his constable corps scoured South Carolina for Eleanor Clubs and stock-piles of weapons, Governor Jefferies headed to Washington to ward off a more immediate threat. In early fall 1942, the Senate held hearings on the proposed bill to abolish the poll tax in the handful of Southern states that still required it. Defenders claimed that the practice provided needed funds for education, but few denied its effectiveness as a disfranchisement tactic. For poor Southerners, black and white, a tax of one or two dollars represented a sizable chunk of their weekly income. In several Deep South states, the tax was cumulative. An older voter might have to pay fifty dollars or more to cover the previous decades' unpaid levies.[27]

The fight to end this practice had become a liberal cause célèbre, with the National Committee to Abolish the Poll Tax coordinating a campaign that brought together civil rights organizations, labor unions, and progressive church groups. Opponents of the practice pointed out that, in non-poll tax states, two-thirds of the voting-age population cast ballots in the 1940 elections. In the poll tax states, less than a quarter of adults voted. While defenders of the poll tax argued that turnout was higher in primary elections, the only races that actually mattered in the solidly Democratic South, Southern journalist Stetson Kennedy dispelled that line of argumentation by demonstrating that voter participation was even lower in those elections.[28]

In addition to disfranchising an estimated 11 million potential voters, the poll tax ensured that conservative Southerners enjoyed a disproportionate influence in national politics. As poll tax opponents pointed out, more Rhode Islanders cast ballots for their two representatives in the House than the combined voters of Mississippi, Alabama, Georgia, and South Carolina cast for their thirty-two. Once the seventy-eight poll tax congressmen reached Washington, their road to seniority was much easier that that of their colleagues. In the three congressional elections between 1938 and 1942, the turnover for congressmen from "free voting states" was 70 percent greater than for poll tax representatives. With their seats safe and their seniority ensured, Southern solons enjoyed disproportionate control of congressional committees. Poll tax Democrats headed seventeen of forty-three committees in the House and ten of thirty-three in the Senate. As conservative Southern Democrats turned against Roosevelt and the New Deal, they used their lopsided influence on Capitol Hill to kill progressive legislation. "When Polltaxia is 'agin' a bill," lamented Stetson Kennedy, "the United States is often forced to do without it."[29]

The poll tax embodied for many Americans the fundamentally undemocratic nature of Jim Crow politics, but the campaign to abolish it provided a call to arms for Southern conservatives. At the Senate hearings on anti–poll tax legislation, South Carolina's governor invoked patriotism and states' rights in defense of voting restrictions. "I respectfully submit," declared Jefferies, "that the eight poll-tax States are inhabited by true Americans willing and ready to make every sacrifice for the protection of our national existence." At the same time, Jefferies argued that the South stood ready to defend its sovereignty. By abolishing the poll tax, he warned, Congress would be headed down a slippery slope towards totalitarianism. "When you get through with that then South Carolina will have no rights whatsoever," argued Jefferies, "we might as well turn over the elections to the Federal Government." South Carolina was "sort of democratic," Jefferies argued, and that was good enough.[30]

The poll tax controversy revealed the continuity between charges of outside agitation and demands for local control. When Congress passed a bill in September 1942 that waived poll tax requirements for American servicemen, fears of emboldened black soldiers collided with resentment of federal encroachment. The Soldier Voting Act of 1942 passed several weeks after the Southern primaries and thus posed no immediate threat to Democratic incumbents in poll tax states. But the dangerous precedent invited howls of protests. Alabama congressman Sam Hobbs deemed the bill "an attack on our Southern way of life and on white supremacy" and an attempt "to cater to the soldier vote at the expense of the very foundation of our democracy." The average white soldier, he contended, "does not wish to vote at such a price." The House's most notorious Negrophobe, John Rankin of Mississippi, blamed the bill's poll tax amendment on "a long range communistic program to change our form of Government and . . . to take the control of our elections out of the hands of white Americans."[31]

After Rankin and company failed to derail the bill, National Negro Council president Edgar Brown hoped to make the infamous race-baiter its first victim. Since the number of active-duty black servicemen from Mississippi's First Congressional District outnumbered the votes cast for Rankin in the recent primary, Brown announced a write-in campaign to oust the congressman. Hailing the soldier vote bill as "the greatest contribution to democracy since Lincoln signed the Emancipation Proclamation," Brown nominated a black Mississippian fighting under General Douglas MacArthur in the South Pacific: Private Abraham Lincoln Brooks.[32]

Despite the high hopes of civil rights advocates, the practical impact of the soldier vote bill fell far short of its promise. Rankin's hometown paper chided "misleaders" for giving false hope to local African Americans. Denouncing the write-in campaign as "Utter Foolishness," the *Tupelo Daily Journal* warned that it would be "many, many years before Negroes will even vote—much less elect congressmen." The paper's stance seemed moderate compared to Rankin's white supremacists tirades, which grew shriller as the poll tax fight raged on Capitol Hill. Just five weeks after exempting soldiers from the levy, the House of Representatives voted overwhelmingly to abolish the requirement altogether. "You are now creating a second front," Rankin warned his colleagues moments before the vote. "You are waging war against the white people of the Southern States."[33]

Unbeknownst to Rankin, a few whites had already struck back. The same day that the House approved the anti–poll tax bill, newspapers across the country reported a brutal double lynching in Mississippi. Early in the morning of October 12, vigilantes had stormed the Clarke County jail and seized two black fourteen-year-olds charged with attempted rape. The next morning, authorities found the boys, Ernest Green and Charlie Lang, hanging from a bridge near Shubuta. Just five days later, a much larger mob dragged forty-nine-year-old Howard Wash from a jail in nearby Laurel. An all-white jury had just convicted Wash of murdering his white employer but had declined to recommend the death penalty. That same night, one hundred armed men hung Wash over a local creek.[34]

Mob violence refocused national attention on the state long regarded as the lynching capital of the South. Yet even as regional and national press blasted the state's ambivalent reaction to mob violence, many white Mississippians blamed Northern politicians and civil rights activists for the lynchings. "Chickens come home to roost!" declared the *Meridian Star*, arguing that "cheap and dirty national politics" had inspired the vigilantes. The *Star* pointed out that the lynchings followed Rankin's warnings that an anti–poll tax bill would spark violence across the South. "Vote-hungry national leadership has purposefully stirred up the issue of race prejudice," the editor declared. "Washington is sowing tragic seed. We must harvest bitter fruit."[35]

Civil rights activists agreed that the poll tax fight on Capitol Hill had spurred mob violence, but they blamed Southern white supremacists. The *New Amsterdam Star-News,* a Harlem weekly, deemed the lynchings a "Poll Tax Rout." The editor deemed no Southern blacks safe from the white supremacist onslaught. "On the eve of the congressional action on the Anti-Poll Tax bill to 'enfranchise' some 4,000,000 Negroes in eight Southern States," the lead story began, "the South opened the first gun of its reprisal by lynching two 14-year-old colored boys." Alongside reports of the Mississippi lynchings, the paper reported that white supremacists in Georgia had launched "the Vigilantes, Inc.," in response to the poll tax vote. This secretive new organization, the paper warned, would "take over the unfinished work of the Klan."[36]

While black newspapers blamed white reactionaries for the violence, Birmingham newspaperman John Temple Graves pointed the finger at the wartime belligerence of civil rights advocates. For months, the syndicated columnist had warned his readers that the "no-compromise leadership among the Negroes" was goading white Southerners into a race war. In his 1943 book, *The Fighting South*, Graves attempted to reconcile the region's patriotic fervor with its allegiance to the segregated status quo. The white South, Graves explained, perceived no conflict between fighting Hitler and defending Jim Crow. By pushing racial reform, Graves argued, in the wake of the Mississippi lynchings, civil rights advocates invited a backlash. "I think the impartial historian," Graves concluded, "will place the greater blame for the disgraceful scene on the incorrigible domestic crusaders who forced the poll tax issue, with all the bitter irreconcilables it involved, at a time of greatest war."[37]

The poll tax controversy, which erupted amidst mounting fears over the domestic implications of World War II, inspired a white supremacist understanding of Double Victory. As Graves explained on a nationally broadcast radio forum, the United States was not fighting "for democracy" but rather "for states' rights, for the right of individual lands not to be invaded by outsiders, not to be dictated to or aggressed against." In response to fellow panelist Langston Hughes, who deemed white supremacy "one of Hitler's cornerstones," Graves lauded "states' rights" as the cornerstone of a budding white countermovement. "Even as we win a war for that principle," Graves warned, "a great political reaction in America is directed at the same principle." White Southerners, Graves warned, regarded their struggle as the domestic arm of a global war against totalitarian aggression. "Rightly or wrongly," he concluded, "they feel that something as vital as this war, as dear as life itself, is involved for them."[38]

The formidable Southern Senate bloc, whose filibuster ultimately killed the anti–poll tax bill, took their white supremacist interpretation of Double Victory to Capitol Hill. Mississippi senator Theodore Bilbo, while personally opposed to a disfranchisement tactic that cut into his support base of hill-country whites, joined with other pro–poll tax Southerners to decry federal interference in state elections. Fashioning himself as a freedom fighter, Bilbo aligned the filibuster with the war effort. "In making this fight against the unconstitutional anti–poll tax bill," he declared, "I feel that I am as much a soldier in the preservation of the American way and American scheme of Government as the boys who are fighting and dying on Guadalcanal."[39]

Such a declaration might have seemed laughable had enthusiastic supporters not echoed the sentiment. "You are receiving these congratulations," declared a Mississippi legislator, "from one who over a month ago joined the United States Marines, and who is willing to fight and die for his country, but who does not want his country depriving him of the freedom he is fighting for." White Southerners' enthusiasm for the global struggle against the Axis powers echoed their traditional hostility to outside interference. Even as civil rights advocates compared lynch mobs to Nazi storm troopers, some white Southerners considered the anti–poll tax bill as perilous as a Panzer division rolling across the Mason-Dixon line. "Such legislation is so very dangerous," an Alabama lumber dealer argued, "in that it seeks to destroy the individual state and make Federal control over all things." Racial reforms, he feared, would "rapidly lead to the destruction of individual rights and Liberties and make of us a Dictator controlled people, the very thing which we are now supposed to be fighting to destroy in other Nations and to keep America free."[40]

In their descriptions of the wartime threats facing the South, the defenders of white democracy often cursed African Americans and the Axis in the same breath. Some even tried to link them together in a grand conspiracy. But given that Hitler sympathizers were no more numerous on the Southern home front than committed integrationists, many white Southerners simply regarded Nazism and NAACP-ism as a dual threat to the Southern way of life. Faced with a homegrown campaign for interracial democracy, some whites flatly admitted that they would rather take their chances with the Nazis. "We the people of the south are as patriotic and determined to win this World War as any body, and are working diligently to cooperate with all groups to win the war," declared one Mississippian, "but we might as well be under Hitler rule as to be under the rule of these boneheaded niggers here."[41]

As Southern conservatives assessed the wartime threats to their political and economic power, they pondered the racial implications of global war. Some charged that enemy agents exploited domestic racial turmoil to undermine the American war effort, while others predicted that an Axis victory would turn Jim Crow on its head. When a poll tax defender predicted that newly enfranchised black voters, seething with "inborn hate of the white man," would elect Hitler president, he revealed the connection that racial conservatives drew between Axis totalitarianism and civil rights agitation. Charles Wade, a Mississippi Delta lawyer, linked black protest to a multi-ethnic Axis alliance. "The Jap side of this war is strictly a race matter," he argued. Given the racially charged conflict in the Pacific, this argument was neither novel nor exclusive to Southern white supremacists. However, Wade's notion of a global "race war" provided a counterpoint to African American attempts to parallel Axis totalitarianism with Southern segregation. "The negro question in the South is not as local as the Government wishes to believe," he warned his senators. "It's going to be a world wide race movement, and you people who call the turns had better get your ears to the ground if you wish to continue to enjoy the advantages of white supremacy."[42]

In the majority-black Mississippi Delta, white elites took such warnings to heart. Even in an area long regarded as a bastion of white domination, any hint of black initiative represented a threat. When a committee of the elite Delta Council sponsored an interracial meeting in early 1943, some alarmed locals protested the concession. "I see nothing good to come out of such meetings," argued a Delta Council executive, "except further demands for social and political equality . . . which they are craving and we all know it." Deeming blacks "unfit at this time to exercise the ballot from both a mental and cultural standpoint," the Delta lawyer argued that whites should continue to decide policies and reforms "without having to be goaded by the negroes."[43]

Unnerved by black assertiveness, Delta whites quickly organized "active Vigilance Committees to protect our rights, our civilization and our way of life." Committee leaders in Leflore and Sunflower counties stood ready to assist other Delta communities in forming their own chapters. Hoping to discourage Delta blacks from pushing for racial change, white elites also launched the Southern Crusaders to "Keep America Safe for Americans." Carrying endorsements from the governor as well as prominent planters and businessmen, the Southern Crusaders advocated "teaching the negroes the advantages of the American form of government" while warning them "to shun that class of persons who would have them accept some foreign teachings." By urging their black neighbor "to keep his ear to the ground and his eyes open," the organizers hoped to enlist a network of "Crusaders" who could help keep racial agitators at bay.[44]

Southern senators could protect the poll tax, but they could not prevent the federal judiciary from ruling on an explicitly racial disfranchisement tactic: the white primary. By legally barring blacks from participation in the Democratic primary, Deep South states effectively nullified any black political challenge. The Supreme Court had previously upheld the white primary, ruling that the Democratic Party was a private organization that could restrict membership by race. But in 1943, the NAACP took up the case of Lonnie Smith, a black Houston dentist who had sued a Texas election official for denying him a ballot in the state's 1940 Democratic primary. Southern African Americans anticipated the Supreme Court's decision with unprecedented organization. Hopeful but not counting on a favorable court ruling in *Smith v. Allwright*, the Negro Citizens Committee of South Carolina raised $300,000 for future court battles. Meanwhile, black activists in the state organized a pro-Roosevelt "Colored Democratic Party" as a grassroots challenge to whites-only politics. Renamed the Progressive Democratic Party, the organization enlisted 45,000 members, sent protest delegates to the Democratic National Convention, and ran a black Senate candidate. While neither the seating challenge nor the Senate campaign succeeded, grassroots activists served notice that the political status quo faced internal as well as external threats.[45]

The reality of homegrown protest primed white South Carolinians for a particularly strident condemnation of *Smith v. Allwright*. The state legislature preempted an unfavorable decision by adopting a resolution demanding "the damned agitators of the North leave the South alone" and proclaiming "our belief in and our allegiance to established white supremacy." Like previous wartime protests, the resolution linked the defense of the racial status quo with the struggle against the Axis. The resolution accused Northern politicians and civil rights activists of "taking traitorous and treasonous advantage" of wartime upheaval and adopting a "Nazi philosophy of conquest." When the Supreme Court struck down the Texas white primary on April 3, 1944, sitting governor and Senate candidate Olin Johnston urged South Carolinians to employ all "necessary methods" to exclude blacks from the Democratic Party. "White supremacy will be maintained in our primaries," he vowed. "Let the chips fall where they may!"[46]

After *Smith v. Allwright*, as one national news magazine put it, "the lid came off the race problem." Combining the wartime threat of enemy subversion with the specter of federal tyranny, Southern conservatives branded the Roosevelt administration as the domestic front in a worldwide totalitarian offensive. With racial tensions at the boiling point, white Southern leaders contrasted their vision of Americanism with the federal activism and social engineering of the New Deal. "The duties and ideals of loyal Americans, true Democrats, and patriotic Southerners are not inconsistent," declared former Mississippi governor Mike Connor after *Smith v. Allwright*. New Dealers, on the other hand, had embraced "un-American and undemocratic philosophies of government." They sought, Connor charged, "to change the very form of our government from a republic to an absolute, totalitarian state of communism or national socialism, which would destroy at home everything our armed forces abroad are fighting to preserve." For Connor, the racial stakes of this struggle had never been clearer. The national Democratic Party, he argued, had become a "New Deal Party" that would continue to "traffic with northern negroes to place the black heel of negro domination on our necks." Connor called on Democrats to reclaim the traditional values of the "white man's party" and reject the New Deal. "America is White, not Red, not Black," Connor declared, "and the time has come for the Democratic Party to tell the New Dealers, with all the force at our command, that we purpose [*sic*] to keep it White."[47]

For Roosevelt's reinvigorated Southern critics, the attacks on the poll tax and the white primary forecast other assaults on Jim Crow. "It is abundantly easingly clear," declared former Louisiana governor Sam Jones, "that Deal high command hopes to use the war as an instrument for forcing al 'equality' of the Negro upon the South." Echoing Jones's warnings, a North Carolina industrialist distributed anti-Roosevelt pamphlets during the 1944 campaign. Concluding that the president "has done more to give [blacks] social equality than all men and political parties combined," the pamphleteer announced, "I Can't Vote for Mr. Roosevelt in November." The front page featured a photograph of an interracial wedding party: "The picture on the front is the result of these teachings and preachings," he warned, " . . . when this white boy gets married, in Connecticut, he gets a negro for best-man."[48]

The racially charged revolt against Roosevelt fueled a broader Southern attack on the New Deal. Clayton Rand, a Mississippi newspaperman, melded his critique of totalitarianism with his take on Southern history. Speaking before civic groups and business leaders in Alabama, Mississippi, and Louisiana in the spring of 1944, Rand warned that the New Deal portended a "New Slavery" far worse than anything the South had imposed on African Americans. "The most humane type of slavery," Rand argued, had existed on the antebellum plantation. The "lenient masters" allowed their slaves "more or less personal freedom," while the New Dealers sought to destroy individual liberty through bureaucracy. "The cruelest form of slavery is that in which the individual is under the complete control of the state," Rand declared. "Much rather would one be owned by an individual than become a chattel under the regimentation of a totalitarian state."[49]

During World War II, the crusade to save "white democracy" evolved from rumor-mongering and scattered protest to an alternate articulation of Double Victory. More than an elite rhetorical strategy but less than an authentic grass-roots rebellion, the attempt to reconcile Jim Crow with the war effort involved and invigorated racial conservatives from all walks of life. From the battlefield to the home front, white Southerners experienced the convulsions that shook the region and confronted the racial stakes of global conflict. Some connected their prewar misgivings about the New Deal to wartime racial upheaval, which they blamed on the federal government's leftward drift and increasing sympathy for racial minorities. They anticipated fiercer confrontations in the postwar years, when emboldened civil rights activists would build on wartime advances in an all-out attack on the color line. In response, Southern racial conservatives organized explicitly in its defense—continuing a long tradition of organized opposition and prefiguring the campaign of massive resistance that would sweep the South a decade later. While World War II undoubtedly raised the expectations of civil rights advocates, it simultaneously embold-ened a countermovement that perceived no conflict between American war aims and the segregated status quo. Thus Southern conservatives, like their adversaries, moved into the postwar years convinced that theirs was the true patriotic crusade.

Notes

1. "Victory Near in the Fight to Get Poll Tax Vote," *Chicago Defender*, September 26, 1942, 4; National Association for the Advancement of Colored People, "On Guard Against Racial Discrimination," February 1942, Folder 52, Richard Manning Jefferies Papers, South Caroliniana Library, University of South Carolina, Columbia, South Carolina [cited hereafter as Jefferies Papers, SCL].

2. W. M. Burt to Theodore G. Bilbo, November 19, 1942, Box 1076, Folder 1, Theodore Gilmore Bilbo Papers, McCain Library and Archives, University of Southern Mississippi, Hattiesburg [cited hereafter as Bilbo Papers].

3. Brinkley Morton to Theodore G. Bilbo, November 19, 1942, Box 1076, Folder 1, Bilbo Papers.

4. O. F. Bledsoe, "Agriculture and the Federal Government," p. 3, Box 29, Folder 5; Walter Sillers and James O. Eastland, May 13, 1943; Walter Sillers to James O. Eastland, February 5, 1943, both in Box 98, Folder 2; all in Walter Sillers Papers, Charles W. Capps Archives and Museum, Delta State University, Cleveland, Mississippi [cited hereafter as Sillers Papers].

5. Homer A. Legg to Richard B. Russell, April 29, 1942; R. F. Hardy to Richard B. Russell, June 26, 1942; Richard B. Russell to Secretary of War, April 29, 1942; all in Series X, Box 139, Folder 3, Richard B. Russell Papers, Russell Library for Political Research and Science, University of Georgia, Athens [cited hereafter as Russell Papers].

6. John W. Martyn to Richard B. Russell, June 29, 1942, Series X, Box 139, Folder 3, Russell Papers.

7. John W. Martyn to Richard B. Russell, June 29, 1942, Series X, Box 139, Folder 3, Russell Papers; "There Is a Race Question," *The Statesman,* June 24, 1943, 2. This editorial was reprinted in a statewide newspaper owned and operated by Georgia governor Eugene Talmadge.

8. Mrs. G. W. Arrington to Richard B. Russell, September 8, 1942; Alice Rogers to Richard B. Russell, August 17, 1942; Giles L. Toole to Richard B. Russell, September 21, 1942; all in Series X, Box 139, Folder 2, Russell Papers.

9. John P. Smith to J. Emile Harley, February 26, 1942, Federal Government Correspondence, Box 1, Folder "U.S. Army, 4th Corp," Gubernatorial Papers of R. M. Jefferies, South Carolina Department of Archives and History, Columbia, South Carolina [cited hereafter as Jefferies Papers, SCDAH].

10. C. L. West to Richard B. Russell and Walter F. George, July 17, 1942, Series X, Box 139, Folder 3, Russell Papers.

11. "White M.P.—Sworn Statement of Corporal Wilbert H. Loesing," July 12, 1942; "White M.P.—Sworn Statement of Corporal Leonard Seidel," July 12, 1942; "Sworn Statement of Private George W. Sutton," July 12, 1942; "Sworn Statement of PFC Johnny T. Terry," July 12, 1942; "Sworn Statement of Pvt. James F. Jackson," July 12, 1942; all in Series X, Box 139, Folder 2, Russell Papers.

12. C. L. West to Richard B. Russell and Walter F. George, July 17, 1942; "Statements Taken at a Called Meeting of Council," July 21, 1942, 3; both in Series X, Box 139, Folder 3, Russell Papers.

13. "Statements Taken at a Called Meeting of Council," July 21, 1942, 4; "Statements Made at Call Session of Council," July 30, 1942, 2; both in Series X, Box 139, Folder 3, Russell Papers.

14. Burnet R. Maybank to R. M. Jefferies, April 28, 1942; R. M. Jefferies to Burnet R. Maybank, October 5, 1942; Burnet R. Maybank to Frank Dixon, April 30, 1942; all in Federal Government Correspondence, Box 1, Folder "Sen. Burnet R. Maybank," Jefferies Papers, SCDAH.

15. Burnet R. Maybank to R. M. Jefferies, April 30, 1942, Federal Government Correspondence, Box 1, Folder "Sen. Burnet R. Maybank," Jefferies Papers, SCDAH; Richard B. Russell to J. D. Nesmith, August 19, 1942, Series X, Box 139, Folder 2, Russell Papers; "Bankhead Says Keep Northern Soldiers North," *Chicago Defender*, August 15, 1942, 7; "Sen. Bankhead of Alabama," *Chicago Defender,* August 15, 1942, 14.

16. W. J. Hall to Richard B. Russell, February 25, 1942, Series X, Box 139, Folder 3, Russell Papers.

17. George Atwood to Theodore G. Bilbo, June 10, 1943, Box 1066, Folder 9, Bilbo Papers.

18. Abner Spiers to Theodore G. Bilbo, February 10, 1942, Box 1084, Folder 8, Bilbo Papers.

19. Dan Shipp to Richard B. Russell, January 1, 1942 [quoted]; Carl F. Hutcheson to Richard B. Russell and Walter F. George, May 26, 1942; both in Series X, Box 139, Folder 3; William E. Colley to Richard B. Russell, September 28, 1942, Series X, Box 139, Folder 2, Russell Papers.

20. Sgt. Moss Simms to Theodore G. Bilbo, September 22, 1945, Box 1085, Folder 1; Major C. Williams to Bilbo, January 5, 1945, Box 1067, Folder 3; both in Bilbo Papers.

21. William Colmer, "Congressional Sidelights," April 7, 1944, Box 421, Folder 15, William M. Colmer Papers, McCain Library and Archives, University of Southern Mississippi, Hattiesburg.

22. J. R. Bryson, "White Supremacy in the South," n. d. [1944], Box 3, Folder "Public, Legis, 1952, Civil Rights," Joseph R. Bryson Papers, South Carolina Political Collections, University of South Carolina, Columbia [hereafter cited as Bryson Papers, SCPC].

23. C. L. McKinnon to S. J. Pratt, September 28, 1942; J. L. Dollard to S. J. Pratt, September 26, 1942; both in Folder 51, Jefferies Papers, SCL.

24. Pamela Tyler, "'Blood on Your Hands': White Southerners' Criticism of Eleanor Roosevelt During World War II," in *Before Brown: Civil Rights and White Backlash in the Modern South*, ed. Glenn Feldman (Tuscaloosa, 2004), 102–105. See also Bryant Simon's discussion of Eleanor Club rumors in his introduction to Howard Odum, *Race and Rumors of Race: The American South in the Early Forties* (Baltimore, 1997), xx–xxi.

25. Stanley F. Morse to W. W. Ball, August 1, 1942, Box 37, Folder "Letters, 1942, August-September," William Watts Ball Papers, Special Collections, Perkins Library, Duke University, Durham, North Carolina [cited hereafter as Ball Papers].

26. R. Phillip Stone, "A Battle for Their Rights: Race and Reaction in South Carolina, 1940–1945," *Proceedings of the South Carolina Historical Association* (1999): 37; T. B. Horton to S. J. Pratt, September 10, 1942; W.W. Brown to R. M. Jefferies, September 10, 1942; both in Folder 50, Jefferies Papers, SCL.

27. Lawson, *Black Ballots: Voting Rights in the South, 1944–1969* (New York, 1976), 56.

28. Stetson Kennedy, *Southern Exposure* (New York, 1946), 95. Alabama, Arkansas, Florida, Georgia, Mississippi, South Carolina, Tennessee, Texas, and Virginia required the poll tax, although South Carolina waived the requirement for the white primary. For a comprehensive study of the poll tax in these states, see Frederic D. Ogden, *The Poll Tax in the*

South (Tuscaloosa, 1958). For an excellent recent account of the poll tax's impact on civil rights activism and national politics, see Glenda E. Gilmore, *Defying Dixie: The Radical Roots of Civil Rights, 1919–1950* (New York, 2008), 336–341.

29. "Poll Tax Dynasty Opposes Bill to Permit Soldier Vote," *Afro-American*, August 1, 1942, 13; Kennedy, *Southern Exposure*, 95. For more on the disproportionate power of Southern congressmen, see Ira Katznelson, Kim Geiger, and Daniel Kryder, "Limiting Liberalism: The Southern Veto in Congress, 1933–1950," *Political Science Quarterly* Vol. 108 (Summer 1993): 283–306. Dewey W. Grantham contends that the South's congressional delegations continued to wield disproportionate power during World War II, carrying out "a kind of dress rehearsal" for future battles over racial reform. See Grantham, "The South and Congressional Politics," in *Remaking Dixie: The Impact of World War II on the American South*, ed. Neil McMillen (Jackson, 1997), 30.

30. "Statements of Senator Burnet R. Maybank, Governor R. M. Jefferies, Attorney General John M. Daniel, State Senator Edgar A. Brown In Opposition to United States Senate No. 1280," October 13, 1942, 19, 6–7, Folder 35, Jefferies Papers, SCL.

31. Congress, House, 77th Cong., 2nd sess., *Congressional Record* 88, pt. 5, p. 7072; "House To Act On Soldier Vote Bill September 9," Norfolk *Journal and Guide*, September 5, 1942, B1.

32. The National Negro Council was distinct from and unaffiliated with the National Negro Congress. "House to Act on Soldier Vote Bill September 9," Norfolk *Journal and Guide*, September 5, 1942, B1; "Soldier Vote Bill Accepted by House," *New York Times*, September 10, 1942, 23. Brown quickly substituted the name of a black Tupelo pastor, James Arthur Parsons, as the write-in candidate to challenge Rankin in the general election. See "Minister to Oppose Rankin in Mississippi Election," *New York Amsterdam Star-News*, September 26, 1942, 5.

33. "This Is Utter Foolishness Which Will Do Harm Rather Than Good," *Tupelo Daily Journal*, September 12, 1942, 4; Congress, House, 77th Cong., 2nd sess., *Congressional Record* 88, pt. 6, p. 8078.

34. "Lynch Week," *Time*, October 26, 1942, 23–24; Walter Atkins, "Shubuta Bridge's Toll Stands at Six Lynch Victims, But Span Is Doomed," Chicago *Defender*, November 7, 1942, 1; "Two Negro Boys Lynched by Mob," Clarke County [Miss.] *Tribune*, October 16, 1942, 1.

35. "The Bitter Fruit," *Meridian Star*, October 13, 1942, 4 [first and third quotations]; "Biddle Orders Probe Lynchings in Mississippi," *Meridian Star*, October 20, 1942, 1.

36. "Defiant Dixie in Poll Tax Rout," *New York Amsterdam Star-News*, October 17, 1942, 1.

37. John Temple Graves, *The Fighting South* (New York, 1943), 125, 239–240.

38. "Let's Face the Race Question," *Town Meeting: Bulletin of America's Town Meeting of the Air* 9 (February 17, 1944): 6–7.

39. A. M. Jones to Theodore G. Bilbo, November 23, 1942, Box 1076, Folder 1, Bilbo Papers. This was Bilbo's standard wartime response to opponents of anti–poll tax legislation.

40. Hunter K. Cochran to Theodore G. Bilbo, November 24, 1942, Box 1077, Folder 2; M. W. Darby to Theodore G. Bilbo, November 24, 1942, Box 1077, Folder 3; both in Bilbo Papers.

41. B. W. Morgan to Theodore G. Bilbo, n.d., Box 1076, Folder 7, Bilbo Papers.

42. E. M. Pace to Roy Porter, November 19, 1942, Box 1077, Folder 1; Charles W. Wade to Theodore G. Bilbo, June 5, 1943, Box 1084, Folder 8, both in Bilbo Papers. For a discussion of the racially charged nature of the war in the Pacific from American and Japanese perspectives, see John Dower, *War Without Mercy: Race and Power in the Pacific War* (New York, 1986). Penny von Eschen argues that African Americans in World War II paid attention to international anti-colonial movements and offered a radical critique of American diplomacy. See von Eschen, *Race Against Empire: Black Americans and Anticolonialism, 1937–1957* (Ithaca, 1997). For a discussion of scattered African American sympathy for the Japanese war effort, and a longer history of black-Japanese interaction, see Gerald Horne, *Race War!: White Supremacy and the Japanese Attack on the British Empire* (New York, 2003), 55–59, 105–109.

43. J. W. Bradford to Walter Sillers, April 2, 1943, J. W. Bradford to The Delta Council, April 2, 1943, both in Box 11, Folder 8, Sillers Papers. Concerns over a shrinking wartime labor supply only heightened white elites' desire to reassert control over the Delta's black majority. See James C. Cobb, *The Most Southern Place on Earth: The Mississippi Delta and the Roots of Regional Identity* (New York, 1992), 198–208; Nan Elizabeth Woodruff, "Mississippi Delta Planters and Debates over Mechanization, Labor, and Civil Rights in the 1940s," *Journal of Southern History* Vol. 60 (May 1994): 263–284.

44. J. W. Bradford to Walter Sillers, April 2, 1943; "Southern Crusaders," n. d.; both in Box 11, Folder 8, Sillers Papers.

45. Lawson, *Black Ballots*, 23–54; "Time Bomb," *Time*, April 17, 1944, 21; Kari Frederickson, *The Dixiecrat Revolt and the End of the Solid South, 1932–1968* (Chapel Hill, 2001), 42–46.

46. "South Carolina House Backs 'Supremacy' of Whites and Warns 'Damned Agitators,'" *New York Times*, March 1, 1944, 13; untitled speech, n.d., p. 2–3, 4, 5, Subject Files, Box 3, Folder "Negro Question (2)," Gubernatorial Papers of Olin D. Johnston, South Carolina Department of Archives and History, Columbia.

47. "Time Bomb," *Time*, April 17, 1944, 20; Mike S. Connor, "The Case Against the New Deal," April 17, 1944, 2, 3, 16–17, 19, Box 29, Folder 5, Sillers Papers.

48. Sam Jones, "Will Dixie Bolt the New Deal?," *Saturday Evening Post*, March 6, 1943, 21; R. M. Prince, "I Can't Vote for Mr. Roosevelt in November," (High Point, N.C.: n.p., 1944), Series X, Box 113, Folder 1, Russell Papers.

49. Rand delivered the speech, which was reprinted and distributed in pamphlet form, on May 16, 1944, at the Alabama Lions Clubs conference in Birmingham, May 17, 1944, before the Mississippi Bankers Association in Biloxi, June 14, 1944, at Southeast Louisiana College, and June 21, 1944, at a meeting of the Mississippi Cotton Seed Crushers Association. Clayton Rand, *The New Deal and the New Slavery* (Gulfport, Miss.: Dixie Press, 1944).

8

The Sexual Politics of Race in World War II America

Jane Dailey

In the late summer of 1938, Mark Ethridge—an outspoken foe of lynching, a progressive journalist, and a leading "Southern white man of good will"— remarked in a speech before the Fourth Southwide Conference on Education and Race Relations that "I have nowhere mentioned the abolition of segregation or so-called 'social equality,' because I have nowhere found these steps to be among the Negro's aspirations. Upon the whole, he is as proud of his race as we are of ours. . . . But even if these were his aspirations, I should consider him foolhardy if he pressed them, because, as friendly as I am, I would consider them against his own interests and against the general welfare and peace." Quoting an Interracial Commission pamphlet, Ethridge explained that "what the Negro wants" was a reorientation of the horizontal race line along a vertical axis, "so that he may have on his side the rights and privileges to which he is entitled, just as the white man on his side enjoys the rights and privileges of American civilization."[1]

Ethridge's words, especially his warning to African Americans who were not asking for social equality to continue to refrain from asking for it, were the words of a man who felt the ground moving beneath his feet. Since the riotous summer of 1919, when significant numbers of white Americans arose to stamp out any hope of equality on the part of black veterans of the Great War, reform-minded whites like Mark Ethridge had worked shoulder to shoulder with African Americans in regional organizations dedicated to improving social and political conditions in the South. The membership of organizations such as the Committee for Interracial Cooperation (CIC), the Young Men's and Young Women's Christian Associations, and the Association of Southern Women for the Prevention of Lynching overlapped, as did many of their goals and ideological commitments. All of these groups functioned within the confines of the Jim Crow system throughout the 1930s, and all without exception subscribed publicly to what might be termed the central myth of progressive Southern race politics: that black Southerners, although unhappy with many of the more grievously discriminatory aspects of racial segregation, had no desire for social or what was sometimes called "full" equality, a condition that included, crucially, sexual equality. In the language of the day, African Americans were "as proud of their racial integrity" as white people were of theirs. Rather than equal rights and integration, African Americans wanted equal rights within a world that would remain, in its most intimate spaces, segregated.[2]

This myth of black dedication to "race purity," this posited lack of interest on the part of the South's oppressed minority in "social equality," was a precondition for moderate white action in the interest of black civil rights in the South in the 1930s. The understanding that "nobody is asking for social equality" balanced claims for other, more obviously political and economic, rights before World War II. Taking "the inequalities out of the bi-racial system" threatened neither Jim Crow nor white supremacy, white sociologist Guy B. Johnson explained at the CIC's annual meeting in 1935. Political equality did not lead to miscegenation. "The races," Johnson contended, "can go the whole way of political and civil equality without endangering their integrity."[3] "It is entirely possible for a southern white man to be uncompromisingly in favor of justice to the Negro and uncompromisingly against intermarriage," is how Richmond author and editor Virginius Dabney phrased it in 1933.[4] The idea that African Americans were profoundly disinterested in sexual contact with whites and eschewed intermarriage was a necessary core belief of politically progressive white Southerners, a belief that put sex at the center of their civil rights politics.

The argument that African Americans rejected the possibility of equal sex and marriage rights with whites helped white and black reformers make enormous strides in the pre–World War II South. Keeping sex out of the equation eased the way of the NAACP, as it began its legal assault on segregated education. Strategic avoidance of the sex issue also helped facilitate the organization of the Southern Conference for Human Welfare, whose voting rights campaign melded with that of the NAACP and informed later efforts to ensure the right to vote to all Americans. In 1942, explicit denial that the Fair Employment Practices Committe had any jurisdiction whatsoever over private social relations was a crucial step in creating the possibility that the wartime economic boom might benefit more than whites alone.

At the same time, the war itself made the myth of African American indifference to full equality increasingly untenable. The Nazi Party's assault on the rights and status of Jewish German citizens in the mid-1930s altered substantially the context of conversations about equal sex and marriage rights in the United States, and exposed Jim Crow laws to a comparative critique. While white reformers continued to insist that African Americans wanted government jobs and voting rights but spurned social equality, the black press identified restrictive marriage laws as a hallmark of fascism and by the middle of the war counted freedom of marriage as an essential democratic right.

The struggle to desegregate the armed forces took place along explicitly ualized lines; when black leaders campaigned for integration of the armed forces, military commanders countered with anti-miscegenation laws to justify segregation in the ranks. On the ground, in the new spaces of wartime America, questions of interracial sexuality sparked discussion and violence from Mississippi to Manhattan.

By the middle of the war, even black colleagues of white Southern reformers attacked not just Jim Crow but the myths that upheld Jim Crow. "While the southern white traditionalist likes to believe that the race system is accepted as natural and proper, in actuality he and all other participants know that it is not," wrote black sociologist and Fisk University president Charles S. Johnson in 1941. With the myth of black accommodation to segregation in great measure shattered, sex became the problem around which the shattered fragments coalesced. What was to be done? The result of this impasse for whites was not, with the exception of a few brave souls, the articulation of a new way but retrenchment. Rather than cementing the bonds of progressive interracial alliance, the Second World War widened the distance between African Americans and many of their white Southern liberal allies of the 1930s until, in the end, white Southern reformers ceased to be a potent force for reform at either the regional or the national level.

Nazis at Home and Abroad

The sudden rise to power of National Socialism in Germany after 1933 created ideological and rhetorical space for critics of American politics and society, critics who labored to make fascism synonymous with racism—and vice versa—and to tie democracy to non-discrimination. Establishing the first half of this equation was increasingly easy, particularly after passage of the 1935 Nuremburg Laws regulating and restricting Jewish German life, which leading Nazis and the black press both pointed out were modeled on American Jim Crow statutes. As one black author put it, "What else are jim-crow laws but Fascist laws . . . it is difficult to believe that Hitler to save time did not copy them directly from the Southern statutes and from the unwritten laws of America against negroes."[5]

Although some white newspapers did note the erosion of Jewish civil rights in Germany, they did not acknowledge the obvious parallels between German *Rassenpolitik* and America's Jim Crow system, and they were uninterested in doing anything about what the *Philadelphia Tribune* (black) called "the Nazis zu Hause."[6] According to Howard University sociologist and mathematician Kelly Miller, the chief difference between the United States and Germany in 1935 was that in Germany "Hitler has decreed that proscription against the Jew is a government function while here, especially in the South, every white man arrogates to himself the monitorship over the behavior of colored Americans."[7] Revisiting the question a year later, Miller recast the comparison in terms of violence: "In America the Negro is often lynched and burned at the stake, not so much for his crime, but on account of his color. The German people have not yet reached such depths of depravity nor reverted to such primitive barbarism."[8] In 1941, *Opportunity*, a magazine published monthly by the National Urban League, editorialized that "all over the world the color line is being erased as nations fight to preserve the democratic form of government—all over the world except in Hitler's Germany, Mussolini's Italy, and the United States of America."[9]

This campaign of moral and practical equivalence of Nazi race policies with Jim Crow was so widespread that as late as 1942 (even as the Polish government in exile reported that the Jewish death toll in their country had reached 700,000), a white liberal could argue that life in the Jim Crow South was only marginally superior to Nazi Germany, wondering if a concentration camp was really worse than a Georgia chain gang.[10] The NAACP also made an open effort to link Nazi race policies and American segregation. "The only essential difference between a Nazi mob hunting down Jews in Central Europe and an American mob burning black men at the stake in Mississippi is that one is actually encouraged by its national government and the other is merely tolerated," lectured the *Crisis*.[11]

In addition to noting the mounting repression of German Jews in all areas of life, America's black press drew attention to three significant markers of degradation propounded by the Nazis during the 1930s: segregated public transportation, segregated schools, and restrictive marriage laws.[12] Segregated education and Jim Crow cars were already high on the agenda of black civil rights organizations by the mid-1930s, although the Nazis' embrace of them underscored for American civil rights organizations the rightness of their cause. "The fact that Hitler has adopted the Jim Crow Car for Jews should be proof enough that it is malicious in intent and repressive in purpose," *Opportunity* editorialized in 1941.[13]

Interracial marriage was different. Despite the fact that W.E.B. Du Bois and other left-leaning blacks had been airing the issue for years, interracial marriage remained a theme most people considered best avoided—until the Nazis transformed restrictive marriage laws into a hallmark of fascism. Frequently noting that racial prejudice was officially outlawed in the Soviet Union, black publications hammered home the point that "Nazi Prejudice Against Jews is Like Dixie's."[14] In a story about the German authorities forcibly separating a non-Jewish man from his Jewish wife, the headline read, "Nazi Virginians Separate Husband from Wife by Court Order."[15] In a 1936 article, Kelly Miller cited anti-miscegenation laws as the centerpiece of the "striking analogy" between German and American race prejudice, and devoted two-thirds of his argument to this topic.[16] After 1935, the Nazi embrace of anti-miscegenation laws made it easier for critics of American marriage laws to portray them as undemocratic—as, indeed, integral to fascism.[17]

Acid Tests of Democracy

The black campaign for the right to serve as combat troops in the Armed Forces also brought sexual tensions to the fore. When he wanted to demonstrate the degraded status of free blacks in America in order to deny them citizenship rights, Chief Justice Roger Taney—in his decision in the *Dred Scott* case in 1857—pointed to two facts: black men were excluded from state militia, and African Americans were forbidden to marry whites. After quoting a number of state anti-miscegenation laws, Justice Taney turned to white-only state militias:

> Nothing could more strongly mark the entire repudiation of the African race. The alien is excluded, because, being born in a foreign country, he cannot be a member of the community until he is naturalized. But why are the African race, born in the State, not permitted to share in one of the highest duties of the citizen? The answer is obvious; he is not, by the institutions and laws of the State, numbered among its people. He forms no part of the sovereignty of the State, and is not therefore called on to uphold and defend it.[18]

The connection between bearing arms in defense of a community and being vested with full rights within it is ancient and enduring; as Justice Taney noted, the issues had been linked in America since the nation's founding. Members of a community are expected to defend it; by the same token, those who defend the people may expect whatever rights are enjoyed by the people. This reciprocity was understood by African American leaders and the United States government alike, which is why Secretary of War Henry Stimson preferred America to fight the Second World War with an all-white Army and Navy backed up by all-black service brigades. That this rational and efficient option was not, in the end, politically feasible was thanks, Stimson complained, to "the deliberate effort . . . on the part of certain radical leaders of the colored race to use the war for obtaining . . . race equality and interracial marriages." Making precisely the same link between marriage and military service as Justice Taney had, both Stimson and those he deemed "radical leaders of the colored race" realized that civil equality at home would depend, in great measure, on whether or not African Americans were trained as combat troops. For America's 13 million black men and women, *serving* their nation would not be enough: the campaign for equal rights could not be won by legions of heroic latrine-diggers and gracious Navy stewards. Black America needed its black men to *fight.*[19]

The struggle for equal representation within the Armed Forces occupied a position of growing importance for black leaders throughout the 1920s and

1930s. The Committee for Participation of Negroes in the National Defense was founded in 1938 in order to stave off the "wholesale regimentation" of black soldiers "to the service of supply." Trying to explain the depth of feeling among American blacks on this issue, the editor of the *Crisis*, Roy Wilkins, wrote to Secretary of War Harry H. Woodring in 1940 that there was "no other single issue—except possibly lynching—upon which there is a unanimity of opinion among all classes in all sections of the country." But it was Du Bois who best articulated what was at stake in the struggle for unrestricted participation in the armed forces. "This is no fight merely to wear a uniform. This is a struggle for status, a struggle to take democracy off of parchment and give it life."[20]

Democracy in one sphere, as black leaders knew well, could sometimes encourage the growth of democracy elsewhere. Loyal to Roosevelt when it came to the New Deal but uninspired by what one biographer of the president has termed his "benevolent neutrality" when it came to race issues, black newspapers made discrimination in the armed forces an issue in the 1940 presidential election. In no danger of losing his position, the president was nonetheless troubled by the extent of black criticism of defense policies. Against the War Department's unbending position that "the Army is not a sociological laboratory," Roosevelt asked repeatedly what steps could be taken toward inclusion of black Americans in the military without actually ending segregation. The fact that the president's own beloved navy was the racist outlier even within the armed forces was inconvenient. Prodded by Roosevelt to "invent something that colored enlistees could do," the navy—which refused to enlist black men in any position other than as messmen—answered that their policy was no more discriminatory than the general society's. Under pressure from both the president and the secretary of war, Secretary of the Navy Frank Knox finally abandoned lesser arguments and explained that as long as "the white man refuses to admit the negro to intimate family relationships leading to marriage," the navy was under no compulsion to breach its own racial barriers of intimacy.[21]

Committed to the navy's argument in reverse, African Americans were, nonetheless, skeptical about the possibility of using the war to further full equality at home. The NAACP's official reaction to American entry into World War II acknowledged African American ambivalence toward fighting another European war when memories of the last war and its unfulfilled promise for American blacks lingered so bitterly. "We all know that the attitude towards the colored people of the nations fighting Hitler, Mussolini and Hirohito leaves much to be desired," Executive Secretary Walter White admitted. But he insisted that African Americans had special interests at stake in this war: "If Hitler wins, every single right we now possess and for which we have struggled here in America for more than three centuries will be instantaneously wiped out. . . . If the allies win, we shall at least have the right to continue fighting for a share of democracy for ourselves" and added that African Americans must "continue to be the spearhead and the acid test of democracy in the United States."[22]

To this end, black Americans added a fifth freedom—"Freedom from Segregation"—to the "Four Freedoms" already denominated by Roosevelt (freedom of speech and religion, freedom from fear and poverty).[23] The black press, ever skeptical, urged black Americans to remember what had happened the last time America went to war.[24] When Vice President Henry Wallace insisted in a speech on war aims before the Free World Association in New York in May 1942 that "the four freedoms must apply to all nations and all races," the *Afro-American* responded, "We Think He Includes Us, but We Thought Woodrow Wilson Did, Too."[25]

Separate Wars

If leading whites were irritated by black demands for equality, seeing them as untimely, many progressive white and black commentators were disgusted by the reaction of white Southerners to the military crisis, which seemed to be primarily to shore up the domestic racial caste system under wartime conditions and only secondarily to win the war.[26] Believing that they were fighting for things "as they have been in America" and haunted by "revolting visions of what the new society may be like," white Southerners often seemed to be fighting their own, separate war. "When you go South and hang around a while, asking questions and drinking beer and cokes with new-found friends, you get the uneasy feeling that the war the South is fighting isn't the same war that the rest of the country is fighting," reported white Northerner Victor Bernstein in September 1942.[27]

The campaign that many white Southerners were most interested in pursuing was a rear-guard action against African American efforts to erode Jim Crow. Chatting with the Secretary of the Chamber of Commerce in Birmingham, Bernstein received a lecture on the looming dangers of social equality. "There's one thing you can put in your pipe and smoke," Bernstein was told. "There's no white man down here goin' to let his daughter sleep with a n—, or sit at the same table with a n—, or go walkin' with a n—. The war can go to hell, the world can go to hell, we can all be dead—but he ain't goin' to do it." Insisting that "nobody down South is asking for the colored man's right to sleep with a white woman," Bernstein dismissed the Alabaman's concern as "the artificially contrived bugaboo of almost every Southerner. You talk to him about giving the colored people a fair break with a job, or better housing, or better schools, and somehow the argument winds up with threatened rape and the sanctity of Southern womanhood."[28]

But with leading black newspapers now openly advocating intermarriage as "the quickest way to solve the racial problem" and the NAACP's assistant secretary Roy Wilkins calling for "absolute political and social equality" and rejection of the racial status quo,[29] Southern whites were not wrong to interpret black war aims as incompatible with their own. Even if African Americans had been more reticent, Lillian Smith's observation that "whenever, wherever race relations are discussed, sex moves arm in arm with the concept of segregation" remained accurate and to the point.[30]

Consider the potential for both sex and integration in a new setting that arose in response to the mass mobility occasioned by the war: USO canteens. The United Service Organization (USO) was established in February 1941 to provide safe settings in which to entertain soldiers. Civilian-run and funded, the USO was staffed entirely by volunteers, most of whom were women, whose work consisted of socializing with soldiers far from home. Most canteens, following local custom and the example of the military, were segregated by race.[31]

A significant exception to the pattern of segregated USOs was the Stage Door Canteen in midtown Manhattan, where servicemen swung to the tunes of Benny Goodman, Tommy Dorsey, and Count Basie on a fully integrated basis. Making the same connection between civil rights and military service as Chief Justice Taney, Secretary of War Stimson, and the Committee for Participation of Negroes in the National Defense, the operating principle of the Stage Door Canteen was that "a Negro serviceman who was good enough to die for a white girl was good enough to dance with her." Writer Margaret Halsey and the other volunteers considered it a part of the job to upset segregationist thinking on race and sex, particularly the seamless progression from dancing to sex and marriage. It wasn't easy. As Halsey recalled:

> One of the most monotonous aspects of race relations in the United States is the blind acceptance—by otherwise sensible people—of any wild, half-baked, fragmentary, unsubstantiated or even patently absurd cock-and-bull story that comes along, provided it has to do with Negroes and sex. . . . Nobody on God's green footstool could sell these people stock in a phony gold mine, but when the issue is sex and Negroes, they sit with their mouths open like fledgling birds and swallow whatever is dropped in.[32]

Educating these fledglings in racial camaraderie under arms was the task of the Junior Hostesses, young black and white women volunteers ranging in age from eighteen to twenty-five, who agreed to dance with any serviceman who asked, and all of whom were taught, Halsey was at pains to explain, that "courtesy is not copulation."[33] Known worldwide for its stance on non-discrimination, the Stage Door attracted a self-selecting group of young women: NAACP head Walter White's daughter Jane worked there, for example. Even so, many of the white Junior Hostesses cherished prejudices that needed to be addressed. To this end, Halsey wrote and distributed a Memo to Junior Hostesses, which outlined the canteen's policy on African Americans (which, she explained, was based on the Fourteenth and Fifteenth Amendments to the Constitution), and addressed frankly but with humor the root fear of white women asked to dance with black men. "What worries you more [than how to make conversation with black GIs]," Halsey wrote, "is the fear of rape. You unconsciously, but very arrogantly, assume that no male Negro can so much as glance at you without wanting to get you with child. The truth is," the older woman informed the girls under her wing, "that while you are an extremely attractive group of young women, there isn't one single one of you who's *that* good."[34]

Halsey seemed to be right that interracial civility need not lead to interracial concupiscence. The Stage Door Canteen entertained more than 3 million servicemen from all over the world over the course of four years. During that time, there was only one major racial contretemps on the dance floor, when a white Marine tried to pull a black sailor away from the sailor's white partner. There was never, as Margaret Halsey put it dryly, an occasion for one of the white Junior Hostesses "to go home to Papa with an interracial baby wrapped up in an old plaid shawl." In fact, there was not all that much crossing of the color line at the canteen: as Halsey recollected, the black servicemen generally asked the black Junior Hostesses to dance, and white GIs shied away from the African American girls. What America's black men in arms liked, Halsey remarked, "was not dancing with white girls, per se. What they liked was being free to choose with whom they would dance."[35]

The possibility that the war would bring that freedom worried many whites, especially but not exclusively in the South, who responded to the social dislocation caused by military mobilization by rearticulating their commitment to white supremacy under markedly changed conditions. If not officially under siege by the government, which refused to desegregate the armed forces during the war, the South's social system was nevertheless challenged more directly, and more systematically, than it had ever been before. Military installations became, after 1941, a chief site of such challenges. Most of the armed forces' new training bases were located in the South, because of its climate and the power of its congressional delegation. The war brought money South, but it also brought strangers, including young men unprepared to accept local custom when it came to race. Southern social conventions worked out painstakingly via elaborate municipal laws and local custom came under severe pressure as wartime congestion swelled towns and strained segregated public services. Northern black recruits unfamiliar with the quotidian indignities of Jim Crow clashed on a daily basis with Southern white GIs and war workers, and chafed against the strictures of segregation.

The military bases erected hastily on soil previously occupied by share-croppers now building ships and airplanes became a chief site for the violent reassertion of white supremacy.[36] In the three months following Pearl Harbor, there were two army camp riots; by May 1942 fourteen black men in uniform had been killed by civilian police in adjacent communities. At Fort Benning, Georgia, Private Felix Hall was found hanging from a tree, his arms and legs bound. Black soldiers stationed at Luke Field near Pheonix, Arizona, spent Thanksgiving Day 1942 shooting it out with white military police from Pagago Park; three were killed and eleven wounded, and twenty-seven black GIs faced courts martial. The previous January, white MPs and civilian police wounded twenty-one black soldiers and killed ten in a riot in Alexandria, Louisiana, that began when an MP slapped a black soldier's girlfriend. Not all the violence occurred in the South, although white Southerners, particularly white military police, were usually involved. Private James Greggs, a white Southern MP, shot and killed Private David Woods, a black soldier from Chicago, outside a movie theater at Fort Dix, New Jersey, when Woods refused to go to the end of the line. All in all, wartime America saw six civilian race riots, more than twenty military riots and mutinies, and between forty and seventy-five lynchings. As Howard Donovan Queen, a black officer in the Regular Army who eventually rose to the rank of colonel, recalled years later, "The Negro soldier's first taste of warfare in World War II was on army posts right here in his own country."[37]

Much of the violence in and around Southern military bases was triggered by perceived competition over women.[38] A riot at Camp Stewart, Georgia, was traced to a rumor that a black soldier's wife from New York had come to see him, and that she was white. "How much was truth I really don't know," a black GI recalled, "but it was enough to turn Stewart upside down."[39] Hoping no doubt to limit the possibility of interracial tension among his troops, in January 1942 Captain A. D. Robbins of the 77th Anti-Aircraft Regiment defined interracial sex as synonymous with rape and therefore punishable by death under military law. Denounced by the NAACP as "Funny War Order No. 1" and disavowed and revoked by the War Department, it is noteworthy that Robbins's order included *all* interracial relationships, including those between white men and black women, "whether voluntary or not."[40]

By the end of the war, having fought alongside black soldiers and relied on African American logistical support, many white officers and GIs alike seem to have realized that black soldiers had earned certain rights through their participation in the war—but they nonetheless drew strict boundaries around those rights. "I don't think it is possible for anyone outside of the U.S. to understand just what the general attitude of the white people is toward the negro," wrote one white corporal in response to an interview with Walter White published in the *London Sunday Dispatch*. "In the first place it is not as bad as most outsiders seem to believe. The fact is that we are not opposed to the negro 'getting ahead in the world' if he goes about it in the right way. We do object, however, to negro men sexing with white women," the author explained. "Even the most ardent race equality advocates in the States would be highly browned off if they suspected that any of their women folks were fraternizing, mating, marrying, or otherwise having truck with negro men." Complaining that white GIs in Britain felt "*forced* to accept race equality" by the absence of Jim Crow laws, this American soldier concluded that "the white GIs just can't stand to see [a] nice looking white girl necking with a big black negro. We're not fighting for that kind of 'democracy.' We could have it without fighting if we wanted it."[41]

Not all white Southern GIs were as grudging or as nervous as this one, however. Toward the end of the war, the Stage Door Canteen's Margaret Halsey received this letter from a white lieutenant from the Deep South. Describing himself as one of those "who seek democracy in a nation where it is sometimes hard to find," the lieutenant continued:

> Even I am not sure how far I would go to insure that democracy. I want my colored friend to vote; I want him to be free from prejudice in the courts; I want him to go to college; I want him to have the best of living conditions; I want him to be paid what he is worth; I want him to be an active and respected member of any union he desires; I want him to know and enjoy the Four Freedoms. I will work and work hard to see that he—or his sons—get these things, but—I do not want him to live next door to me; I do not want him to be my house guest; and I do not want him to dance with my daughter. How can I reconcile these conflicting desires?

> Halsey responded that she did not think the lieutenant, or most white southerners of this generation, could reconcile them: they would just have to live with the tension these conflicting desires produced. Recommending that the lieutenant join an organization dedicated to working for racial justice when he returned to the States, Halsey suggested as well that the white man "stock up on bicarbonate of soda and try not to think of posterity."[42]

The FEPC

Men in uniform were not the only ones to connect the war with sexual rights. Racialized sexual tension was exacerbated not simply by the military effort on the battlefield, but also on the factory floor and in the politics of the lucrative defense industry. In June 1941, when African American leaders threatened mass action over discriminatory hiring in the defense industries, Franklin Roosevelt issued Executive Order 8802, which stipulated equal hiring practices in defense industries but did not desegregate the armed forces. To administer the order, the president created the Fair Employment Practices Committe (FEPC), and installed at its helm the progressive and well-connected Louisville journalist Mark Ethridge.

Endowed with investigatory but not enforcement power, the FEPC illuminated but was unable to alter the racially stratified war economy. The agency's chief weapon was moral suasion, which might have worked had white Southern employers had any scruples about their discriminatory hiring practices, or shared the same moral premises as the committee. Instead, FEPC hearings on wartime Southern industrial practices, to which leading Southern whites came as if summoned before the Grand Inquisitor, crystallized white opposition to the African American agenda for the war. For white Southerners, the FEPC represented a clear federal response to black political power, which was reason enough to despise it. The vitriolic denunciations of the FEPC by Mississippi senator Theodore Bilbo, a Roosevelt loyalist and strong supporter of most New Deal programs, earned him the title "Prince of the Peckerwoods." In public hearings in Birmingham in 1942, Alabama governor Frank Dixon denounced the FEPC as a "kangaroo court obviously dedicated to the abolition of segregation."[43]

Hoping to head off the likes of Dixon and Bilbo, Ethridge explained in a statement at the Birmingham hearings that the FEPC's goal was not to dismantle segregation, but to make it "as painless as possible"; to uphold segregation while trying, somehow, to address discrimination.[44] Nevertheless, Deep South whites kept turning to the question of social equality. Whereas Louisiana senator John Overton spoke broadly, insisting that "this war would bring not only political but social equality," Senator Bilbo connected the dots, and lectured white Southerners that they should not forget that federal support for equality in one realm led irresistibly to demands for equality across the board. Framing his claims as broadly as possible and in terms that connected hiring and marital practices, Bilbo intoned, "Every Negro in America who is behind movements of this kind . . . dream[s] of equality and inter-marriage between whites and blacks."[45]

As the head of the FEPC, Mark Ethridge was not in a position simply to denounce this sort of rhetoric: he had to engage it. In his statement at Birmingham, Ethridge acknowledged and tried to allay white Southern fears that the FEPC intended to reorganize Southern social relations. He began by speaking to the white men and women in the room. "No white Southerner can logically challenge the statement that the colored man is entitled, as an American citizen, to full civil rights and to economic opportunity," Ethridge asserted. In a conscious effort to defuse the "social equality" question, Ethridge denied that the FEPC had any influence in the private sphere. Admitting that "individual members of the committee have their own ideas" about desegregation (indeed, black committee members Earl Dickerson, Chicago's first African American alderman and Milton Webster, first vice president of the Brotherhood of Sleeping Car Porters [BSCP], showed no signs of bowing to Jim Crow conventions), Ethridge insisted that the committee "recognized that the President was not endeavoring, in Executive Order 8802, to write a social document. . . . I believe it is perfectly apparent that Executive Order 8802 is a war order, and not a social document." Had this not been the case, Ethridge added, he would not have agreed to serve on the committee, because he "would have considered a Federal fiat demanding, for instance, the abolition of social segregation against the general peace and welfare."

Turning his attention to the African Americans present and to the black press and organizations monitoring the Birmingham hearings, Ethridge warned them not to press too far, too fast, in their urge toward equality, and spoke the words to which he would be forever tied in civil rights memory: "The Southern colored man . . . must recognize that there is no power in the world—not even in all the mechanized armies of the earth, Allied and Axis—which could now force the Southern white people to the abandonment of the principle of social segregation."[46]

It is easy to read Mark Ethridge's comments in Birmingham as evidence of the inflexibility and virulent racism of white Southern liberals: in the midst of a world war, the white Southern administrator of the first federal anti-discrimination program took the opportunity to articulate his region's commitment to Jim Crow in apocalyptic terms. What this perspective misses is Ethridge's redrawing of Jim Crow's territory, the narrowing of his realm. Standing stoutly on the rock of social segregation, Mark Ethridge conceded almost everything else on the black reform agenda.

But even this reformist possibility was insufficient to the new day. Lectured by Ethridge, African Americans talked back. Calling for his resignation as head of the FEPC, the *Afro-American* declared that the social equality question needed public airing, not repression. "The average Southern white . . . becomes so emotional and noisy" over the "social equality" question, the editors noted, "that we ought to talk about it a little. We begin by saying that the AFRO believes in social equality if it is anything other citizens have. We think we are entitled to all the public rights of citizens and therefore need no special arrangements made for us." Running down Ethridge's list of the rights of citizenship, the editors added marriage. "If intermarriage is social equality, we are for it. Free people choose their own life-time companions without any interference from the State." It was the editors' belief, in short, "that in every human relationship government can have but one standard—citizenship. . . . The only spot reserved for social equality is in the home, or private club which requires no public license to operate." The Prince of the Peckerwoods may have exaggerated the sexual fantasy life of American blacks—but his analysis of the trajectory of African American politics was on the mark.[47]

Nearer and Nearer the Precipice

From a segregationist point of view, the overcrowded conditions of the wartime South, with so many strangers of uncharted genealogy in town, made it both more important than ever to keep everybody in their allotted racial spaces and much harder to do so. By 1942 there was no mistaking the new belligerency of black bus and tram riders in the wartime South, particularly young black men, who moved the "white" and "colored" dividers, refused to vacate seats when instructed to, and hung over white women, sharing their breath and body odor. Southern whites linked such behavior with the new opportunities that the war and the FEPC had brought to black workers. The *Richmond Times-Dispatch* was not alone in interpreting black insistence that whites respect their own segregation rules and vacate seats reserved for blacks as part of African Americans' new "nation-wide fight for full citizenship." An official of the Virginia Electric and Power Company complained that there were fights on the buses and streetcars almost every day, because "the Negro . . . is making good money now and feels that he is as good as the white man." Bus drivers in Mobile, Alabama, and Alexandria, Louisiana, shot and killed black servicemen in quarrels over segregation.[48]

Southern reformers were not blind to this crisis. In November 1943 Virginius Dabney, the progressive white editor of the *Richmond Times-Dispatch*, a man widely respected among blacks for his editorials in the 1930s denouncing lynching and decrying the miscarriage of justice at Scottsboro, made a modest proposal. The city of Richmond should repeal its laws segregating streetcars and buses. Originally passed to lessen racial friction, the laws, Dabney argued, no longer worked and actually heightened racial tensions because of war-related overcrowding and attendant jostling for position. Under these circumstances, Dabney considered segregated public transportation counterproductive and a danger to the broader system of segregation, which he embraced.

Dabney's argument was entirely expedient, his goals ameliorative. As he explained to Louis Jaffé, the left-leaning editor of the white Norfolk *Virginian-Pilot*, he eschewed moral arguments against segregation because if it were true that segregation was undemocratic, as many argued, "it is just as logical to argue against it in the public schools, for instance." Dabney was concerned both to prevent violence and to preserve segregation where it worked and was necessary. "I am entirely opposed to the elimination of segregation as a general proposition," Dabney wrote in another letter, "but this is one area where segregation doesn't segregate." Many white Richmonders seemed to agree with Dabney's piecemeal approach to reforming Jim Crow: letters to the *Times-Dispatch* ran three to one in favor of his suggestion, and the Virginia League for the Repeal of the Segregation Laws was formed in Richmond in December 1943.[49]

Dabney's attempt at limited desegregation came to nothing, but his goal of preventing violence and shifting the defense of Jim Crow to those areas where he thought segregation mattered most, such as schools and the marital bed, remained. As he had already written in a noted article published in *The Atlantic Monthly*, America seemed on the brink of an interracial explosion that could make the race riots of the First World War "seem mild by comparison."[50] Wartime social and economic transformations could not by themselves explain the heightened racial tension. Rather, black-white relations had been brought to the brink through the demands of "extremist Negro leaders and Negro newspapers" for "an overnight revolution in race relations," and the rabid response by "tub-thumping demagogues" like Georgia's Eugene Talmadge and the congressional "white trash bloc" led by John Rankin of Mississippi. Sounding for all the world like his friend Mark Ethridge, Dabney warned that if the NAACP did not cease its campaign for "absolute political and social equality" with whites, then "the white leaders in the South who have been responsible for much of the steady progress of the Negro in the past, and who can bring about a great deal more such progress in the future, will be driven into the opposition camp." Angry that men like Ethridge were being assailed by the black press as "spiritual kinsmen of Hitler," Dabney testified to the rhetorical power of the African American campaign for equality and spoke for himself as well when he complained that white Southern reformers unwilling to dismantle segregation root and branch were being "attacked as traitors to democracy who ought to be fighting beside the Nazis."[51] As far as men such as Dabney and Ethridge were concerned, African American rights could be gained only through the intercession of progressive white Southerners, who remained the strategic lynchpin of reform.

What the Negro Wants

Halfway through the war, William Terry Couch, the director of the University of North Carolina Press, suggested to Howard University historian Rayford Logan that he assemble a collection of essays representing "the personal creed of 10 or 15 prominent Negroes." Left-leaning enough to have been tagged a "parlor Bolshevik" in the 1930s and active in North Carolina interracial reform circles, Couch was by 1943 a fully credentialed white Southern liberal.[52]

Couch's intent in commissioning *What the Negro Wants* was to assess the state of American, but particularly Southern, race relations during the war, and to spark a lively discussion of the future of segregation. As he would later explain in his "Editor's Preface" to the book, in which he assumed the role of Pontius Pilate to Logan's assembled High Priests and Elders, Couch hoped to further discussion of how the white South could disentangle itself from the worst excesses of a social system that, he allowed, imposed "numerous unnecessary burdens" on its minority black population. Having carefully balanced the contributors among conservatives, moderates, and known rabble-rousers, Couch was appalled and Logan astonished by the authors' unexpectedly unanimous opinion that what the Negro wanted was absolute equality and an end to legal segregation in all areas of life.

From Right to Left, the contributors spoke with one voice. What the Negro wanted was equality under the law and an end to racial segregation. To Logan's demand for "First-Class Citizenship" was added "The Negro Wants Full Equality" (the NAACP's Roy Wilkins), "The Negro Wants Full Participation in the American Democracy" (educator Frederick Douglass Patterson), "Count Us In" (poet Sterling Brown), and "'Certain Unalienable Rights'" (National Youth Administration director Mary McLeod Bethune). *Pittsburgh Courtier* columnist George Schuyler's tart rearticulation of the book's organizing logic as "The Caucasian Problem" transposed the key, but not the leitmotif, of the volume. Most shocking was the openness with which the authors of *What the Negro Wants* addressed the fundamental question of sexual equality and intermarriage.[53]

Of the fourteen essayists, half called for the abolition of restrictive marriage laws. Three others spoke in code through references to "*absolute political and social equality*" (Wilkins), "the abrogation of every law which makes a distinction in treatment between citizens based on religion, creed, color or national origin" (the BSCP's A. Phillip Randolph), and calls for full "equality before the law" (Bethune).[54] Without demanding an end to what Schuyler referred to as "racial pollution laws barring marriage because of so-called race," Langston Hughes nonetheless noted that "nobody as a rule sleeps with or eats with or dances with or marries anybody else except by mutual consent," and poked fun at the "ballot box to the bedroom" logic of Southern whites. "Millions of people of various races in New York, Chicago, and Seattle go to the same polls and vote without ever co-habiting together," he announced. Following on Hughes's heels, Sterling Brown ridiculed the notion that "crowded buses and street cars and cafeterias are marriage bureaus" and remarked that "Negroes have long recognized this as the hub of the argument opposing change in their status."[55]

Bill Couch had hoped to publish a thoughtful book with practical suggestions about how to make the postwar Jim Crow South more humane: the sort of book that Virginius Dabney could recommend to the readers of the *Times-Dispatch*. *What the Negro Wants* was not that book. Suddenly unsure of his ability to comprehend, much less predict, what the Negro wanted, Couch wrote to Rayford Logan looking for solace, or at least affirmation. "For years I have been . . . telling people the Negro . . . is not interested in social equality," Couch complained. The fault lay, obviously, with the essayists and not with Couch. "The things Negroes are represented as wanting seem to me far removed from those they ought to want. Most of the things they are represented as wanting can be summarized in the phrase: complete abolition of segregation. If this is what the Negro wants, nothing could be clearer than what he needs, and needs most urgently, is to revise his wants." Until that happened, Couch could not—would not—publish this book.[56]

When Couch rescinded his offer of publication, Logan threatened to sue. Panicking slightly, Couch took his troubles to a trio of leading white liberals: Jackson Davis (an officer of the General Education Board, which was funded by the Rockefeller Foundation), Mark Ethridge, and Virginius Dabney. Cognizant of the explosive nature of the book, Davis and Ethridge nonetheless urged publication, as did Dabney, who alone seemed to understand how Couch had backed himself into such a corner. Couch's trouble, Dabney wrote, was that "you were under the delusion, when you arranged for this book, that the Negro does not want the abolition of segregation, establishment of complete social equality, etc." Dabney had thought the same in 1941. But his wartime experiences in Richmond and his close reading of the black press had taught him otherwise in the intervening years. The book would be published, but with a disclaimer by Couch.[57]

Writing in the waning weeks of 1943, as the *London Times* reported soberly that evidence from Berlin and Poland gave the "bleakest possible picture" of the fate of European Jewry and warned that "the worst of Hitler's threats are being literally applied," W. T. Couch agonized in his "Editor's Preface" that all theories of racial hierarchy were in danger of being completely discredited by the Nazis.[58] "Is there any sanity in the view now often stated that no one but a Fascist or Nazi can believe one people or race superior to another?" he asked. Regretful of the more arbitrary and mean-spirited aspects of segregation, Couch agreed that many of the burdens that white Southerners placed on the region's African American minority should be removed. But the Jim Crow barrier itself—by which Couch meant the anti-miscegenation laws that were meant to guarantee racial identity and hence make segregation possible—must remain. Such a barrier could not be made completely effective, Couch realized, "but the fact that some people may cross it in secret does not mean that the barrier ought to be torn down." Social and sexual segregation, he admitted, "may be a tremendous handicap on the Negro; but removing it would result in something worse."[59]

Since the early 1930s, Couch continued, numerous books, articles, and pamphlets had argued "that racial notions are responsible for Nazism, that race is a 'modern superstition,' a 'fallacy,' 'man's most dangerous myth,' that the concept of race has no scientific basis, that there is no scientific evidence of differences of ability among races, that mental tests have proved substantial equality, that custom, tradition, prejudice, rather than genuine differences in capacity are responsible for the status of the Negro in the South."[60] The apogee of this trend had been reached at precisely the moment that Couch wrote his introduction to *What the Negro Wants*, in the form of Gunnar Myrdal's *An American Dilemma: The Negro Problem and Modern Democracy* (1944). Couch attacked Myrdal for his argument "that the United States must either give up the 'American Creed' and go fascistic, or accept an equality which would permit amalgamation." The issue, ultimately, was sex, and racial reproduction, which Couch considered tantamount to cultural reproduction. Lashing out at Myrdal for his cultural relativism and his refusal to take white Southern abhorrence of miscegenation seriously, Couch argued that the solution to the Southern race problem was not to be found in integration but in the ability of Negroes and whites to "remain racially separate and distinct and at the same time avoid inflicting disabilities on each other." Could not the white man, Couch asked, "separate cultural from biological integration, and help the Negro achieve the first and deny him the second?"

Although he framed his introduction as a response to *An American Dilemma*, Couch was arguing as well with his own authors in *What the Negro Wants*, most notably with W.E.B. Du Bois, whose "Evolving Program for Negro Freedom" included a brief for interracial marriage.[61] Insisting that "equality" meant "the right to select one's own mates and close companions," Du Bois conceded that "Naturally, if an individual choice like intermarriage is proven to be a social injury, society must forbid it. It has been the contention of the white South," he continued, "that the social body always suffers from miscegenation, and that miscegenation is always possible where there is friendship and often where there is mere courtesy." Joining his voice to those sociologists and anthropologists denounced by Couch in his Preface, Du Bois insisted that "modern science has effectively answered" this belief. "There is no scientific reason why there should not be intermarriage between two human beings who happen to be of different race or color."[62]

African American reviewers, predictably, raved about the collection, and attacked the argument, common among Southern whites, that its views were unrepresentative. Casting a different net, the Hampton Institute's J. Saunders Redding advised readers of the *New Republic* in his review of the book. "Ask any expert—and any expert would be any literate Negro. Indeed, the validity of the book is derived from the undisputable [*sic*] fact that the editor might have chosen fourteen other contributors and achieved the same general result."[63]

White reviewers received *What the Negro Wants* with more equanimity than its publisher did, although they did not fail to note the call for social equality. In a review published in the *New York Times Book Review*, William Shands Meacham—chairman of the Virginia State Board of Parole and a trustee of the Hampton Institute—stated forthrightly that "what the Negro wants is first-class American citizenship without any reservations." This included, Meacham explained, equal marriage rights. Although he understood the logical progression in the demand for full equality, Meacham worried about the effects of such a "frontal approach" for the amelioration of Southern race relations, which, he noted, "must count upon the support of the dominant race." "[W]hen a Negro leader implies that the breaking down of the legal barriers to mixed marriages is an essential part of the democratic process, he risks poisoning the atmosphere in which countless white Americans of good-will would like to eliminate needless differentials."[64]

An American Dilemma

By 1944, all hope of consensus between white and black Southerners about the definition of needless differentials and necessary differentials—about, in essence, the limits of equality—had vanished, a casualty of "the war against racism," as J. Saunders Redding defined it, and the clear answer provided by African Americans to the eternal white Southern question, "What does the Negro want?" Let all who would hear, hear, Redding advised. "The black South believes in equality now. The black South wants segregation laws abolished now. The black South wants an end now to the economic tyranny exercised over it. The white South would not know this if it could."[65]

The truth of Redding's final remark is underscored by the fact that even those few whites who were willing to advocate complete equality and the abolition of all segregation laws could only articulate that willingness on the grounds that sex with white women was not, in the end, what the Negro wanted. Although he argued in *An American Dilemma* that sex was "the principle around which the whole structure of segregation of the Negroes . . . [was] organized," Gunnar Myrdal nonetheless assured his readers that American blacks wanted good jobs above all else and that "the marriage matter, finally, is of rather distant and doubtful interest" to black Americans. Eleanor Roosevelt—considered an over-the-top radical on the race question by rank-and-file white Southerners—equated opposition to racial intermarriage with Nazism, and argued that marriage was a question best left "to individuals to handle." At the same time, the First Lady addressed the root fear of Southern whites and dismissed it. "There is no more reason to expect that there will be more intermarriage if the four fundamental basic rights of citizens [including equality before the law] are granted to all people in this country than there will be if they are withheld," she opined. "In fact, I think it probable that there would be less."[66]

With the war winding down and the myth of black Southern acquiescence in segregation shattered, white Southern reformers self-consciously faced the question of what to do next. In June 1944 white Mississippian David Cohn, who considered himself a liberal, tried to parse the race issue for other Americans in an article written originally for the *Atlantic Monthly*, "How the South Feels about the Race Problem." Cohn began with three "candid acknowledgments" about the race problem in the South: first, that it was insoluble, in the sense that it was a complicated social problem and no "final solution can be found and the whole matter neatly disposed of." Second, Cohn asserted that "it is at bottom a blood or sexual question. The whites are determined that no white in their legal jurisdiction shall marry a Negro, and this is the law of all the southern states." Under these circumstances, Cohn concluded, "there can never be 'social equality' between the races. . . . It is useless to tell Southerners that their fears are groundless; that Negroes say they do not want 'social equality' or intermarriage with whites," Cohn continued, appealing to the by-now tattered myth of Southern race politics. "Instinctively the Southerner argues that sex is at the core of life—that it is one of the most profound instincts or desires that animate the human body, and that it is capable of evoking primitive fears and demoniac passions. Southern whites, therefore, will not at any foreseeable time relax the taboos which keep the races separate. They fear and believe that once a small crack is made in the walls of social segregation, the walls will eventually be breached."[67]

Because it was condensed and reprinted in *Reader's Digest*, David Cohn's article reached many thousands of readers, who in turn shared their thoughts on the topic in letters to Cohn. Although some letter-writers objected to the frankness of Cohn's remarks, others took up the position regarding black equality articulated by Mark Ethridge in 1942. As "A Texan" wrote, "The Southerner is broad-minded enough to see that intermingling with the Negro could result in inter-marriage. That is the main reason the Southern White man wants the Negro to keep his place, and we'll keep ours. We do, however, believe the Negro is entitled to civil rights." William J. Frazier, Jr., agreed. "In our manner of doing, it will not be in our life time, nor our children's, but the negro will someday enjoy these freedoms *without intermarriage.*" How, exactly, this limited equality was going to come about remained something of a mystery, and two students from the Florida State College for Women requested further advice. "For those of us who know how right you are," Vivian Thomas and Phyllis Freeman wrote, "won't you publish a follow-up of *How the South Feels* with an article about 'What the South can do, in spite of How the South Feels?'"[68]

There was no follow-up article. But the organization of a group of Southerners, a group that included Mark Ethridge and Virginius Dabney, offers insight into what these leading white Southern men thought could be done about the race issue, in spite of how the white South felt about interracial sex and marriage. In March 1944 a new publication, *The Southern Frontier*, announced the creation of another interracial Southern reform organization. Pledging to "try honestly and courageously to take the inequalities and inequities out of the biracial civilization of the South," the Southern Regional Council (SRC) dedicated itself to devoting its "very best statesmanship and untiring energy for the next twenty years to the realization of this goal." Thinking not in terms of months and years but rather in terms of "all the centuries that may lie ahead," the SRC sought to establish "a blue-print for the shape of things to come," a "more democratic, a more abundant South."[69]

Dedicated to removing "the inequalities which violate the law in letter and spirit" but not the segregation laws themselves, the SRC was attacked immediately by those who advocated an immediate end to Jim Crow. "Until [the SRC], or any similar group, comes clean on the question of segregation, I haven't much hope for it," wrote the editor of the liberal magazine *Common Ground* to Virginius Dabney in January 1944.[70] Declining the invitation to join the SRC's board of directors, prominent white author Lillian Smith explained that she "would not feel comfortable as a member of any organization working for racial democracy that does not deem it important to take a firm and public stand in opposition to segregation and in defense of human equality."[71]

Forced onto the defensive before the organization was even fairly launched, the SRC's supporters portrayed out-and-out opponents of segregation such as Lillian Smith and J. Saunders Redding as "a few lonely souls who denounce segregation and are powerless to do anything about it," and declared with suitable humility that if the SRC fails, "we shall not have done worse than Democracy and Christianity and Humanity itself."[72]

Operating from the premise that the best defense is a strong offense, leading African American "lonely souls" continued throughout the final year of the war to articulate their demand for full equality as American citizens. As the war wound down in May 1945, a panel of experts was asked to discuss the question, "Are We Solving America's Race Problems?" on the popular radio show *America's Town Meeting of the Air*. Novelist Richard Wright spoke directly to the point:

> At once let's define what we mean by a solution of the race problem. If the race problem were solved, we would have no Black Belts, no Jim Crow army or navy, no Jim Crow Red Cross blood banks, no Negro institutions, no laws prohibiting inter-marriage, no customs assigning Negroes to inferior positions. We would all simply be Americans, and the nation would be the better for it.[73]

This was a sentiment with which very few Southern whites could agree, even those—perhaps most especially those—who had dedicated years of their lives to bettering the conditions in their region. Increasingly, the question that arose was the one raised by William T. Couch and echoed by William Shands Meacham: Was freedom of marriage a right? Was the breaking down of barriers to intermarriage an intrinsic part of the democratic process? How far would the advocates of the competing responses to these questions go in defense of their position? Who would hold the line, and how?

At the beginning of America's war in 1941, Charles S. Johnson had predicted that an outcome of that war would be change, if not necessarily progress, in race relations. Thanks to the war, black Southerners had traveled the globe; as veterans, they would return from London, Berlin, Rome, and Burma determined to share the fruits of democratic victory and with a hard-earned appreciation of what men working in concert can achieve. Drawing nourishment for their fight from "the global struggle for freedom," as Richard Wright described it on the radio that day in May 1945, black GIs swelled the ranks of the NAACP, transforming the association into a mass organization, and positioning it to take the lead in the movement for black equality in America. The torch previously carried by regional interracial organizations was not so much passed as dropped. In consequence, the NAACP, not the Southern Conference for Human Welfare, the Commission on Interracial Cooperation, or the Southern Regional Council, led the struggle for full equality after 1945. Unable to bring themselves to attack the heart of segregation, many white Southern race reformers assaulted what were, at best, its extremities. No longer able to dictate the content of "what the Negro wants" to African Americans, "white Southern men of goodwill" like Mark Ethridge and Virginius Dabney did not become overnight conservatives: but they moved from the front of the revolution in race relations to the rear just as the real battle was heating up.

Notes

1. Speech, "America's Obligation to Its Negro Citizens," August 4, 1938, p. 11, folder 108 in the Mark F. Ethridge Papers #3842, Southern Historical Collection, Louis Round Wilson Special Collections Library, University of North Carolina at Chapel Hill.

2. To call white Southern belief in black accommodation to the segregationist core of Jim Crow a "myth" is not to deny its social power. On the contrary: as anthropologist Bronislaw Malinowski theorized at precisely the same time as Adolph Hitler composed *Mein Kampf*, myth is a "vital ingredient of human civilization; it is not an idle tale, but a hard-worked active force." Myth justifies the present by providing a link to the past; often it strengthens tradition by tracing it back to a supernatural reality. "Every historical change creates its mythology," Malinowski concluded. "Myth is a constant by-product of living faith, which is in need of miracles; of sociological status, which demands precedent; of moral rule, which requires sanction." Bronislaw Malinowski, "Myth in Primitive Psychology," *Magic, Science and Religion and Other Essays* (Chicago, 1960; 1948; 1926): 93–148; quotes from 100, 126, 146, 145; originally a lecture from 1925, the year *Mein Kampf* was published. Ernst Cassirer, *The Myth of the State* (New Haven, 1950), 47 ("Myth is an objectification of man's social experience, not of his individual experience.").

3. Johnson quoted in John T. Kneebone, *Southern Liberal Journalists, 1920–1944* (Chapel Hill, 1985), 91, 150. Working mainly from white sources, Kneebone argues that "the consensus on vertical segregation made interracial cooperation possible," 92.

4. Dabney quoted in Kneebone, *Southern Liberal Journalists*, 91.

5. As *Opportunity* editorialized in 1939, "Germany is modeling its program of Jewish persecution after American persecution of Negroes." *Opportunity*, January 1939, 2; *Pittsburgh Courier*, October 17, 1936, section 2, 2. Cf. Johnpeter Horst Grill and Robert L. Jenkins, "The Nazis and the American South in the 1930s: A Mirror Image?" *Journal of Southern History*, Vol. 58 (November 1992): 667–694, 675. See also the compilation from black newspapers by Lunabelle Wedlock, "Comparisons by Negro Publications of the Plight of the Jews in Germany with that of the Negro in America," in Maurianne Adams and John Bracy, ed., *Strangers & Neighbors: Relations Between Blacks and Jews in the United States* (Amherst: University of Massachusetts Press, 1999), 427–433.

6. *Philadelphia Tribune*, May 10, 1934, 4; *Afro-American*, June 4, 1938, 1. Grill and Jenkins, 668, note that "white southern newspaper editorials condemned Nazi racism but refused to acknowledge the obvious similarities between the German racial system and that of the South in the 1930s." Cf. Kneebone, 181, who goes further than Grill and Jenkins and says that liberal Southern journalists made racial prejudice (but not segregation per se) "unrespectable" by identifying it with the Klan and the Nazis.

7. "U.S. Pot Can't Call German Kettle Black, Says Miller," *Afro-American*, November 30, 1935, 4. Cf. "Germany and Dixie," *Afro-American*, May 2, 1936, 4. *Opportunity* noted in 1939 that "the German Reich has decided to model its program of racial repression on the prevailing laws and customs in the Southern part of the United States." "On Racial Prejudice at Home and Abroad," *Opportunity*, Vol. 17 (January 1939): 2.

8. Miller, "Race Prejudice in Germany and America," *Opportunity*, April 1936, 105.

9. "A Negro Pursuit Squadron," *Opportunity*, Vol. 19 (April 1941): 98.

10. Alabaman quoted in Barbara D. Savage, *Broadcasting Freedom: Radio, War and the Politics of Race, 1938–1948* (Chapel Hill, 1991), 110. On white Southern interventionists, see

Kneebone, *Southern Liberal Journalists*, 176–186. On Poland, see Deborah E. Lipstadt, *Beyond Belief: The American Press and the Coming of the Holocaust, 1933–1945* (New York, 1986), 162.

11. *Crisis* quoted in Harvard Sitkoff, "African Americans, American Jews, and the Holocaust," in William Chafe, ed., *The Achievement of American Liberalism* (2003): 181–203, 188.

12. For schools, see "Nazi Prejudice Against Jews Is Like Dixie's," *Afro-American*, September 21, 1935, 12. For Jim Crow cars, see *Philadelphia Tribune*, December 29, 1938, 1. For marriage see *Philadelphia Tribune*, July 5, 1934, 4; *Afro-American*, June 18, 1938, 1–2.

13. "A Negro Pursuit Squadron," *Opportunity*, Vol. 19 (April 1941): 99.

14. *Afro-American*, September 21, 1935, 12; September 9, 1939, 4. Du Bois quoted Stalin on the absence of racial prejudice in the Red Army in "A Chronicle of Race Relations," *Phylon,* Vol. 3, No. 2, (2nd Quarter 1942): 206–220, 208.

15. *Afro-American*, June 18, 1938, 1–2.

16. Kelly Miller, "Race Prejudice in Germany and America," *Opportunity*, April 1936, 102–105.

17. Glenda Elizabeth Gilmore also makes this point about democracy, in *Defying Dixie: The Radical Roots of Civil Rights, 1919–1950* (New York, 2008), 159–160.

18. *Dred Scott v. Sandford*, 60 U.S. 393 (1857).

19. Henry L. Stimson Diary, June 24, 1943. Quoted in Richard M. Dalfiume, *Desegregation of the U.S. Armed Forces: Fighting on Two Fronts, 1939–1950* (Columbia: University of Missouri Press, 1969), 31.

20. *Afro-American* survey of black leaders, September 16, 1939, 1–2; "For Manhood in National Defense," *Crisis,* Vol. 47 (December 1940), 375; Dalfiume, 26–27 (including Wilkins quote).

21. Roosevelt and Knox quoted in Dalfiume, 54–55.

22. *Afro-American*, December 20, 1941, 1–2.

23. *Afro-American*, May 23, 1942, 4; Samuel A. Stouffer et al., *The American Soldier* (2 vols., Princeton, 1949), v. I, 516–517.

24. This skepticism was reciprocated: Franklin Roosevelt considered the *Chicago Defender* and the *Afro-American* seditious, and tried to get Attorney General Francis Biddle to intimidate them. Adam Fairclough, *Better Day Coming: Blacks and Equality, 1920–2000* (New York, 2002), 193–194. Circulation of black newspapers increased 40 percent during the war. See Ralph N. Davis, "The Negro Newspapers and the War," *Sociology and Social Research*, Vol. XXVII (May-June 1943): 373–380, and Thomas Sancton, "The Negro Press," *New Republic,* Vol. 108 (April 26, 1943), 557–560.

25. *Afro-American*, May 23, 1942, 1.

26. *Afro-American*, February 7, 1942, 1, 4.

27. Pete Daniel, "Going among Strangers: Southern Reactions to World War II," *Journal of American History,* Vol. 77, No. 3 (December 1990): 886–911, 892; Victor H. Bernstein, "No Belief in Democracy," *Afro-American*, September 19, 1942, 17.

28. Ibid.

29. *Afro-American*, September 27, 1941, 4; Wilkins' keynote address to the NAACP's convention in Los Angeles in July 1942 quoted in Virginius Dabney, "Nearer and Nearer the Precipice," *The Atlantic Monthly,* Vol. 171 (January 1941): 94–100, 94.

30. Smith quoted in Nancy MacLean, "The Leo Frank Case Reconsidered: Gender and Sexual Politics in the Making of Reactionary Populism," *Journal of American History,* Vol. 78 (December 1991): 948.

31. In addition to the men roaming the country in uniform, 3.2 million people left Southern rural areas during the war, most of them heading for the centers of the wartime defense industry in the North and West. During the war it is estimated that 300,000 black Southerners migrated to the border and Northern states, a further 100,000 blacks from the border states moved further North or West, and an additional 250,000 African Americans moved to the West Coast. Statistics from Carey McWilliams, *Brothers under the Skin* (Boston: Little, Brown, 1964; 1942), 7. On the USO, see http://www.skylighters.org/canteen. Not all the segregated canteens were in the South: one black girl tried to volunteer at the White Plains, NY, canteen, but was rejected as unnecessary because the canteen did not admit black soldiers. See *Negro Digest*, Vol. 2, No. 5 (March 1944), 3.

32. Eleanor Roosevelt story from Patricia L Sullivan, *Days of Hope: Race and Democracy in the New Deal Era* (Chapel Hill, 1996), 160–161. Halsey quotes from Margaret Halsey, *Color Blind: A White Woman Looks at the Negro* (New York: Simon & Schuster, 1946), 69, 36–37. Second Halsey quote from "Memo to Junior Hostesses," *Negro Digest*, Vol. 1, No. 12 (October 1943): 51–53, 3.

33. *Color Blind*, 20.

34. *Color Blind*, 55; for Jane White see *Negro Digest*, Vol. 2, No. 5 (March 1944): 3.

35. *Color Blind*, 20 (first quote), 70–71 (quote from 71). On white soldiers' disinclination to dance with black hostesses, see Michael Carter, "Trouble in the Canteen," *Negro Digest*, Vol. 2, No. 6 (April 1944), 7–9, 8.

36. Description from John Dos Passos, *State of the Nation* (Boston: Houghton Mifflin, 1944), 67.

37. *Afro-American*, March 21, 1942, 4; *Afro-American*, February 13, 1943, 12 (Phoenix); December 12, 1942, 1 (Fort Dix); November 21, 1942, 1, January 24, 1942, 3 (Alexandria, LA). On Williams, see Bruce Nelson, "Organized Labor and the Struggle for Black Equality in Mobile during World War II," *Journal of American History,* Vol. 80, No. 3 (December 1993): 952–988, 967; Mary Penick Motley, ed., *The Invisible Soldier: The Experience of the Black Soldier, World War II* (Detroit: Wayne State Univ. Press, 1987), 40. Cumulative statistics from Daniel, "Going among Strangers," 893–894. The Social Science Institute at Fisk University reported 242 racial battles in 47 cities; cited in Sitkoff, "Racial Militancy," 671, who also notes, 668, that at least fifty black soldiers were killed in race riots. The most complete treatment of wartime interracial violence remains James A. Burran III, "Racial Violence in the South during World War II" (Ph.D. diss., University of Tennessee, 1977).

38. *Afro-American*, February 13, 1943, 2 (Re: Phoenix).

39. *Invisible Soldier*, 57.

40. "Army Voids Death Penalty Order for Mixing of Races," *Afro-American*, January 10, 1942, 1; "Stupid Army Orders," 4.

41. "Extracts on Negro Morale, March 1–15, 1944," file 218 (Negro Troops), Entry 578, RG 498, NARA, College Park, Maryland.

42. Halsey, *Color-Blind*, 124–125.

43. Kari Frederickson, *The Dixiecrat Revolt and the End of the Solid South, 1932–1968* (Chapel Hill, 2001), 33 (Bilbo); Dixon quoted in Fairclough, *Better Day Coming*, 186. On the FEPC, see Merl E. Reed, *Seedtime for the Modern Civil Rights Movement: The President's Committee on Fair Employment Practice, 1941–1946* (Baton Rouge, 1991).

44. The *Pittsburgh Courier,* June 19, 1943, characterized the FEPC as a "surrender to Nazi racial theory." Southern Democrats finally succeed in strangling the FEPC in 1946.

This wasn't the South's first experience with wartime efforts by the federal government to ameliorate conditions for black workers. During World War I, the National War Labor Board intervened on the side of black workers in disputes with white employers. Memories of the NWLB may help explain the hysterical white Southern reaction to the FEPC. On the NWLB, see Robert Zieger, *America's Great War: World War I and the American Experience* (New York, 2000), 131–134, and Elizabeth Haiken, "'The Lord Helps Those Who Help Themselves': Black Laundresses in Little Rock, Arkansas," *Arkansas Historical Quarterly,* Vol. 49 (Spring 1990): 20–50 (for an example of the NWLB intervening on behalf of the laundresses).

45. Quote from Louis Ruchames, *Race, Jobs, and Politics: The Story of FEPC* (New York: Columbia UP, 1953), 94.

46. Ethridge speech at Birmingham printed in its entirety in *Afro-American*, July 11, 1942, 14. Text of Durham Statement quoted in J. Staunders Redding, "Southern Defensive," *Common Ground*, Spring, 1944, 36–45, 37.

47. CIC fact sheet, June 30, 1943, in folder 6, Series II—No. 12, Clip Sheets, Department of Field Work, Commission on Interracial Cooperation, Inc., Alfred H. Stone Collection, Special Collections, J. D. Williams Library, University of Mississippi, D-15, 76–78. *Afro-American*, July 18, 1942, 4. Ethridge did, in fact, resign shortly thereafter, although more out of frustration that the FEPC had no power to achieve even the limited goals he had outlined in Birmingham than out of a sense of obligation to the *Afro-American*'s readers.

48. Virginia E&P Co. and Birmingham quotes from Nelson, 967. *Times-Dispatch* quoted in the *Afro-American*, May 9, 1942, 20. On public transportation as a special site of resistance to Jim Crow during the war, see Robin D.G. Kelley, "The Black Poor and the Politics of Oppression in a New South City, 1929–1970," in Michael B. Katz, ed., *The 'Underclass' Debate: Views from History* (Princeton, 1993): 293–333, 305–309. On Norfolk, where blacks mounted a successful legal challenge to the way in which bus segregation was implemented, see Earl Lewis, *In Their Own Interests: Race, Class and Power in Twentieth-Century Norfolk, Virginia* (Berkeley, 1991), 189–192. Fairclough, *Better Day Coming*, 191–192, reports that in the police in Birmingham recorded "fifty-five incidents in which black passengers defied white drivers by refusing to give up their seats or by sitting in the white section" in 1941–1942; see 193 for murders of black servicemen.

49. "To Lessen Race Friction," *Richmond Times-Dispatch*, November 13, 1943; Dabney to Louis Jaffe, November 16, 1943; Dabney to Warren M. Goddard, November 19, 1943; clipping, "Virginians Speak on Jim Crow," *Crisis*, February 1944, 47, all in file "Segregation Correspondence 1943," box 4, Papers of Virginius Dabney (hereafter Dabney Papers), #7690, Alderman Library, University of Virginia. According to the Thernstroms, only 4 percent of white Southerners were of the opinion that there should not be "separate sections for Negroes on streetcars and buses." Stephan Thernstrom and Abigail Thernstrom, *America in Black and White: One Nation, Indivisible* (New York, 1997), 141.

50. Virginius Dabney, "Nearer and Nearer the Precipice," *Atlantic Monthly*, Vol. 171 (January 1943): 94–100.

51. Dabney, "Nearer and Nearer the Precipice," 94, 96, 95.

52. Background on Couch from John Egergon, *Speak Now Against the Day: The Generation before the Civil Rights Movement in the South* (New York, 1994), 133–134.

53. *What the Negro Wants* (1944; 1982), Kenneth R. Janken, ed. (Notre Dame, IN, 2001), xxxiii.

54. *WTNW*, 117, 133, 161, 254. Randolph's formulation drawn from the demand of the March on Washington Movement, as quoted by Du Bois, "A Chronicle of Race Relations," *Phylon*, Vol. 4, No.1 (1st quarter, 1943): 73–84, 82.

55. *WTNW*, 297, 305, 328, 326.

56. Janken, introduction, xvi-xix.

57. Virginias Dabney to William Couch, January 10, 1944, UNC Press Records; quoted in Janken, xxii, and in Singal, 299.

58. *London Times* quoted in Lipstadt, *Beyond Belief*, 189–190.

59. *WTNW,* xii; Janken, introduction, xxiii.

60. Couch referring to work by Ruth Benedict, Melville J. Herskovits, John Dollard, Ashley Montegue et al.

61. W.E.B. Du Bois, "My Evolving Program for Negro Freedom," *WTNW*, 31–70, 65.

62. Du Bois, *WTNW*, 66. The "great gift to mankind" reference is to Alexander Dumas and his siblings.

63. J. Saunders Redding, "Fourteen Negro Voices," *The New Republic*, November 20, 1944, 665–666.

64. William Shands Meacham, "The Negro's Future in America," *NYTBR*, November 5, 1944.

65. J. Saunders Redding, "Southern Defensive," *Common Ground*, Spr. 1944, 36–45, 41.

66. Gunnar Myrdal, *An American Dilemma: The Negro Problem and Modern Democracy* (New York, 1944), 60–61; quote from 61; Eleanor Roosevelt, "The Four Equalities," *Negro Digest*, Vol. 1, No. 11 (September 1943): 81–83.

67. "How the South Feels about the Race Problem," *Reader's Digest*, June 1944. In Folder 36, Box 9, David L. Cohn Papers, Special Collections, J. D. Williams Library, University of Mississippi. Thanks to Neil McMillen for drawing my attention to this collection. For more on Cohn, see James C. Cobb, ed., *The Mississippi Delta and the World: The Memoirs of David L. Cohn* (Baton Rouge, 1995), especially the Editor's Afterword, 183–213.

68. "A Texan," n.d. (1944); Wm. J. Frazier, Jr., June 1, 1944; Vivian Thomas and Phyllis Freeman, May 2, 1944, folder 36, box 9, David L. Cohn Papers, Special Collections, J. D. Williams Library, University of Mississippi.

69. Editorial, *Southern Frontier*, March 1944.

70. Margaret Anderson to Virginius Dabney, January 21, 1943, "Southern Regional Council, 1943–44" folder, box 8, Virginius Dabney Papers, Alderman Library, University of Virginia.

71. Lillian Smith to Dr. Guy B. Johnson, Executive Director of SRC, June 12, 1944, "Southern Regional Council, 1943–4" folder, box 8, Virginius Dabney Papers.

72. Quotes from Guy B. Johnson, "Southern Offensive: A Reply to Mr. Redding and Miss Smith," in the Spring 1944 edition of *Common Ground*, and from Gordon B. Hancock to Margaret Anderson, May 6, 1944, "Southern Regional Council, 1943–4" folder, box 8, Virginius Dabney Papers.

73. Letter, L. C. Christian, Houston, TX, May 5, 1945, in box 26, Critical T.M., Moderator, Speakers file, "America's Town Meeting of the Air," and transcript for May 24, 1945, Town Hall Inc., Records, New York Public Library. In addition to Wright and Voorhis (Democrat of California), the panel included Elmer A. Carter, the former editor of the Urban League's magazine "Opportunity" and a member of the Unemployment-Insurance Appeals Board of the New York State Department of Labor; and Irving M. Ives, the Majority Leader of the New York state assembly and co-author of a recent anti-discrimination bill.

9

Civil Rights and World War II in a Global Frame

SHAPE-SHIFTING RACIAL FORMATIONS AND THE U.S. ENCOUNTER WITH EUROPEAN AND JAPANESE COLONIALISM

Penny Von Eschen

In Ousmane Sembéne's 1987 film *Camp de Thiaroye*,[1] Senegalese Sergeant-Major Diatta, who has fought with the 1st Free French Army against the Italians and Germans, first in the Libyan desert into Tripoli, and then in the liberation of Paris, sits in his room at Camp de Thiaroye, playing recordings of jazz saxophonist Charlie Parker. The camp, located in Senegal, is a staging ground for the demobilization of African colonial troops who have disembarked in Dakar at the conclusion of their service with French forces. Many are arriving from recently liberated German prisoner of war camps. But Camp Thiaroye itself is little better than a POW camp, and it fuels Diatta's growing disillusionment with French colonial racism. The solace that he finds in jazz, and the audaciously inventive horn of Parker, heard through recordings acquired during the war, suggests the new knowledge presented through contact with black American soldiers. The film also suggests that new black diasporic sensibilities had emerged from such wartime contacts. Jazz, as well as the American-accented English that Diatta learned during the war, symbolizes the alternative black subjectivities that inform his rebellion against French colonial authority. As Diatta grapples with the recalcitrant French empire, he learns of a 1942 massacre in his village carried out by French authorities, but now disavowed by his superior officer as having occurred under the Vichy regime.

This chapter considers Sembéne's film as a point of departure to offer a cautionary tale about the importance of World War II as a catalyst for U.S. civil rights struggles and global challenges to racial hierarchies. At first glance, there is much in the film to support conventional views that the war was a catalyst for the expansion of American civil rights and global anti-colonial movements. After all, as dramatized in *Camp de Thiaroye*, Allied claims to support democracy while denying civil and political rights to people of African descent sharpened colonial peoples' critiques of colonialism and racism. Encounters between peoples from different parts of the colonized world and between black and brown peoples in the metropoles and colonies opened new avenues for the circulation of cultural and political manifestations of rights-consciousness. Such alternative perspectives encouraged and enabled challenges to colonial and racist regimes. Nazism and the horrors of the Holocaust discredited racism, and Europe's empires faltered under the pressures of war. Colonizers faced vigorous challenges as the war created vacuums of power and posed urgent questions about who and what would fill them. The tumult and transformations of war permeated the global stage on which civil rights and anti-colonial struggles would play out. Surely, World War II was a powerful stimulus for global demands for freedom, an end to racial hierarchies, and self-determination.[2]

But far from being a simple celebration of black diasporic ties, Sembéne's film unfolds as a tragedy and a historical critique of postwar colonialism, as Diatta's anger at the realization that Vichy collaborators are being put in charge of the colonies leads to his demise. The story of Sergeant-Major Diatta in *Camp de Thiaroye* suggests the shared racism of colonial authorities, whether French or German. Indeed, Sembéne draws viewers' attention to the reinstatement of colonialism after the war, serving as a reminder that the positive impact of World War II on global race relations coexisted with the dogged persistence of systemic racial subjugation. An early postwar critique of French imperial racism anticipated the disillusionment portrayed in Sembéne's film. In his 1948 manifesto *Discourse on Colonialism*, Aimé Césaire argued that World War II emphatically did not democratize metropolitan culture. Particularly in France, but throughout the colonized world, one found a persistence of the belief in the "civilizing mission" and of rhetoric of benevolent paternalism, which sought to obscure the murderous exercise of colonial violence, such as the 1948 French massacre in Madagascar.[3]

At the war's end, Senegalese soldiers returned to broken promises. They were denied pay and pensions, and were forced to endure menial to brutal working conditions. Across the Atlantic, black American soldiers and civilians soon learned that not only did their wartime contributions go unappreciated, but even worse, black veterans in uniform inspired violent rage rather than respect, resulting in physical assaults and lynchings in the South. Such indignities during and after the war offered bitter testimony that the war had not democratized the allied nations who claimed to have fought to save democracy from the fascists. As was acknowledged in the belated U.S. government recognition in 2007 of the surviving members of the Tuskegee Airmen—black air force combat veterans who distinguished themselves during the war—their heroism and patriotism was no match for the endemic insults of a segregated society.

Situating World War II in the context of colonial conquest, anti-colonial struggle, and attendant challenges to regimes built on racial hierarchy is critical to understanding the stakes of the war and the postwar world. By looking first at the war and then the postwar developments through centering questions of colonialism, time lines shift and multiple temporalities emerge. The United States ended the war as the dominant global power, but its claim to support anti-colonial movements was belied by its backing of European allies as they tried to hold onto colonial possessions. The United States further showed a reluctance to make a clean break from colonialism with its occupation of former Japanese colonies such as Korea and Micronesia. Rather than renouncing the colonial histories of Europe and Japan, even as officials came to disavow older legal forms of discrimination, the United States extended colonial racial hierarchies in unprecedented and unpredictable ways.

However much Nazism had discredited ideas of race, far from abandoning racial formations, the extension of U.S. power depended on the social production of new forms of racial thinking as well as the unthinking "commonsense" employment of previously held assumptions. Global politics in the post-war world cannot be understood without attention to the ways in which race and racism were made and remade during and after the war. Historians have explored multiple ways in which racialized readings of the geopolitical order informed postwar interventions and conflicts (from Korea and Vietnam, to Algeria, Iran, the Congo, and Guatemala), along with efforts to garner public support and the self-justification of such policies and objectives, depended in part on tried and true forms of racial thinking.[4] For example, even as the State Department embraced racial integration as the solution to America's "Achilles' heel," the Eisenhower administration viewed Congolese prime minster Patrice Lumumba through the racialized optics of political immaturity and irrationality. Yet the efforts of U.S. liberal internationalists to "lead the free world," from assertions of "soft-power" to the hyper-extraction of mineral and other resources of the global South and widespread covert and overt military interventions, also depended on and indeed produced new modes of racial formation and thinking.

From a global view, vast numbers of formerly colonized peoples were locked into the under-examined extractive dimension of the global economy, with suppressed wages that severely curtailed access to consumer benefits. Indeed, Fordism is typically characterized as mass production/mass consumption, virtually ignoring the extractive process. The latter part of this chapter suggests a frame for considering the remaking of race and the new social and political production of difference in the encounter of the United States with postwar independence movements, as well as in the political and military protection of the extractive nodes of the global Fordist economy on which the increasing wealth and relative equality of the West depended. Discussing production of new inequalities in the wake of the war is not intended to diminish or underestimate the vibrant social and political movements of that era. To the contrary, the complex dimensions of such movements are better appreciated with a fuller portrait of their milieu and challenges, as they faced emergent structures that cannot be grasped through notions of continuity versus change.

World War II and Colonialism

Scholarly and popular accounts typically date World War II from 1939 to 1945, with the beginning cited as the German invasion of Poland on September 1, 1939, and the British and French declaration of war against Germany two days later; and for the Pacific war, the Japanese attacks on China and the United States. But for many African American and colonized observers of the war, World War II had begun with the 1935 Italian invasion of Ethiopia, and the indifference of the Western powers to this blatant fascist attack was an egregious act of racism.[5] Reading World War II through the longer history of colonialism—Ethiopia had successfully repulsed invading Italian armies in 1896 as part of Africans' military resistance to European colonialism—situates Italy's invasion within the colonial scramble for land touched off by the 1884–1885 European partition of Africa in Berlin, as well as the first in a wave of foreign invasions spurred by the global economic crises of the 1930s. Indeed, Germany, although tacitly constrained as its southern African colonies became League of Nations mandates after World War I, was thoroughly steeped in the policy of colonialism. In August 1941, Hitler told a group of his officers "what India was for England, the eastern territories will be for us."[6] In another declaration of the colonial nature of the war, Erich Koch, the Reich commissioner in the Ukraine, said that he had waged a colonial war "as among Negroes."[7] Scholars of Germany have increasingly argued that Nazi technologies of violence and genocide were developed in the laboratory of German colonialism.[8]

The war brought the importance of colonies to Europe into sharp relief as it fomented debates about colonialism. Winston Churchill objected to the idea that the 1942 Atlantic Charter would extend democratic freedoms to the colonies. "We mean to hold our own. I have not become the King's first minister in order to preside over the liquidation of the British empire." Churchill understood clearly what was at stake in the war, and he insisted on distinguishing strategic and tactical war considerations—such as that of the Atlantic Charter—from their clear implications for colonial and racial subject peoples for equality, self-determination, and anti-colonial freedom. African American and anti-colonial activists seized on President Franklin Delano Roosevelt's support for extending the freedoms of the charter to colonized peoples, and sought to exploit the split between Churchill and Roosevelt. With his inimitable sarcasm, the writer George S. Schuyler noted in his *Pittsburgh Courier* column that:

> Soft-hearted people may feel that these African, Asiatic, and Malaysian people should come under the provision of the Atlantic Charter. They

do not stop to think how many companies would go into bankruptcy, how many aristocratic Nordic families would be reduced to working for a living, how impoverished all the missionaries, explorers, archaeologists, artists and others who live off the bounties of colonialism would be.[9]

The African American political cartoonist Jay Jackson portrayed England as too drunk from imbibing white supremacy to see that immediate independence for colonized peoples would be the best Allied wartime strategy.[10]

The temporality of war in the Pacific also appears differently when viewed through the lens of colonialism. From the perspective of the Chinese, for example, the war would begin with the 1931 Japanese invasion of northeastern China."[11] For Korea, Vietnam, the Philippines, and the Marshallese islands, the war was part of the long struggle for national liberation from colonialism (Japanese, French, and U.S.), beginning long before World War II and continuing long after its conclusion.[12]

People throughout Asian and African diasporas watched the war in the Pacific with great interest, with many arguing that the rapidity with which European and American colonies fell to the Japanese in the Pacific war can only be explained by the unwillingness of local populations to fight to preserve colonial rule. From Burma to French-controlled Vietnam (Indochina) and Dutch-ruled Indonesia, colonies quickly fell to the Japanese. As the *Chicago Defender* journalist John Badger succinctly put it, "colonialism is incapable of defending a territory [or] population under its control."[13] Reporting on a colonial conference in Britain at which speakers discussed the collapse of Malaya, Singapore, and Burma, the Trinidad-born, U.S.-educated, and London-based journalist George Padmore explained that native peoples either "remained passive, considering the war as a struggle between two sets of imperialism which did not concern them," or as in Burma, "joined up with the invader in the hopes of getting the land back which had been appropriated from them." Reflecting a pervasive discourse on race and colonialism among African Americans, the NAACP's Walter White argued that British policy was making India as much a pushover for the Japanese as Burma, whose long-suffering people wondered, "If we are going to be exploited, what matters if our exploiters be yellow or white?"[14]

In India, the dominant position was the non-cooperation with Britain advocated by Mohandas Gandhi and Jawaharlal Nehru. But Subhash Chandra Bose, another leader of the Indian National Congress, took the alternative position that "the enemy of my enemy is my friend." Arrested eleven times by the British Raj, Bose fled India for Germany, where he hoped to gain support from Hitler to raise an army that would attack the British in India. In German POW camps, Bose recruited roughly 3,000 Indian soldiers who had joined the British fight against fascism but now switched their allegiance to Germany. Bose, a leftist, quickly became disillusioned when Hitler's armies invaded the Soviet

Union and he suspected that the British were using him. He fled to Japan and recruited Indian POWs in Malaysia and Burma. The recent release of British government documents reveals that British officials were profoundly shocked by such widespread defections and that Bose's efforts sparked a crisis in British confidence in their ability to maintain the empire.[15]

The refusal of Indian leaders to support the British in the war against Germany without the immediate guarantee of independence was widely celebrated throughout the colonial world and the African diaspora. A 1942 survey by the *Pittsburgh Courier* of 10,000 black Americans reported that 87.8 percent supported India's insistence on self-rule as a necessary condition for support of Britain. In a stark demonstration of the anti-colonial priorities of black leftists most often assumed to be closest to the Communist Party, Paul Robeson and Max Yergan, leaders of the Council on African Affairs, directly challenged the Comintern and CPUSA position that anti-imperialism needed to be put on the back burner until fascism was defeated, by organizing a 1942 "Rally for the Cause of Free India."[16] Indeed, in an era when much of popular front politics became caught up in the wartime politics of unity with the Soviet Union, the independence of anti-colonial leftists from Soviet as well as American policies remains striking.[17] The dominant views expressed among leaders in the London-based International African Service Bureau and among African American opinion leaders were strongly anti-fascist but insisted that freedom from colonial and racial subjugation was the necessary precondition and litmus test for democracy. Journalists and activists alike extended the "Double-V" campaign of victory over fascism and racism to a triple-V campaign against, fascism, racism, and *colonialism*.

Like the position taken by Bose in India, some African Americans, especially on the West Coast, overlooked Japanese imperialism and supported Japan as a non-white power fighting white imperialism. Whether Malcolm X's statement to U.S. Army induction officers that he was "frantic to join the Japanese army" may have been a strategic ploy to get out of service or in part naive, it was clearly an indictment of U.S. racism and a refusal to fight to maintain a Jim Crow society.[18] A black "counter-narrative" of internationalism was formed, centered on Japan, that reached back to 1905 and celebrations of Japan's defeat of Russia, and remained a significant influence through the 1930s and into the war years.[19]

From the vantage point of colonialism and the Pacific theater of war, scholars have also viewed Pan-Asianism as a complicating factor in World War II, but with a greater emphasis on the history of Japanese empire and colonialism. People living under Japanese colonial rule viewed Japan's ideological propagation of the Greater East Asia Co-Prosperity Sphere during the 1940s with a skepticism born of previous and ongoing experience of Japanese invasions, massacres, and colonial rule, resulting in wary, strategic, and hardly freely chosen collaborations.[20] Wartime collaboration in Korea, for example, must be understood in the context of Japan's annexation of Korea in 1910 and sustained Korean protests against Japanese rule. The Provisional Government of the Republic of Korea, which had operated in exile since the 1919 Korean Declaration of Independence and the Japanese suppression of the March 1919 protests against Japanese rule, took advantage of wartime disruption to reorganize in Korea. Among those who had experienced multiple colonial rulers—European and Japanese—as in the case of Micronesia, or who now faced Japanese occupation after decades of European rule, a "wait and see" attitude prevailed. Indeed, Japanese aggression prompted the Bengali poet and passionate advocate of cultural Pan-Asianism, Rabindranath Tagore, to abandon the position.[21]

U.S. policymakers were keenly aware of the potential power of Japanese racial propaganda, and never separated this issue from what, in their perspective, was the aim of winning the peace through the reincorporation of Japan into the U.S. hegemonic sphere. The frequently remarked viciousness and brutality of the war in the Pacific was, in part, a product of the two-sided racial demonization of the opponent. It was also the result of the clash of two empires that had long been competing in the Pacific as the Japanese colonized Korea, Micronesia, and parts of China, and the United States made incursions into China, annexed Hawaii, and colonized the Philippines and Guam.

During World War II, U.S. officials argued that employing Japanese Americans in global propaganda efforts, especially through service in the armed forces, could counter Japanese charges that the "war was a racial conflict."[22] This strategy was realized in President Franklin Roosevelt's public announcement of the 442nd Regimental Combat Team in early February 1943.[23] In a highly instrumentalist approach to Japan, strategists advocated launching psychological war with the Japanese in tandem with their argument for establishing a postwar "puppet emperor system in Japan." Indeed, the U.S.-Japan conflict was intertwined with the broader history of competing Japanese and U.S. imperialisms. Until mid-1941, Japan was a junior hegemon in its Asian sphere of influence, still dependent on U.S. power in the region. When U.S. leaders shocked Japanese officials by an oil embargo, Japanese leaders concluded that the only alternative was war. Yet by 1942, shortly into the war, "a small cadre of internationalists in the American State Department and in Japan began moving on remarkably parallel lines to reintegrate Japan into the postwar American hegemonic regime."[24] Thus the 1952 McCarran-Walter Acts—making it possible for Japanese to become naturalized U.S. citizens— and the earlier trans-war extensions of the right to naturalize to Chinese immigrants (1943) and Filipino and Asian Indians (1946) were part of a larger strategy of containing race in a U.S.-run world. The remaking of race vis-à-vis Japan took place on multiple levels, as the new advocacy of "model minorities" went hand in hand with the reintegration of Japan as the junior capitalist partner in Asia.

The U.S. position as a victor in Japan and the prolonged military presence through occupation and military bases enabled the reconstruction of Japan as a dependable U.S. Asian ally. Metaphors of maturity and gender were important in the American shift from imagining Japan as a racialized brutal enemy to the rapid acceptance of Japan as a worthy postwar ally. General Douglas MacArthur, who oversaw the U.S. occupation of Japan from 1945 to 1951, described Japan as "like a twelve year old boy." Such images allowed Americans to see Japan as an unthreatening dependent and therefore, as a worthy cold war ally once it matured under U.S. guidance.[25]

As dominant understandings of race shifted from overt racism grounded in claims of innate biological difference to claims of difference rooted in modernization models, Japan's aggression could be explained as an earlier immature warlike state of a people now fast developing under proper democratic tutelage into worthy allies. Unlike the mature Germany, which should have known better and was therefore responsible for its actions, Japan could be forgiven for childish impulses. The work of Yuka Tsuchiya on the U.S. occupation of Japan explores the occupation in the context of continuities with earlier Japanese as well as American modernizing projects and in light of both nations' imperial ambitions in Asia. Exploring CIA and United States Information Agency films produced for Japanese audiences, Tsuchiya demonstrates that not only did Japanese filmmakers use these productions for their own ends, but the image of a classless society typically conveyed in the films served Japanese economic reconstruction as well as U.S. hegemony.[26] Thus, both nations benefited enormously from Japan's reintegration into the global capitalist economy as the junior partner of the United States, and their mutual investment in the denial of their imperial histories in Asia and the Pacific.

Considerations of these entangled imperial histories once again call into question the temporality of the war. The date of August 15, 1945, was decisive only for Japan. Five days earlier, when American policymakers divided the Korean peninsula at the 38th parallel, without the consultation of the Korean Provisional government that had formed during the war, Japanese colonialism was replaced by American occupation. While U.S. historians tend to see the Korean War as the first major U.S. intervention in the cold war, in the frame of colonialism, as for the Viet Mihn Central Committee that met on August 16, 1945, and called for a Vietnamese general insurrection, the war was another phase in a long struggle against foreign occupation.[27]

Remaking Race in the American Century

The consolidation of the U.S. position as the ascendant world power at the dawn of the cold war had a profound impact on the future of the struggle for civil rights and global challenges to white supremacy. In the United States, successful wartime alliances and support for the United Nations provided a forum for a range of African American activists and intellectuals, who viewed the abolition of colonialism as a necessary condition for a democratic and just world.[28] These observers were thus chagrined, first by Winston Churchill's Iron Curtain speech and then, when the Truman Doctrine ended the wartime alliance between the United States and the Soviet Union. For such African Americans as W.E.B. Du Bois, the cold war usurped prospects of a democratic world order as embodied in the hopes of anti-colonial activists sparked by the formation of the United Nations. A *Baltimore Afro-American* editorial argued that Churchill's proposed Anglo-American alliance would assure "[a] continuation of imperialism and eventually plunge us into war with Russia on the other side."[29] Arguing that British interests were in jeopardy in Greece, Egypt, India, and Indonesia, the editorial concluded: "We shudder to contemplate the fate of colonials already oppressed under the British heel should such an imperialist partnership become a reality."[30]

If, as Césaire observed, colonial metropolitan societies had resisted democratization under wartime conditions, in the United States the wartime struggles for the expansion of democracy also met with indecisive and uneven outcomes. The most far-reaching demands for political and economic equality, including the linking of civil rights to anti-colonial struggles abroad were abruptly altered and in many cases thoroughly repressed during the early cold war.

The acceptance by Walter White and other key African American leaders of the proposition that the United States, as leader of the free world, was engaged in a fundamental struggle with the Soviet Union, had a profound impact on anti-colonial and civil rights struggles. Civil rights politics narrowed during the Truman administration as a result of the contraction of public discourse and the collapse of the Left during the early cold war years. With the formation of Truman's Committee on Civil Rights, White and others began to craft the dominant argument of the anti-communist civil rights liberals. The new argument seized on international criticism of American racism to argue that anti-discrimination measures were necessary for the United States in its struggle against communism. The dominant liberal argument against racism, using anti-communism to justify the fight against racism and for civil rights, conceded the high ground to anti-communism.[31]

The marginalization of the global black Left at the very moment of the postwar resurgence of the U.S.-led Fordist economy deepened a racialized global division of labor. Cold war anti-communism and the powerful remobilization of business between 1946 and 1948 blocked the social agenda of labor evident during World War II; and the narrowing of labor's agenda had a direct and powerful impact on global labor politics and on anti-colonial movements.[32] In a fusion of domestic and foreign policies, as communists were expelled from unions in America, American labor supported anti-communist unions abroad, even when that meant collaborating with former Nazis and other fascists.

In 1949, CIO unions left the World Federation of Trade Unions, and both the AFL and CIO took the lead in setting up the new anti-communist International Confederation of Free Trade Unions. CIO support for African labor during World War II had been an important feature of the globally inflected civil rights politics that had embraced anti-colonialism. But after the CIO's departure from the WFTU, the role of U.S. labor in Africa, as well as in the well-documented European cases, would be filtered through the close liaison of the AFL and the State Department—with support from the CIA. Domestically, the rising conservatism of the labor movement—demonstrated by the pulling back of labor's efforts to organize the South and labor's abandonment of a civil rights agenda—was intimately tied to the curtailment of the wartime civil rights movement.[33]

American labor's collaboration with former Nazis and other fascists stands in ironic contrast to the central rhetorical place of Nazism in discrediting racism. And as many grew uncomfortable with overt racism reminiscent of the Nazis, the rewriting of race in this repressive political environment turned out to be a double-edged sword for racialized populations. Altered political and rhetorical strategies in the fight against discrimination during the cold war era had far-reaching consequences for the definitions and meanings of racism. Throughout World War II, African Americans and many in the colonized world had portrayed Nazism as one consequence of imperialism and one manifestation of racism, seeing anti-fascism as a critical component of democratic politics but not to the exclusion of anti-colonialism. After the war, some activists continued to point to similarities between racism and Nazism for their legitimacy. According to the new syllogism, Hitler became the standard of evil and thereby un-American, Hitlerism equals racism, and therefore racism is evil and un-American. The actions of Alabama police against black Americans were called "Gestapo tactics." However powerful the argument, it took the case against racism out of its American context and out of the context of colonialism as well. And in positing Nazism and racism as unique, ahistorical evils, it took both out of the context of history.[34]

Not only did this argument sever fascism from the history of colonialism, but in stark contrast to wide-ranging analyses of the political economy of colonialism and racism promoted by black Americans during World War II, by the early 1950s racism was consistently portrayed as a primordial trait of "backward" countries and peoples (such as rural white Southerners), not a modern development located in specific social and economic practices. Like the functionalist modernization paradigm that emerged in the social sciences, the popular notion of racism as an outmoded, dysfunctional practice that would gradually disappear as nations progressed, obscured human agency and responsibility in the creation and maintenance of racialized political, economic, and social institutions. Far from "outmoded" in the popular language of the day, "race" was made anew in the complex political and social work of war and U.S. economic expansion in formerly colonized areas.

U.S. Power and Shape-Shifting Racial Formations

Despite U.S. policymakers' desire to dissociate themselves from European co-lonialism, as seen in the tragic examples of Vietnam and the Congo, the United States nearly always backed up its colonial allies and acted to protect mutual economic interests through direct or covert interventions, thus tying the United States in these cases, respectively, to French and Belgian colonialism. Thus, at the very moment when U.S. officials attempted to combat global criticism of American race relations—the "Achilles' heel" in the cold war battle for hearts and minds—deepening encounters of the United States with postwar inde-pendence movements entailed the social production of new forms of racial thinking as well as the employment of previously held assumptions.

To better appreciate how the United States became entangled in colonial wars, it is worth outlining attempted strategies that sought to distinguish the United States from colonial powers. U.S. policymakers first sought to defend their claim to lead the "free world" by distancing themselves from European co-lonialism. In publisher Henry Luce's "American Century," formulated during World War II and profoundly influencing U.S. wartime and postwar objec-tives, policymakers envisioned an American-led, globally integrated capitalist economy. In theory, colonialism had no place in that vision. Policymakers not only objected to the privileged access to resources and markets that colonialism afforded the European powers, but understood the benefits of promoting racial liberalism in an effort to combat worldwide criticisms of U.S. racism. For the most part, they did not seek to take over European forms of colonialism. Asserting instead the right of the United States to lead the "free world," they pursued a project of global economic integration through modernization and development. Those American policymakers committed themselves to making sure that the West had privileged access to the world's markets, industrial infra-structure, and raw materials.

Yet in the many areas where the accelerated anti-colonial activity of World War II carried into armed conflict between independence movements and colo-nial powers, ultimately the United States nearly always backed up its colonial allies when they faced challenges to their rule. Only in rare cases, such as Indo-nesia, where the United States judged the Dutch to be so intransigent as to be driving the Indonesians into the hands of the communists, and the 1956 Suez crisis, when the United States defied Britain and France, did the United States directly challenge its European allies in matters of colonial control.

In the face of persistent attempts on the part of formerly colonized peo-ples to regain control of their resources, the United States became extensively involved in colonial wars such as that of the French in Vietnam and Belgium's instigation of the Kantanga secession and ensuing crisis in the Congo. U.S. policymakers made repeated use of (often covert) military force, making the term "cold war" a misnomer for the peoples of Asia, Africa, Latin America, and the Middle East, where democratic challenges often met with violent suppression by either proxies or covert operatives, or both.[35] By the mid-1950s, the CIA had already carried out covert actions in Iran, Indonesia, and Guatemala.[36] Certainly many policymakers viewed these actions as a necessary evil. Support for covert action depended on a worldview that saw the Soviet Union as a dangerous enemy that fundamentally threatened "the American way of life." But in confronting a seemingly ubiquitous Soviet threat, American policymakers repeatedly conflated nationalism and communism.

The consistent conflation of nationalism and communism, the overthrows of governments, and the willingness to support colonial powers depended on new racialisms that were developed as U.S. policymakers confronted Asian and African heads of state, as well as on racial hierarchies that devalued African, Asian, and Latin American lives. The ouster of leaders throughout these regions depended on ethnocentric assumptions about non-Western leaders that prevented American policymakers from viewing them as independent political agents. From the CIA overthrow of Mussaddiq in Iran, fueled in part by *Time-Life* magazine portrayals of him as effeminate and fanatical, to the ouster and assassination of Patrice Lumumba in the Congo in 1961, U.S. policymakers tended to see leaders in these regions as pawns or potential pawns of the Soviets.[37] Despite the complexity of America's global relationships, when control over crucial strategic resources such as oil and uranium were at stake, American policymakers brooked no ambiguity when it came to assessing the allegiances of national leaders, and cast these leaders as untrustworthy in highly racialized terms.[38] In both Iran and the Congo, aborted democracies were immediately replaced with pro-Western dictatorships that would stay in power for decades, allowing the destructive exploitation of resources and people for the benefit of pro-Western elites, and severely undermining civil and human rights.

The American war in Vietnam is a devastating example of the tendency of the United States to support its colonial allies. The war has been considered as an inevitable outcome of cold war assumptions and even as an example of the sheer excess of liberal ideology. Historians have less often seen it as an ill-advised outgrowth of the U.S. commitment to colonial France. Although the United States was initially sympathetic to Ho Chi Minh's revolution, when the de Gaulle government found itself both embattled by the communist Left and incapable of defending its colonial empire, the United States reversed its position and came to the aid of France, taking on the job of propping up successive South Vietnamese governments tottering precariously atop an inherited colonial state structure.[39]

As France fought to hold Algeria in its prolonged war for independence, and as the United States continued to defend colonial regimes in southern Africa, U.S. officials were contemptuous of the non-aligned politics advocated by Jawaharlal Nehru in India, Gamal Abdel Nasser in Egypt, and Kwame Nkrumah in Ghana.[40] From the early 1950s, nations around the globe announced with growing frequency that they would not be subjugated by either the West or the East and declared their intentions to be neutral, "non-aligned states," forming their own "Third World." For example, in 1954, when the United States, in order to combat communism, established the Southeast Asian Treaty Organization (SEATO) and wanted to include all the states in the region, India, Burma, Ceylon, and Indonesia resisted pressure to join and asserted their resolve to remain "neutral" in the cold war. A year later, U.S. Secretary of State John Foster Dulles condemned the meeting of Asian and African nations in Bandung, Indonesia, as "an obsolete, immoral, and short-sighted conception."[41] U.S. hostility toward India and non-alignment contrasted sharply with U.S. support for Pakistan's military since partition, which continued into the twenty-first century.[42]

New forms of racial inequality were produced in the context of unprecedented U.S. and Western confrontations with new African, Asian, and Middle Eastern nation-states. Relationships in combat zones and on military bases, as well as those spawned by postwar corporate ventures, produced new forms of racial subjugation. The sexual and racial violence endemic to U.S. military base communities, as wartime bases were consolidated and expanded in the postwar period, has been widely documented by scholars. The gendered and racialized exploitation that developed around the "archipelago empire" of U.S. bases dotting the globe built on and extended practices that developed during World War II (and earlier wars), as in the enslavement of Korean women to serve Japanese men in brothels during World War II, and the postwar sex trade sanctioned by the South Korean government and U.S. military.[43]

Beyond the bases, U.S. corporations not only continued to extend Jim Crow–based labor relations throughout the Western Hemisphere, but also extended such arrangements into former parts of the British and French empires. U.S. corporations, such as the Arabian American Oil Company (ARAMCO), formed in 1944, imposed Jim Crow–style segregationist labor and housing laws for Arab workers in the oil fields and refineries of Saudi Arabia. The owners of ARAMCO—Texaco, Chevron, Exxon, and Mobil—had decades of experience in setting up similar camps with segregated labor forces and workers paid differently according to race, in localities from Mexico, to Venezuela, to Texas. ARAMCO, like other U.S.-based companies, portrayed itself as a private enterprise version of the Marshall Plan, one that acted as a modernizing and developing force that treated its workers better than those in other oil fields. Yet in Iran, *prior* to the 1953 CIA coup overthrowing the democratically elected government of Musaddiq, the democratic institutions of parliament, the press, and unions all facilitated reforms in the oil industry that reached further than those of ARAMCO in Saudi Arabia.[44]

As indicated by the U.S. export of inequities in the oil industry, in order to understand postwar racial formation, it is critical to pay attention to the structural relationship of formerly colonized peoples to the Fordist economy at its productive height, and the multiple ramifications of Western commitment to these industries. In the post-1945 period, the raw materials necessary for U.S. wealth and power were densely concentrated in sub-Saharan Africa and the Middle East. In ensuring the uninterrupted flow of raw materials to the West, U.S. support of dictators in the Congo also ensured the development and elaboration of notorious Belgian colonial labor practices. The resulting impoverishment of the population of the most resource-rich country in the world, along with the extensive arming of the country for Western cold war objectives, produced the conditions for later wars of genocide. As these wars reproduced images of "primitive Africa," and posited Africa as fundamentally a "problem," it is critical to recognize these particular racial formations not simply as a persistence of older racial hierarchies but rather as formations that were produced in a murderous alchemy of colonialism and that were cast as the economic and political imperatives of the "post-colonial" leader of the free world.

In the final scene of *Camp de Thiaroye*, in a truck full of Senegalese soldiers, one soldier plays "Lily Marlene" on a harmonica. A melancholy German love song popular among Allied troops, the song's performance by a Senegalese soldier expressed both his disaffection from French colonialism, and his awareness, on returning to an unchanged colonial status, that for him, the war was not over. In the context of the tragic developments of the film, this is a stark reminder that the democratic hopes of wartime would be sorely tested in a world of colonial intransigence. The historian Utsumi Aiko has also invoked the harmonica as a symbol of the war in his childhood Tokyo. "We played the harmonica," Utsumi remembered, and "we would hear the harmonica in the street as well." Wounded soldiers who stood in front of train stations soliciting money played the harmonica while singing sorrowful war songs: "here in Manchuria hundreds of miles from our honorable country. . . . That tune overlapped with images of mutilated bodies of soldiers playing harmonicas for the crowd, leaving an impression of the war's tragedy."[45] For Utsumi, the haunting image of impoverished veterans playing war-era songs on the streets led to the discovery and grappling with the conscription of Koreans and other Japanese colonials, who were later stripped of Japanese nationality and left without support.

Whether in the European, North African, or Pacific theater for colonized people the democratic hopes of wartime were betrayed in the aftermath of war. From the colonial violence and massacres during and after World War II dramatized in Sembéne's fictional account of Diatta's return to Senegal, to the stripping of Korean soldiers' ability to receive government compensation, colonial and imperial power, along with the racial hierarchies that had been contested during World War II, took on new life in often strange and unexpected ways in the postwar world. Indeed, the prolonged wars for national independence and the conflicts of the later part of the twentieth century—too often lumped under the rubric of cold war—are incomprehensible without first reading World War II through the long history of colonialism and the strange careers of political and social worlds built on racial hierarchies in America and abroad.

Notes

1. Thierno Faty Sow shared director and screenwriter credit.

2. On African American interaction with the anti-colonial world, see, Penny M. Von Eschen, *Race Against Empire: Black Americans and Anticolonialism 1937–57* (Ithaca, 1997); Brenda Gayle Plummer, *Rising Wind: Black Americans and U.S. Foreign Policy* (Chapel Hill, 1996); Winston James, *Holding Aloft the Banner of Ethiopia: Caribbean Radicalism in Early Twentieth-Century America* (London, 1998); James Meriwether, *Proudly We Can Be Africans* (Chapel Hill, 2001); and Kevin K. Gaines, *American Africans in Ghana: Black Expatriates in the Civil Rights Era* (Chapel Hill, 2006).

3. Aimé Césaire, *Discourse on Colonialism*, first published in France, 1955 (New York, 2001).

4. For recent important framings of global politics through a focus on colonialism, see Odd Arne Westad, *The Global Cold War* (Cambridge, 2005), and Erez Manela, *The Wilsonian Moment: Self-Determination and the Origins of Anticolonial Nationalism* (Oxford, 2007).

5. William Scott, *The Sons of Sheba's Race* (Bloomington, 1993).

6. Enzo Traverso, *The Origins of Nazi Violence* (New York, 2003), 71.

7. Traverso, *The Origins of Nazi Violence,* 72.

8. Isabel V. Hull, *Absolute Destruction: Military Culture and the Practices of War in Imperial Germany* (Ithaca, 2005).

9. Quoted in Von Eschen, *Race Against Empire*, 27.

10. Von Eschen, *Race Against Empire*, 24.

11. T. Fujitani, Geoffrey M. White, and Lisa Yoneyama, introduction to *Perilous Memories* (Durham, 2001), 3.

12. Arif Dirlik, "Trapped in History on the Way to Utopia: East Asia's Great War Fifty Years Later," in *Perilous Memories: The Asia-Pacific Wars,* 320. On the Marshallese Islands, see Laurence M. Carruci, "The Source of the Force on Marshallese Cosmology," in Geoffrey White and Lamont Lindstrom, eds., *The Pacific Theater.*

13. Quoted in Penny M. Von Eschen, *Race Against Empire: Black Americans and Anticolonialism 1937–57,* (Ithaca, 1997), 23.

14. Von Eschen, *Race Against Empire,* 23.

15. Christopher Alan Balay and Timothy Norman Harper, *Forgotten Wars: Freedom and Revolution in Southeast Asia* (Cambridge, Mass., 2007), 19–23. On the release and implications of these documents, see Mike Thompson, "Hitler's Secret Army," BBC Now, September 23, 2004.

16. Von Eschen, *Race Against Empire*, 29.

17. Most of the recent scholarship in black internationalism, including the work of such historians as Martha Biondi, Kevin Gaines, Gerald Horne, Robin Kelley, James Meriwether, and Nikhil Singh, bears out this observation of a richly contested and critical black anti-colonial Left.

18. George Lipsitz, "Frantic to Join . . . the Japanese Army": Soldiers and Civilians Confront the Asian Pacific War."

19. Marc Gallicchio, "Memory and the Lost Relationship Between Black Americans and Japan," in Marc Gallicchio, ed., *The Unpredictability of the Past: Memories of the Asian-Pacific War in U.S.-East Asian Relations* (Durham, NC., 2007), 255–286; Gallicchio, *The African American Encounter with Japan and China: Black Internationalism in Asia* (Chapel Hill, 2000).

20. Naoki Sakai, "Two Negations: The Fear of Being Excluded and the Logic of Self-Esteem," in Richard Calichman, *Contemporary Japanese Thought* (New York, 2005), 164, 170.

21. Stephen Hay has argued that Pan-Asianism was untenable because its promoters projected what they understood as the essence of their own societies onto the rest of Asia; *Asian Ideas of East and West: Tagore and His Critics in Japan, China, and India* (Cambridge, 1970).

22. Ibid.

23. T. Fujitani, "The Reischauer Memo: Mr. Moto, Hirohito, and Japanese American Soldiers," *Critical Asian Studies*, Vol. 33, No. 3 (2001): 379–402, 390.

24. Akira Iriye, *Power and Culture: The Japanese-American War, 1941–1945*, 1981; Bruce Cumings, "Archaeology, Descent, Emergence: Japan in the British/American Hegemony, 1900–1950," in *Japan in the World*, ed. Masao Miyoshi and H. D. Harootunian (Durham, 1993), 109.

25. Naoka Shibusawa, *America's Geisha Allies: Reimagining the Japanese Enemy* (Cambridge, 2006).

26. Yuka Tsuchiya, "Imagined America in Occupied Japan: Re-Educational Films Shown by the U.S. Forces to the Japanese," *The Japanese Journal of American Studies*, Vol. 13 (2002): 193–213; John Dower, *Embracing Defeat: Japan in the Wake of World War II* (New York, 1999).

27. Dirlik, "Trapped in History," 302.

28. For an excellent discussion of the range and depth of the work of the NAACP at the United Nations, see Carol Anderson, *Eyes Off the Prize.*

29. Von Eschen, *Race Against Empire*, 98–99.

30. ibid.

31. Von Eschen, *Race Against Empire*, 109–110. See also Mary Dudziak, *Cold War Civil Rights: Race and the Image of American Democracy* (Princeton, 2000).

32. Robert Korstad and Nelson Lichtenstein, "Opportunities Found and Lost: Labor Radicals and the Early Civil Rights Movement," *Journal of American History*, Vol. 75, No. 3, (1988): 811.Von Eschen, *Race Against Empire*, 112–114; Robert L. Zangrando, *The NAACP Crusade.* As the historian Robert L. Zangrando has shown, the campaign promises of 1948 failed to translate into legislation.

33. George Lipsitz, *Rainbow at Midnight*, 190–192; Barabar S. Griffith, *The Crisis of American Labor: Operation Dixie and the Defeat of the CIO* (Philadelphia, 1988); Michael

K. Honey, *Southern Labor and Black Civil Rights: Organizing Memphis Worker*, (Urbana, 1993); Patrick Renshaw, *American Labor and Consensus Capitalism*, 123–124; Von Eschen, *Race Against Empire*, 114: Stoner, Yvette Richards, Gaines.

34. Von Eschen, *Race Against Empire*, 153.

35. See Bruce Cumings, "The Wicked Witch of the West Is Dead. Long Live the Wicked Witch of the East," 87, and Walter LaFeber, "An End to Which Cold War?" in *The End of the Cold War: Its Meanings and Implications*, ed. Michael J. Hogan (New York, 1992).

36. Ibid., Uadrey R. Kahin and George McT.Kahin, *Subversion as Foreign policy: The Secret Eisenhower and Dulles Debacle in Indonesia* (New York, 1995); Robert J. McMahon, *Colonialism and the Cold War: The United States and the Struggle for Indonesian Independence, 1945–1949* (Ithaca, 1981).

37. Thomas Borstelmann, *The Cold War and the Color Line* (Cambridge, Mass., 2001); Michael Hunt, *Ideology and American Foreign Policy* (New Haven, 1987).

38. Klein, *Cold War Orientalisms*.

39. For stellar examples of books that view America's war in Vietnam in the context of colonial history, see Marilyn B. Young, *Vietnam Wars: 1945–1990* (New York, 1991); and Mark Bradley, *Imagining Vietnam and America: The Making of Postcolonial Vietnam, 1919–1950* (Chapel Hill, 2000).

40. On U.S. views of Middle Eastern non-alignment, see Douglas Little, *American Orientalism: The United States and the Middle East since 1945* (Chapel Hill, 2002); on U.S. diplomacy and views of non-alignment in Ghana and Africa, see Kevin K. Gaines, *American Africans in Ghana: Black Expatriates in the Era of Civil Rights* (Chapel Hill, 2006).

41. Lauren, *Power and Prejudice*, 214.

42. Mahmood Mamdani, *Good Muslim: Bad Muslim, The Cold War and Roots of Terror* (New York: Pantheon, 2004). See also Odd Arne Westad, *The Global Cold War and the Making of Our Times* (Cambridge, 2005), and David F. Schmitz, *The United States and Right Wing Dictatorships, 1965–1989* (Cambridge, 2006).

43. Sandra Sturdevant and Brenda Stoltzfus, *Let the Goodtimes Roll: Prostitution and the U.S. Military* (New York, 1993); Yoko Fukamura and Martha Matsuoka, "Redefining Security: Okinawa Women's Resistance to U.S. Militarism," Choe Sang-Hun, "Ex-Prostitutes Say South Korea and U.S. Enabled Sex Trade Near Bases," *New York Times*, 7 January 2009.

44. Robert Vitalis, *America's Kingdom: Mythmaking on the Saudi Oil Frontier* (Palo Alto, 2006).

45. Utsumi Aiko, "Korean 'Imperial Soldiers': Remembering Colonialism and Crimes against Allied POWS," in *Perilous Memories*, 197.

10

Race, Rights, and Nongovernmental Organizations at the UN San Francisco Conference

A CONTESTED HISTORY OF "HUMAN RIGHTS . . . WITHOUT DISCRIMINATION"

Elizabeth Borgwardt

The entrance to Garden Room of the Fairmont Hotel in San Francisco bears an unusual commemorative plaque, which reads as follows:

25 April–26 June 1945

In this room met the Consultants of forty-two national organizations assigned to the United States Delegation at the Conference on International Organization in which the United Nations Charter was drafted. Their contribution is particularly reflected in the Charter provisions for human rights and United Nations consultation with private organizations.

According to its designers, this artifact memorializes both the entire eight-week conference in the spring of 1945, where delegates of dozens of nations met to negotiate and sign the United Nations Charter, as well as a particular meeting that took place on May 2. Accounts describe a dramatic confrontation over the role of human rights in the draft UN charter between Secretary of State Edward R. Stettinius, Jr., head of the U.S. delegation to the UN conference, and representatives of the forty-two nongovernmental organizations (NGOs) chosen by the State Department and designated as the delegation's official "consultants."[1]

There are several iconic accounts of this encounter, in memoirs by participants such as Frederick Nolde of the Federal Council of Churches and Joseph Proskauer of the American Jewish Committee, as well as in later secondary sources by human rights scholars. They sketch a scenario where ordinary citizens who happened to be leaders of grassroots civic organizations spoke truth to power, focusing on their dissatisfaction with the absence of strong human rights provisions in the draft UN charter.[2]

Each of the forty-two official consulting organizations—which would today be called NGOs but at the time were often known as "pressure groups"—was represented in San Francisco by one consultant and two associates. Represented groups included religious, labor, and professional associations, ranging from the National Lawyers' Guild to the National Association of Manufacturers, along with veterans' groups and other civic organizations such as the Rotary Club and Kiwanis, capturing an ideological span that was relatively wide by American standards. Only one African American NGO was represented: the NAACP, with Walter White as the consultant and Mary McLeod Bethune and W.E.B. Du Bois as the associates. A smattering of women's organizations alongside this lone African American contingent highlight how relatively few inclusions on this NGO roster would fit into contemporary parsings of "diversity."[3]

Alerted in advance to the high-profile opportunity for advocacy, during the afternoon of Wednesday, May 2 several of these groups had hastily written a letter demanding that the draft UN charter include a number of explicit human rights provisions, as well as provisions for the creation of a human rights commission. The letter asked for language pointing to "the dignity and inviolability of the individual" in the draft UN charter, suggesting that one of the charter's enumerated purposes should be "to promote respect for human rights and fundamental freedoms." The letter also demanded a more detailed assertion of human rights–related principles: "All members of the Organization . . . shall progressively secure for their inhabitants without discrimination such fundamental rights as freedom of religion, speech, assembly and communication, and to a fair trial under just laws," amounting to "the equivalent of an International Bill of Rights."[4]

At the 5 P.M. meeting that same day, Secretary Stettinius initially offered his pessimistic assessment of this human rights agenda, noting that he and others "had struggled exceedingly hard the previous summer to get as much into the Dumbarton Oaks proposals [an early draft of the UN charter] on the question of human rights as was possible," as Nolde wrote in his memoir. "[Stettinius] felt that there was little hope of securing anything more."[5]

According to Nolde and other NGO representatives present at the meeting, an inspiring speech from another grassroots leader, Judge Joseph Proskauer, transformed this discouraging dynamic. As Proskauer himself rather breathlessly recounted:

> I said that the voice of America was speaking in this room as it had never before spoken in any international gathering; that that voice was saying to the American delegation: "If you make a fight for these human rights proposals and win, there will be glory for all. If you make a fight for it and lose, we will back you up to the limit. If you fail to make a fight for it, you will have lost the support of American opinion—and justly lost it. In that event, you will never get the Charter ratified."

Then other NGO leaders spoke, including Walter White, who urged that a reference to "colonies and other dependent peoples" be included in the "human rights proposals." Nolde, who had submitted the letter, explained that these provisions would be a way of getting "our toe in the door."[6]

At the conclusion of these speeches, Stettinius "rose to his feet impulsively," according to Proskauer, "and exclaimed that he had no idea of the intensity of feeling on this subject." The Secretary of State then committed to try to persuade the rest of the U.S. delegation, and to use American leverage to secure agreement from other key delegations. "I have never seen democracy in action demonstrated so forcefully," observed Walter Kotschnig, a Stettinius aide who was present at the meeting, to other NGO leaders later on in the conference: "It is the participation meeting we had in this room when Mr. Nolde first introduced the matter, which really changed history at this point."[7]

Ultimately, according to this traditional narrative, somewhat watered-down versions of the requested human rights provisions triumphed in later drafts of the charter, along with new, explicit provisions acknowledging the important consultative role of NGOs, as Secretary Stettinius himself had explained in his own description of the role of the "consulting organizations" at San Francisco.[8]

A more critical and textured counter-narrative of the Fairmont Garden Room meeting specifically, and the role of NGOs at San Francisco generally, depicts a more cynical and savvy State Department staff that had been busily co-opting internationalist NGOs since at least the autumn of 1944.[9] It seems most unlikely that these staffers and their superiors would have changed course at the eleventh hour, except at perhaps the most superficial and cosmetic level, based on a meeting lasting less than half an hour. These analyses suggest that Stettinius's team was already committed to those human rights provisions depicted as dramatic "concessions" flowing from the Garden Room meeting, such as the creation of a human rights commission as part of the UN system. The State Department saw advantages in letting the NGOs take credit for an eleventh-hour intervention, right down to the little brushstroke of having Archibald MacLeish, then serving as Assistant Secretary for Public Affairs, sit down next to Frederick Nolde at the consultants' meeting and urge Nolde to speak.[10]

Not coincidentally, these recent counter-narratives connect the silences, tensions, and internal contradictions in the process of negotiating the UN charter—and in the final version of the charter itself—with issues of race. Any possibility of "progressively secur[ing] . . . without discrimination" a variety of "fundamental rights," in the language of the Consultants' May 2 letter to Stettinius, would presumably have rather stark implications for America's domestic Jim Crow regime, as well as for the design of "trusteeships" for colonial territories and for the link between imperialism and exploitation more generally.

Such race-related connections were obvious to the African American activists in San Francisco, many of whom made common cause with other NGOs and delegates of color at the UN conference. Various U.S.-based organizations such as the Council of African Affairs, while disappointed to find themselves "officially" represented by the more moderate NAACP, were nevertheless present and active in San Francisco in unofficial capacities (and during the war, Du Bois had served as deputy to the CAA's president, Paul Robeson). The three designated NAACP representatives also readily linked NGO human rights–related advocacy to questions of American segregationism and colonial autonomy. W.E.B. Du Bois in particular had rejoined the NAACP leadership in the summer of 1944 in order to "revive the Pan-African movement and to give general attention to the foreign aspects of the race problem."[11]

The lens of race accordingly helps us explain the UN charter story, but what about the story of what came next? Despite some inspiring rhetoric in wartime documents such as the 1941 Atlantic Charter, the United Nations Organization that emerged from San Francisco had no place for individual petitioners and seemed tailor-made to further enshrine colonialism.[12] After all, Du Bois was immediately told that the UN could take no action on his dramatic 1946 petition, "An Appeal to the World: A Statement on the Denial of Human Rights to Minorities in the Case of Citizens of Negro Descent in the United States of America and an Appeal to the United Nations for Redress," as a nonconforming NGO effusion, embarrassing to a Security Council power.[13] The afterlife of Du Bois's petition, however, shows instead how the power of NGO advocacy infused new life into domestic identity politics, contributing as it did to the ferment around Truman's 1947 Report by the President's Committee on Civil Rights, *To Secure These Rights*. At the international level, moreover, African peoples had a new forum which, however flawed, "offered new opportunities for a politics imbued with a sense of [nationalist] identity," in Von Eschen's assessment. In contrast to the traditional Cold War narrative of retrenchment, the UN charter's flaws, tensions, and silences contributed in their own way to what historian Jason Parker has recently called "the global race revolution of the twentieth century."[14]

A World Charter Without "Social Uplift Frills": The Dumbarton Oaks Proposals

The first multilateral draft of what would become the United Nations charter resulted from the Dumbarton Oaks conference of August to October 1944. In the late summer of 1944, the main mansion at the Dumbarton Oaks estate in Washington, D.C., became the site for a series of "conversations" to plan a postwar organization for collective security. The proposal that came out of this meeting of the United States, Britain, the Soviet Union, and rather belatedly, China, was then circulated for comment as the "Dumbarton Oaks proposals."[15] The State Department had billed the meeting as an informal and exploratory exchange among military and foreign affairs experts. This focus on professional expertise was meant to contrast with the amateurish proceedings of the Paris Peace Conference a generation before. The Dumbarton Oaks planners believed that they had learned the essential lessons from the First World War on how to devise a postwar multilateral order: start planning while hostilities are still continuing; make the plan identifiably and organically American-led; use "experts" and "technicians" to make the process appear less politicized; and separate the actual peace treaty from the machinery for resolving later disputes. Despite some initial Soviet resistance, the Dumbarton Oaks negotiators agreed to use a set of detailed, pre-circulated proposals generated by the Americans as a basis for discussion. The participants agreed that the most powerful nations, which was to say themselves, must take the most active role in enforcing any kind of world peacekeeping scheme. FDR's earlier idea of a regionally oriented system of "Four Policemen" had been the starkest expression of this orientation.[16]

This initial discussion draft contained only a single, vague reference to human rights, contemplating that the General Assembly could "initiate studies and make recommendations for the promotion of the observance of basic human rights." The General Assembly might also choose to create future subsidiary organizations that could address economic and social questions, as well as take on these advisory-type human rights functions. Roosevelt had approved this draft through his chief of staff, Admiral William D. Leahy, and Leahy indicated that he was opposed to any "social uplift frills" woven into the future collective security institution, because "the real job of the organization [was] to prevent war." Even this tepid proposal was shunted aside for a time during the negotiations after Soviet representative Andrei Gromyko objected to formalizing proposals for subsidiary bodies.[17]

Stettinius and his delegation offered the first human rights–related proposal debated at Dumbarton Oaks, yet tellingly, this same proposal emphasized protecting domestic jurisdiction—a protective "veil of sovereignty" over a state's internal practices, such as Jim Crow laws in the case of the United States—even as it advocated human rights.

"The international organization should refrain from intervention in the internal affairs of any state," the proposal began, drafted by Benjamin Cohen, FDR's lawyer and personal representative at the conference. States must be responsible for arranging their domestic affairs so as not to "endanger international peace and security and, to this end, to respect the human rights and fundamental freedoms of all of its people." Eventually this only slightly firmer reference migrated to become part of the mission of the Economic and Social Council, which was added at American insistence. Overcoming British and Soviet objections, the Economic and Social Council was to "promote respect for human rights and fundamental freedoms." On the same day, in timing that may not have been entirely coincidental, Britain, the United States and the Soviet Union agreed on a provision prohibiting the Security Council from intervening in matters falling primarily within the domestic jurisdiction of member states.[18]

In the short and perfunctory "Chinese phase" of the talks, V. K. Welling-ton Koo, the urbane, Columbia-educated head of the Chinese delegation, had decided that he had little choice but to play the largely ceremonial role allocated to him by the Big Three. The United States had insisted on inviting China over British and Soviet objections—Churchill famously referred to Chinese partici-pation as a "faggot vote for the United States"—and the Soviets had departed before the official Chinese phase had even started. Upon receiving the initial invitation to participate in formal conversations for postwar planning, Chinese diplomats had responded with a letter of acceptance over Jiang Jieshi's (Chiang Kai-shek's) signature, noting that "[w]ithout the participation of Asiatic peo-ples, the conference will have no meaning for half of humanity." The Chinese also sent a proposal in advance suggesting that a fundamental tenet of the new organization should be that "the principle of equality of all states and all races shall be upheld."[19]

The British, Soviets, and Americans opposed this racial equality inclusion so strongly—remembering as everyone did the similar Japanese petition from the wake of World War I—that the Chinese agreed to delete the proposed statement of principle in advance, realizing that the structure of the conference meant that they would have little scope for having controversial provisions de-bated and incorporated. Even so, the three powers spoke among themselves in the earlier "Soviet" phase regarding what they might do if the Chinese so much as raised the issue of racial discrimination at the talks. At Dumbarton Oaks, Koo's negotiating team instead offered suggestions at a higher level of gener-ality, urging that the existing draft be supplemented with a statement of moral principles that could serve as a touchstone for the rest of the document.[20]

The new Chinese modifications proposed that "the Charter should provide specifically that adjustment or settlement of international disputes should be achieved with due regard for principles of justice and international law." The Chinese delegation also suggested that the new organization should play a leading role "with respect to the development and revision of the rules and principles of international law"—in other words, that the UN should build in mechanisms for adjusting to a changing status quo, rather than merely serving as one more ossifying force in international politics. The British supported Stet-tinius when he dismissed even this watered-down list of concerns as "extremely idealistic."[21]

The final version of the Dumbarton Oaks proposals kept a lone and pallid reference to human rights in the Economic and Social Council, a subsidiary organization that was excluded from the list of the proposed organization's major components. The list of the organization's purposes and principles did not mention human rights, there was no dedicated human rights commission as one of the subsidiary organizations, and no human rights role was outlined for the General Assembly. Nor was there any language relating to "trusteeship" or the future status of colonized areas.[22]

In a diary entry from early in the negotiations, the Secretary of State wrote a little wanly of "our hope" that a reference to human rights and fundamental freedoms "can be included somewhere in the document." A handwritten correction in the unpublished version of this diary entry distills this dynamic of shrinking expectations: the line of the original typescript which read "Promise of respect for human rights and fundamental freedoms" was altered in Stettinius's own hand, rather poignantly substituting the word "Promotion" for the crossed-out word "Promise."[23]

"Operation Soapbox"

Determined "not to pull another Woodrow Wilson," in the words of State Department public relations consultant John Sloan Dickey, the State Department sought actively to develop a public consensus in favor of the Dumbarton Oaks proposals while the talks were still unfolding. A campaign of co-opting a variety of nongovernmental organizations appealed to the State Department, where more forthright advocacy would likely have triggered unfavorable scrutiny from what would at the time have been termed "isolationist" constituencies. Such a strategy emphasized alliances with willing NGOs such as the NAACP, the American Federation of Labor, and the Federal Council of Churches, and especially, with overtly internationalist groups such as the Universities Committee on Post-War Problems or Americans United for World Organization and the Commission to Study the Organization of Peace.[24]

These associations could, in turn, be relied upon to mobilize individuals, a responsibility that these groups took very seriously. As the president of the Kiwanis International explained at a January 1945 meeting celebrating his organization's thirtieth anniversary, "the task of all Kiwanians and like service groups" was "to build a strong and vocal public opinion that demands a lasting peace. We must use our [2,250] Kiwanis Clubs as forums and platforms to mold in each community a public opinion that will be powerful and insistent . . . in this fateful year."[25]

To advance this public relations offensive, a reorganized State Department that had never before systematically concerned itself with its public image planned to use its newly created Office of Public Information in order to "take out the word" on the content of the Dumbarton Oaks proposals. What the historian of international relations Michael Leigh describes as a "consultative-educative process" unfolded during late 1944 and early 1945, and "by stressing the tentative nature of the proposals [Stettinius] tried to give the public a sense of their own capacity to influence the final outcome." The State Department convened an off-the-record briefing and meeting in October 1944 with representatives of more than ninety NGOs. Stettinius's address underlined the Department's oft-repeated assertions that the Dumbarton Oaks proposals needed a phase of "critical and candid" public debate, fueled by a "substantial and informed body of public opinion."[26] The Department had hosted an additional four such NGO summits by the end of 1944, and between October 1944 and June 1945, State had sent representatives to over 335 individual meetings with NGOs nationwide. These strenuous efforts yielded gratifying results, culminating in the "National Dumbarton Oaks Week" of April 17, 1945. The attendant parades, rallies, shop-window exhibits, school projects, radio programs, and religious services unfolded in the emotional atmosphere of the aftermath of Roosevelt's sudden death on April 12. State Department opinion polls suggested that roughly 60 percent of the U.S. public knew at least something about the Dumbarton Oaks proposals by late April, as the San Francisco conference was opening. Over 80 percent of those questioned also answered "yes" to the question: "Do you think the United States should join a world organization with police power to maintain world peace?" Of these affirmative responses, over 80 percent thought it was "very important" that the United States participate.[27]

After 1935, moreover, the advent of scientific public opinion polling meant that internationalist voices were amplified in the policy-making process. Vocal and articulate "pressure groups," as they were often called in the 1940s, functioned with new confidence that their voices would register, and the State Department designed its public relations processes accordingly.[28] More than this: the State Department saw liaisons with international NGOs as a way of amplifying the Roosevelt and later Truman administration's impact on the development of American internationalism. Bolstering the impact and reach of international NGOs through the State Department Office of Public Affairs was a way of disseminating and reinforcing the administration's positions on international institutions without directly incurring the ire of isolationist constituencies, in the Senate and elsewhere.

An image-conscious senator considering how to vote on international issues in late 1944 and early 1945 thus encountered a very different landscape from the one he would have seen in 1919 or even 1935. But that landscape was being cultivated and shaped even as it was being surveyed.

"The Dumbarton Oaks provisions do not give assurance to the non-white peoples . . . that a new page of history is about to be written"

Strong unilateralists—often referred to as "isolationists" in this era and who tended to prefer the moniker "nationalists"—were predictably horrified by the assumptions regarding collective security embodied in the Dumbarton Oaks proposals. Their criticisms tended to center around the perceived giveaway of American sovereignty to a gang of Old World exploiters. Protestors such as the Reverend L. K. Smith, a rabble-rousing advisor to the late Governor Huey

Long of Louisiana, marched outside the iron gates of the Dumbarton Oaks estate with his wife, arguing that Roosevelt should be impeached for, among other offenses, setting up a "superstate" that would serve as a "world police force." The Smiths were joined by self-appointed "Constitutional Crusader" Collis O. Redd, who distributed weekly diatribes as leaflets, which he also sent to the State Department, complaining that:

> through deliberate planning and scheming America and England's government-political-religious leaders have steeped the world in wrong religious, economic, financial and government theories. We do not need any more New Deal educational propaganda.

(One of Redd's pamphlets is dedicated to "Wellington Foo [*sic*] Chairman Chinese Delegation" at Dumbarton Oaks, as well as the "oppressed nations of the world").[29]

In common with Redd and the Smiths, criticism from the Right often had an anti-imperialist overlay. As early as 1943, unilateralist Senate leader and perennial presidential hopeful Robert A. Taft, senator from Ohio, dismissed the possibility of turning the resources of sovereign states over to "President Whoozis of Worlditania," a program which, he observed scornfully, "may appeal to the do-gooders who regard it as the manifest destiny of America to confer the benefits of the New Deal on every Hottentot."[30] Voices on the Left were just as dismissive. The National Council of Negro Women insisted, "The world powers, now preparing the blueprint of the post-war world, must recognize that no lasting peace can be possible until the world is purged of its traditional concepts and practices of racial superiority, imperialist domination and economic exploitation."

What was most extraordinary about this prescient statement was not so much its content—which would have been familiar to any follower of various African American press outlets in this era—but rather that this critique was reprinted in full in a compilation of "Statements of National Organizations" from a pamphlet circulated by a rather mainstream and moderate group, Americans United for World Organization (AUWO), and was based on a State Department–sponsored meeting with that and other groups. The AUWO pamphlet also included statements by the U.S. Chamber of Commerce and the YMCA. The NCNW assessment continued:

> The non-white populations of the world, the oppressed and underprivileged of every complexion, who have contributed unstintingly to the inevitable victory, must be liberated and given full opportunity for development. The character of the new world organization must include provision for the ultimate self-government of the dependent peoples, and for full political, economic and social emancipation of racial and cultural minorities. . . . The Dumbarton Oaks proposals do not give assurance to

the non-white peoples, the dependent peoples, and the minority groups of the world that a new page of history affecting their welfare is about to be written.

W.E.B. Du Bois also attended this meeting as a representative of the NAACP, where he observed with dismay that the proposal's exclusive focus on "nations and states and the indifference to races, groups or organizations indicate that the welfare and protection of colonial peoples are beyond the jurisdiction of the conference's proposed governments."[31] A number of groups focused on proposals for appending an "International Bill of Rights" to any proposed international charter.

NGOs that issued supportive statements, such as the National Farmers' Union and the YMCA, nevertheless offered rather more idealistic assessments than the Dumbarton Oaks text could really support. The Farmers' Union approved "full participation by the United States in a world organization based on political and economic justice," while a YMCA statement supported "an international organization composed of representatives of all people whose nations accept the rule of law" and "an international judiciary devoted to attainment of political and social justice."[32]

Most reactions fell somewhere in the middle of this already rather narrow spectrum of anti-imperialist suspicion and idealistic one-worldliness, with criticisms and suggestions converging on a desire for more transparency in the decision-making process and more protections for sub-national groups and even individuals, again often under the rubric of a proposed international bill of rights. Most critics conceded that the proposals were "a good beginning," in the words of a resolution adopted by the National Council of Catholic Women, "although it is incomplete and has defects which, lacking the right spirit, can be most serious."

Internationally inclined religious groups often urged leading roles for their affiliates. Conference discussion groups of the Federal Council of Churches of Christ in America supported an "unconditional endorsement of Dumbarton Oaks," while at the same time "reserv[ing] the right of the Conference and of churchmen in general to continue their efforts at improvement." Or in the primly schoolmasterish assessment of the Reverend Frank Nolde, "Pleasing progress, but should try harder."[33]

"That all the men in all the lands may live out their lives in freedom from fear and want"

Many of the so-called "smaller states" also expressed disappointment over the timidity of the Dumbarton Oaks draft, and their concerns paralleled many of the critical voices within the United States. Members of the British Commonwealth offered their suggestions after meeting in early April 1945 in London, as did representatives of Egypt, Greece, Lebanon, and Turkey, among others, all of which asked for more expansive language on the role of international law in the new institution. Australia and New Zealand met in Wellington in November 1944 and developed a joint proposal calling for a greater role for smaller powers and for expanded human rights provisions, particularly regarding social and economic rights. In February 1945, nineteen Latin American states met in Mexico City and drafted the "Act of Chapultepec," asking for a stronger voice for Latin American countries, along with strengthening the charter's provisions for human rights and "reaffirming the principle of equal rights without regard to race or religion." Poland and Denmark offered proposals to append the text of the 1941 Atlantic Charter—an eight-point, Anglo-American statement of war and peace aims—to a revised version of the UN charter.[34]

The story of how the war and peace aims of the Atlantic Charter became a human rights instrument is in large part a story of unintended consequences. Some of these consequences flowed from the charter's largely rhetorical role as a putative "blueprint" for planning the postwar international order. (At fewer than 400 words, the charter's aspirational provisions were pitched at too high a level of generality to offer concrete guidance—and quite deliberately so.) The "principles of the Atlantic Charter" accordingly could mean virtually whatever invested constituencies wanted them to mean, shaping them simultaneously into the "founding instrument" of the United Nations Charter, the Bretton Woods Charters, and the Nuremberg Charter, according to some of the designers of those institutions.

But this very quality of malleability in turn generated another, even more wide-ranging set of unintended consequences linked to race and colonialism. While FDR is on record at the Atlantic conference as goading Churchill with puckish anti-colonialist comments, in context it is clear that the American president was primarily concerned with dismantling the imperial preference system and opening up international trade—and certainly not exposing domestic racial hierarchies in the United States to United Nations interference. Over the course of his political career Roosevelt had developed a wider analysis of imperialism as a source of wars and injustice, but as with many of FDR's notorious inconsistencies, such a vision existed side by side with a patrician vision of colonized areas as needing extended periods of "tutorial"-style relations with an imperial power.

As for Winston Churchill, the Atlantic Charter's other primary progenitor, he was predictably horrified by reactions suggesting that the Atlantic Charter had implications for the status of the colonies—to the prime minister, the charter was targeted exclusively at "the nations of Europe now under the Nazi yoke," in his own words. One of FDR's speechwriters observed, however, that "it was not long before the people of India, Burma, Malaya, and Indonesia were beginning to ask if the Atlantic Charter extended also to the Pacific and to Asia in general," while Nnamdi Azikiwe, the editor of the Lagos-based *West African Pilot*, inquired whether "the Atlantic Charter would benefit the coloured races as well as white."[35]

Several of these commentators referenced a particular clause in the Atlantic Charter stating that one of the objectives of the war was the creation of a peace where "all the men in all the lands may live out their lives in freedom from fear and want"—the turn of phrase "all the men" suggested that individuals might be situated in a more direct relationship with a wider international order in the postwar world. Such an angle of analysis had an obvious appeal to subjects of oppressive regimes the world over. Nelson Mandela, in 1941 a young lawyer in South Africa, noted later that the Atlantic Charter "reaffirmed faith in the dignity of each individual"—which it manifestly did not on its face, except through a rather attenuated reading of this one phrase. In the United States, the Council of African Affairs published a pamphlet titled "What of Africa's Place in Tomorrow's World?" and calling for "speedy economic and political development within the framework of the United Nations and within the spirit and intent of the Atlantic Charter." Indeed, the contrast between the Atlantic Charter of Winston Churchill's intentions and the charter of Nelson Mandela's or the CAA's aspirations is the pith of what was missing from the UN Charter under consideration at San Francisco.[36]

"Our job was not to take up subjects like the Negro question"

Once the San Francisco conference was underway, the limits of public diplomacy in advancing the kind of human rights agenda articulated by the NGOs were most sharply delineated around the issue of race. Pressure from domestic NGOs and from "smaller" countries for a strong U.S. role in seeking charter revisions favoring human rights, racial equality, augmentation of social and economic provisions, or anti-colonial approaches encountered three formidable obstacles.

Number one was the fact that the U.S. delegation included Texas senator Tom Connally, an ardent segregationist and chair of the Senate Foreign Relations Committee. Connally had been chosen for the U.S. delegation because he would be steering the UN charter—which was of course a treaty—through its all-important Senate ratification process. Mindful that U.S. participation in the old League had foundered on these senatorial shoals, State Department officials understood that "when you had men like . . . Connally [on the U.S. delegation] . . . you didn't go sailing off into the blue. You had to keep your eye all the time on not putting too much limitation on American sovereignty." This meant squelching any kind of charter provision that might result in interference with the states' rights orientation of segregationist Southern senators, to whom the Democratic Party in the mid-1940s was in thrall.[37]

Connally's perspective was of course emblematic of a larger problem: the tension between any kind of human rights–related language and the charter's sweeping provision for protecting a member's "internal" matters from international scrutiny. Charter article 2, paragraph 7 bluntly asserted that "nothing contained in the present Charter shall authorize the United Nations to intervene in matters which are essentially within the domestic jurisdiction of any state or shall require the Members to submit such matters to settlement." Connally noted with satisfaction that this domestic jurisdiction provision "was sufficient to overpower all other considerations," in other words, any vague human rights–related language that might suggest that the internal affairs of a member state were anybody else's business. The Americans had no monopoly on this quest to shield objectionable domestic policies regarding the treatment of minorities from international scrutiny. The British and Soviets were of course especially interested in the workings of domestic jurisdiction, as were the Australians, as part of protecting their "White Australia" immigration policies.[38]

The U.S. military posed another major obstacle to the development of any charter provision emphasizing human rights and the democratic equality of peoples. American negotiators influenced the development of the charter's "trusteeship" system for colonized peoples—a topic that was avoided entirely at Dumbarton Oaks—with an eye to preserving American prerogatives in the territories that the United States had captured from the Japanese in the Pacific. A State Department official explained that the U.S. military needed to have a "free hand" in the Pacific "to use those islands as we saw fit." The ensuing diplomatic machinations involved redesignating these islands as so-called "strategic trust territories" and transferring their oversight from the Trusteeship Council to the Security Council, where the United States held a veto. This set of maneuvers also meant that the U.S. delegation sacrificed whatever moral authority or leadership credibility it might have drawn from FDR's wartime anti-colonialist rhetoric, and forfeited the opportunity to design a trusteeship regime that would support colonized peoples in moving toward independence.[39]

The third major obstacle to the U.S. delegation's advocacy for international human rights provisions was the advent of heightened U.S.-Soviet tensions, which played out in San Francisco in various procedural and substantive disputes over seating delegates from Poland and Argentina, the chairmanship of the conference itself, as well as voting and veto rights. This tense and adversarial atmosphere served to draw the United States closer to European colonial powers as a way of isolating the Soviet Union.

The NGO contingent at San Francisco, however scrappy, well-informed, and motivated, was arguably no match for such a potent combination of domestic political and geostrategic concerns. The presence of these NGO consultants certainly did not change Stettinius's view that the American delegation's "job in San Francisco was to create a charter. . . . not to take up subjects like . . . the negro question." Walter White later lamented that the NGO role in San Francisco was to serve merely as "window dressing."[40]

The final version of the UN charter contained seven human rights–related references, including the lobbied-for language indicating that one of the purposes of the United Nations was "to achieve international cooperation . . . in promoting and encouraging respect for human rights and fundamental freedoms for all without distinction as to race, sex, language or religion." Field Marshal Jan Smuts of South Africa had led the committee drafting a lyrical reference in the Preamble to "faith in human rights and in the dignity and worth of the human person," while Article 13 indicated that the General Assembly was to initiate studies and offer recommendations for "assisting in the realization of human rights and fundamental freedoms for all without distinction as to race, sex, language or religion." The charter also formally acknowledged the role of NGOs.

Just as important as what was included, however, was what was left out. First of all, the charter offered no definition of the terms "human rights" and "fundamental freedoms." Very much in line with other high-flown wartime rhetoric such as the Atlantic Charter, these soaring phrases meant different things to different constituencies. For example, to Field Marshal Smuts, the term "civilization" meant imperial internationalism—clearly a whites-only proposition. The strongly segregationist South African leader likely experienced very little of what we might today call cognitive dissonance in taking the lead in drafting the human rights language in the UN charter's preface, perhaps in the way that Thomas Jefferson may not have tasted his own hypocrisy in drafting the U.S. Declaration of Independence.[41] If Smuts were willing to draft the human rights-related language in the charter, clearly any Southern segregationists who read it need not suffer sleepless nights for fear of its implications for Jim Crow.

A second kind of absence in the charter was the way any hint of commitment was vitiated by the systematic softening of verbs such as "protect," "guarantee," or "safeguard" with watered-down substitutes such as "encourage," "promote," or "assist." These weasel words were deployed in line with Stettinius's earlier wiggling at Dumbarton Oaks.[42] Yet another kind of absence was a dedicated role for individuals or even sub-national groups. As with the Chinese at Dumbarton Oaks, those seeking commitments to equality, justice, or non-discrimination were fobbed off with euphemisms: the charter was not really the spot where "the individual human being first appears in his full stature as endowed with fundamental rights and freedoms," as international legal scholar Hersch Lauterpacht insisted in 1947. Finally, of course, the clear and firm domestic jurisdiction provision in the charter directly contradicted other kinds of vague human rights language.[43]

W.E.B. Du Bois, in his Senate testimony in July 1945, indicated in frustration that the final version of the UN charter had not been altered enough from its "great power" orientation at Dumbarton Oaks, and that the final result was an inadequate compromise among "the national interests, the economic rivalries, and the selfish demands" of these powers. He framed these shortcomings explicitly in terms of racial equality:

> The proposed Charter should, therefore, make clear and unequivocal the straightforward stand of the civilized world for race equality, and the universal application of the democratic way of life, not simply as philanthropy and justice, but to save human civilization from suicide. What was true of the United States in the past is true of world civilization today— we cannot exist half slave and half free.[44]

"Our treatment in America . . . is a basic problem of humanity"

The UN charter was out of date from the moment it was signed, looking backward as it did to problems with the League of Nations and to the relative unity of the wartime "Grand Alliance." As a constitutional system, the charter's general architecture and specific provisions failed to account for the three major factors that were to transform the international politics of the second half of the twentieth century: first, the harshly bipolar and thoroughgoing nature of the already-vigorous cold war; second, the rapid pace and wide extent of decolonization, creating many of the ninety-seven additional member states joining the United Nations Organization before 1980, most of which were not readily able to be manipulated by the United States; and third, the influence of new associations, including but not limited to NGOs, featuring post–San Francisco institutions such as the World Trade Organization or NATO.

The historian Manfred Berg points out that, despite the silences and contradictions in the UN charter, "[n]evertheless, the founding of the United Nations and the declaratory ban on racial discrimination offered political opportunities to expose American racism on the international stage that the civil rights movement was determined to exploit." After UN officials "balked" at the presentation of a petition by the National Negro Congress in June 1946, as Berg tells it, Du Bois pursued his own more ambitious petition project, initiated earlier and purporting "to represent the peoples of Africa before the UNO" as well as the aspirations of African Americans. Even after the NAACP leadership limited the scope of the Du Bois petition to the plight of African Americans exclusively, Du Bois universalized his mission to attack the very foundations of the UN's domestic jurisdiction provision: "Peoples of the World," Du Bois called out in a summary of the petition he had prepared, "we American Negroes appeal to you; our treatment in America is not merely an internal question of the United States. It is a basic problem of humanity."[45]

"An Appeal to the World" was in the end received by the UN Human Rights commission in October 1947, but the commission's leadership, which famously included Eleanor Roosevelt, refused to transmit the petition to the General Assembly. As part of this contretemps, Du Bois leaked the 150-page petition to the press. The NAACP was inundated with requests for copies, to which it responded by releasing the document first as a mimeograph and in 1948 as a booklet, generating maximum publicity. Controversy over the petition led to rifts in NAACP leadership, but even without formal consideration by the General Assembly, "the UN petition had served its propaganda purpose" in galvanizing the domestic civil rights movement, in Berg's assessment. In other words, this NGO document had a significant impact, not least through energizing disappointed constituencies, even if it arguably did not succeed on its own terms. Certainly African American leaders during the protests of the 1960s, including Martin Luther King, Jr., spoke of human rights as much as civil rights.[46]

While the explosive growth of NGOs in the postwar era will likely never challenge the dominant structure of nation-states, nevertheless NGOs have arguably transformed the international landscape and, as sociologist Saskia Sassen notes, are becoming "a force that can undermine the exclusive authority of the state over its nationals," resulting in "significant shifts in the architecture of political membership." Folding in these kinds of transdisciplinary insights offers a supplemental big-picture perspective, and suggests how the spectacular and explosive growth of NGOs in the postwar era might appropriately prompt us to continue to interrogate these micro-level analyses of who was playing whom in the spring and summer of 1945. The San Francisco conference may indeed have marked a kind of turning point for the role of NGOs in international society, but the framework of race offers an important corrective to the linear and triumphalist narratives sketched in participants' memoirs.[47]

We now have a surfeit of "revolutions" unfolding over the course of the postwar era—a race revolution, an advocacy revolution, and a "juridical revolution in human rights," according to commentators such as the ethicist Amy Gutmann.[48] The 1940s in isolation did not mark the inauguration of these movements, much less their consummation. Perhaps instead, the wake of World War II marks a highly visible moment of transformation, and one jumping-off point might be a discussion of what actually transpired in the Garden Room of San Francisco's Fairmont Hotel on May 2, 1945, along with why and whether it might be worth commemorating with a plaque.

Notes

1. For a hagiographic account of this particular meeting and its transformational effect, see Clark Eichelberger's memoir, *Organizing for Peace: A Personal History of the Founding of the United Nations* (New York, 1977), 268–273. Eichelberger's group, the American Association for the United Nations, was also responsible for hanging the commemorative plaque cited above in a 1955 ceremony.

2. In addition to the Eichelberger account cited above, other memoirs and analyses by participants include; Dorothy B. Robins, *Experiment in Democracy: The Story of U.S. Citizen Organizations in Forging the Charter of the United Nations* (New York, 1971); O. Frederick Nolde, *Free and Equal: Human Rights in Ecumenical Perspective* (Geneva, 1968); and Joseph M. Proskauer, *A Segment of My Times* (New York, 1950). Later secondary sources replicating the narrative and tone of the memoirs include William Korey, *NGOs and the Universal Declaration of Human Rights: A "Curious Grapevine"* (New York, 1998); Stephen C. Schlesinger, *Act of Creation: The Founding of the United Nations* (Cambridge, Mass., 2003); Paul Gordon Lauren, *The Evolution of International Human Rights: Visions Seen* (Philadelphia, 2003).

3. "Official List of Consultants," 10 *Department of State Bulletin* (April 22, 1945), 724–725.

4. "Letter Submitted to Secretary Stettinius by Consultants Regarding Human Rights," May 2, 1945, reprinted in the documentary appendix to Robins, *Experiment in Democracy*, 218–220.

5. Nolde, *Free and Equal*. 22; Wilson memo of conversation with O. Frederick Nolde of the Federal Council of Churches of Christ in America, October 31, 1944, Records of the Office of U.N. Affairs, RG 59, Box 30, NARA (complaints about the human rights content of earlier charter drafts); "Charter of the United Nations: Report to the President on the Results of the San Francisco Conference by the Chairman of the United States Delegation, The Secretary of State (June 26, 1945), 27–28, in Truman Papers PSF Folder—Trips—1945, Harry S. Truman Presidential Library.

6. Proskauer, *Segment of My Times*, 225; Nolde and White quoted in Robins at 131.

7. Proskauer, *Segment of My Times*, 225ff; Korey, *NGOs and the Universal Declaration*, especially the first chapter, "Genesis: NGOs and the UN Charter"; Kirsten Sellars's account in *The Rise and Rise of Human Rights* (London, 2002), 1–6; Robins, *Experiment in Democracy*, 109–129–132.

8. Stettinius, "Report to the President," 27–28.

9. For examples, see Carol Anderson, *Eyes Off the Prize: The United Nations and the African American Struggle for Human Rights, 1944–1955* (New York, 2003), 40–55; Sellars, *Rise and Rise of Human Rights*; 3–5; Penny M. Von Eschen, *Race Against Empire: Black Americans and Anticolonialism, 1937–1957* (Ithaca, 1997), 78ff; Borgwardt, *A New Deal for the World: America's Vision for Human Rights* (Cambridge, Mass., 2005), 189–191.

10. Nolde, *Free and Equal*, 22; NARA, RG 59, Records of the US Delegation to the UN Conference on International Organization (UNCIO), 1944–45, Box 208, "Promotion of Respect for Human Rights and Fundamental Freedoms," April 7, 1945.

11. Du Bois quoted in Von Eschen, *Race Against Empire* at p.74; on Du Bois's anti-colonial thought in this later part of his career, see, for example, Gerald Horne, *Black and Red: W.E.B. Du Bois and the Afro-American Response to the Cold War, 1944–1963* (Albany, 1986); on White, see Kenneth R. Janken, *White: The Biography of Walter White, Mr. NAACP* (New York, 2003); the literature is much thinner on Bethune, a situation soon to be remedied by Kim Cary Warren, but see Joyce Hanson, *Mary McCleod Bethune and Black Women's Political Activism* (Columbia, 2003). On making common cause at San Francisco, see Marika Sherwood, "'There Is No New Deal for the Blackman at San Francisco': African Attempts to Influence the Founding Conference of the United Nations, April–July 1945," *International Journal of African Historical Studies* Vol. 29, No. 1, 1996, 71–94.

12. On the relationship between colonialism and the human rights-related politics of the 1940s, see Mark Mazower, *No Enchanted Palace: The End of Empire and the Ideological Origins of the United Nations* (Princeton, 2009).

13. On Du Bois's petition, see Anderson, *Eyes Off the Prize*; Mary Dudziak, *Cold War Civil Rights: Race and the Image of American Democracy* (Princeton, 2000); and Manfred Berg, *"The Ticket to Freedom": The NAACP and the Struggle for Black Political Integration* (Gainesville, 2005), 120–123.

14. Von Eschen, *Race Against Empire*, 70; Jason C. Parker, "'Made-in-America Revolutions'? The "Black University" and the American Role in the Decolonization of the Black Atlantic," *Journal of American History* Vol. 96, No. 3, (December 2009), 727–750; see also Harvard Sitkoff, *A New Deal for Blacks: The Emergence of Civil Rights as a National Issue* (New York, 1978).

15. The few archivally based analyses of the Dumbarton Oaks proposals and their relationship to the final UN charter capture how the structure of the conference relegated China to an inferior, almost ceremonial, position. See, for example, Robert C. Hilderbrand, *Dumbarton Oaks: The Origins of the United Nations and the Search for Postwar Security* (Chapel Hill, 1990), 229–244.

16. "Proposals for the Establishment of a General International Organization (The Dumbarton Oaks Proposals)," reprinted in "Texts of Statements on Dumbarton Oaks and Documents Giving Tentative Security Plans," *New York Times*, October 10, 1944, 12.

17. Stettinius Diaries, August 25, 1944; see also Hilderbrand, *Dumbarton Oaks*, 86–87.

18. Stettinius Diary, September 20, 23, 27, 1944; Informal Record of the meeting of the U.S. Delegation, September 20, 1944, Notter papers; Informal Minutes of Joint Steering Committee, September 27, 1944, Notter Papers; Alger Hiss, Special Assistant to the head of the Office of Special Political Affairs to Stettinius, September 23, 1944; and Stettinius to Hiss, September 25, 1944, Notter Papers.

19. Churchill quoted in Robert Dallek, *Franklin D. Roosevelt and American Foreign Policy, 1932–1945*, rev. ed., (New York, 1995), 223; Jiang Jieshi (Chiang Kai-shek) letter transmitted by Wei Tao Ming for Cordell Hull, June 3, 1944, in U.S. Department of State, *Foreign Relations of the United States (FRUS) 1944* (Washington, DC: USGPO), 1:640.

20. For a discussion of "Big Three" reactions to the original Chinese racial equality proposal, see Paul G. Lauren, *Power and Prejudice: The Politics and Diplomacy of Racial Discrimination*, 2nd ed., (Westview Press, 1996), 158–160.

21. "Chinese Proposals on Dumbarton Oaks Proposals," *Documents of the United Nations Conference on International Organization, San Francisco, 1945*, vol. 3, *Dumbarton Oaks Proposals: Comments and Proposed Amendments*, United Nations Information Organization, London and New York, 1945–1946, 200. Stettinius quoted in Hilderbrand, *Dumbarton Oaks*, 236.

22. "Dumbarton Oaks Proposals for the Establishment of a General International Organization," reprinted in Russell, *History of the United Nations Charter*, appseca1Appendix I, 1019–1029.

23. Stettinius Diary, September 20, 23, 27, 1944; Informal Record of the meeting of the U.S. Delegation, September 20, 1944. Charter of the United Nations, "Report to the President," (June 26, 1945), Appendix A, Charter of the United Nations—Dumbarton Oaks Proposals, (Parallel Texts), 176–232.

24. Michael Leigh, *Mobilizing Consent: Public Opinion and American Foreign Policy, 1937–1947* (Westport, Conn., 1976), 109;

25. Address by the Honorable Ben Dean, Grand Rapids, Michigan, President of the Kiwanis International, Meeting of the Kiwanis Club of Washington, D.C., January 25, 1945, excerpted in Americans United for World Organization, Inc., "America Wants World Organization: Statements of National Organizations" (typed pamphlet), n.d., 14, Dumbarton Oaks Pamphlets, Stettinius Papers; see also Robert A. Divine, *Second Chance: The Triumph of Internationalism in America During World War II* (New York, 1967).

26. Leigh, *Mobilizing Consent*, 117–119, Edward R. Stettinius, Jr., "Remarks," *Department of State Bulletin* Vol. 11 (October 22, 1944).

27. "Postwar Trends in the United States" June 19–July 21, 1945 and "American Opinion on Intellectual Issues," June 16–June 30, 1945, Foreign Office (United Kingdom), U.S. Correspondence 1938–1954, vol. 44608, reel 17, 28–74; "U.S. Daily Survey of Opinion Developments," Box 205, Harley Notter Files, Department of State.

28. Sarah Igo, *The Averaged American: Surveys, Citizens, and the Making of a Mass Public* (Cambridge, Mass., 2007); Susan Herbst, *Numbered Voices: How Opinion Polling Has Shaped American Politics* (Chicago, 1993); Jean M. Converse, *Survey Research in the United States: Roots and Emergence* (Berkeley, 1987).

29. Memorandum of telephone conversation, Breckinridge Long and Mrs. L.K. Smith, and Smith to Hull, August 23, 1944, Breckinridge Long papers, LC; Collis Redd typescripts, n.d., but likely October–November 1944, State Department Dumbarton Oaks Pamphlets, Stettinius Papers.

30. Taft quoted in James T. Patterson, *Mr. Republican: A Biography of Robert A. Taft*, (Boston, 1972), 288–289.

31. "Dumbarton Oaks Proposals Exclude Colonies—Du Bois," Baltimore Afro-American, October 28, 1944, 3 quoted in Von Eschen, *Race Against Empire*, 75. See also W.E.B. Du Bois, *Color and Democracy: Colonies & Peace* (1945); Robert L. Harris, Jr., "Racial Equality and the United Nations Charter," in *New Directions in Civil Rights Studies*, ed. Armistead L. Robinson and Patricia Sullivan (Charlottesville, 1991).

32. National Farmers' Union, from program adopted by the Annual Convention for 1945, *ibid.*, 5; YMCA, plan outlined at National Council, October 1944, *ibid.*, 6.

33. Federal Council of Churches of Christ in America, proposed in a report by Bishop G. Bromley Oxnam of the Methodist area of New York to a session of the National Study Conference on the Churches and a Just and Durable Peace, at Cleveland, Ohio January 18, 1945, *ibid.*, 16–17; Nolde quoted in Nurser, *For All Peoples*, 103.

34. Ruth Russell, *A History of the United Nations Charter*, 569; Olive Holmes, "The Mexico City Conference and Regional Security," *Foreign Policy Reports*, Vol. 21 (May 1, 1945), 44–45; Inter-American Juridical Committee, *The Dumbarton Oaks Proposals: Preliminary Comments and Recommendations*, (Washington, D.C., 1944); Committee II, "An Account of the Essential Comments Made by the Delegates to the Inter-American Conference on Problems of War and Peace Concerning the Bases of Dumbarton Oaks," Records of the Office of UN Affairs, RG 59, Box 30, NARA; "British Commonwealth Conference, *Yearbook of the United Nations 1946–1947*, Department of Public Information, United Nations (Lake Success, N.Y.: 1947), 10.

35. Churchill speech of September 9, 1941, extract from *Hansard* of September 9, 1941, cols. 68–69, NA-Kew, 4/43A/3: 86; Robert Sherwood, *Roosevelt and Hopkins: An Intimate History* (New York, 1948), 362–363; Prime Minister's Personal Telegram, "From Nigeria" (Governor Sir B. Bourdillon to Secretary of State for the Colonies, forwarding Cable No.

1129 of November 15, 1941, from the Editor of the West African Pilot to Mr. Winston Churchill), NA-Kew, PREM 4/43A/3: 85.

36. Nelson Mandela, *Long Walk to Freedom* (Boston, 1994), 83–84; CAA pamphlet cited in Sherwood, "No New Deal for the Blackman," 74.

37. "Address of John Foster Dulles at the Foreign Policy Association Luncheon," June 29, 1945, John Foster Dulles papers, Box 26, Seeley Mudd Library, Princeton; Anderson, *Eyes Off the Prize*, 44; William E. Forbath, "Caste, Class, and Equal Citizenship," *Michigan Law Review,* Vol. 98 (October 1999), 1.

38. UN Charter article 2(7) reprinted in Russell, *History of the UN Charter*, Appendix M, 1035–1054; on domestic jurisdiction, see also ibid. at 900–910; "Minutes of the 51st Meeting of the U.S Delegation," May 23, 1945, in *FRUS 1945*, 1:854;

39. See, for example, the cynical commentary from British diplomat Charles Webster in P. A. Reynolds and E. J. Hughes, eds., *The Historian as Diplomat: Charles Kingsley Webster and the United Nations, 1939–1946*, (London, 1976), 70.

40. Stettinius Diary, Week of April 8–14, 1945; Walter White, *A Man Called White: The Autobiography of Walter White* (New York, 1948), 295.

41. Mazower, *No Enchanted Palace*, 28–43.

42. Asher, et al., *UN and the Promotion of the General Welfare*, 658; for a similar discussion, see Lauren, *Power and Prejudice*, 166.

43. Hersch Lauterpacht, "The International Protection of Human Rights," *Académie de Droit International, Recueil des Cours*, 1947(1), 11.

44. Statement of W.E.B. Du Bois, July 11, 1945, Senate Committee on Foreign Relations, The Charter of the United Nations: Hearings Before the Committee on Foreign Relations, 79th Cong., 1st Sess, July 1945, 218.

45. Quoted in Berg, *Ticket to Freedom*, 120–121.

46. Berg, *Ticket to Freedom*, 121; see also "To Secure These Rights: The Report of the President's Committee on Civil Rights," Washington, DC: US GPO 1947; Thomas F. Jackson, *From Civil Rights to Human Rights: Martin Luther King, Jr., and the Struggle for Economic Justice* (Philadelphia, 2006).

47. Saskia Sassen, *Globalization and Its Discontents* (New York, 1998), 96, 95.

48. Amy Gutmann, "Introduction," in *Human Rights as Politics and Idolatry*, commenting on lectures by Michael Ignatieff (Princeton, 2001) at vii. For references to race and advocacy revolutions in this era, see Parker, "Made-in-America Revolutions," and Thomas W. Laqueur, "The Moral Imagination and Human Rights," in Gutmann, ed., *Human Rights as Politics and Idolatry*. For an analysis discounting the influence of 1940s-era developments, see Samuel Moyn, *The Last Utopia: Human Rights in History* (Cambridge, Mass., 2010), 2, 14, 231.

11

"Did the Battlefield Kill Jim Crow?"

THE COLD WAR MILITARY, CIVIL RIGHTS, AND BLACK FREEDOM STRUGGLES

Kimberley L. Phillips

"The Korean War," *Ebony* magazine observed, "is given credit for hastening integration in the Army." Many white Southerners resisted *Brown*, but "the Army is having a big impact on the South's racial patterns." Some whites-only restaurants near bases quietly served blacks in uniform. "[I]n Columbus, Georgia, soon after Negro and white MP's patrol[ed] the streets, Negroes were added to the city's civilian police force."[1] Walter White linked the military's integration with African Americans' long quest for civil rights. "Once again, as has been true throughout American history, armed conflict and national danger brought the Negro advancement toward his goal of full citizenship." If black Americans lived on the outskirts of democracy, as black journalist and author Roi Ottley concluded in 1951, White argued that the military's integration during the Korean War "demonstrates to the world that the direction of democracy's movement is forward." As American troops occupied Europe and much of Asia, and as the United States launched wars in Korea and military interventions in Vietnam, many African Americans hoped that the integrated military would have far-reaching consequences for their civil rights struggles. White imagined that as blacks and whites bled together in foxholes, as their children attended school and played together on military bases, they would "carry the attitude of respect" into American life. After decades of fighting "for the right to fight," he and other mainstream civil rights leaders interpreted African Americans' expanded roles on the Korean War battlefield as a critical step toward racial equality and a new demonstration of American democracy.[2]

During World War II, the NAACP and other civil rights organizations fought "for the right to fight." A. Philip Randolph's March on Washington had demanded, in addition to the inclusion of black workers in defense employment, the end of discrimination in the army. President Roosevelt initially ducked the army question. Randolph judged the continued discrimination "the war's greatest scandal." Wartime necessity (to mobilize more troops to fight the war, and to stop black and white recruits from fighting each other) saw tentative moves toward the inclusion of black soldiers on an equal footing. President Truman's 1948 Executive Order 9981, which called for "equality of opportunity" regardless of race, appeared to provide a significant victory. Faced with severe shortages in all of the armed services, the Department of Defense considered how it might adapt its "Negro policy" from World War II to the demands of occupation and the cold war. For many civil rights activists, the military's insistence on segregated "manpower" presented a conundrum to President Truman. How could the segregated military represent American democracy? Civil rights leaders believed that the demands for a large military provided an unprecedented opportunity to end segregation not just in the armed services, but in the entire society as well—and, indeed, that the end of segregation in the armed services would lead to the end of segregation in everyday life.

Despite the president's order, however, blacks' fight "for the right to fight" continued when the army remained segregated. It would be combat shortages during the Korean War, not the president's post–World War II order, that accelerated integration of combat troops. Even then, when the army integrated the battlefield, it did so out of need of critical combat labor, not any clear commitment for equality in American life or within its ranks. Meanwhile, the organized violence used to defend segregation across the nation converged with a discriminatory draft that pulled disproportionate numbers of black men into the military. "Why," one soldier asked, "are we in the Army? What have we got to fight for? Can the United States possibly bring freedom to colored people in other countries if we are not free at home?"[3]

William Worthy, an anti-war journalist who wrote for the *Baltimore Afro-American* and the *Crisis*, considered the implications of the cold war civil rights agenda for blacks' freedom struggles. After observing a generation of African Americans who experienced waves of violence at home and participated in wars against "colored peoples" abroad, Worthy concluded that these "GIs have died in vain, utterly in vain." He argued that the NAACP leader Walter White's acquiescence to wars in Asia made blacks' struggles for freedom "narrowly defined and internationally myopic." United States policy "backed every broken down reactionary and all the discredited puppets that have no future. Our Asian policies are wrong A to Z."[4] Black people "entertain illusions about their growing stake of 'equality' in an economic and [a military] social order that is not only doomed but a menace to mankind." Instead of gaining "equality," blacks' participation in wars, Worthy insisted, made them "collaborators" in the new colonialism.[5]

Worthy's indictment of civil rights leaders as collaborators with American imperialism found its genesis in the inequalities of the cold war draft and economic policies that compelled disproportionate numbers of African Americans into successive wars while the nation condoned violence against them. While the nation demanded blacks' labor in the military, it did so within prevailing ideas of racial hierarchies. African Americans questioned the logic that linked military service and full citizenship, especially as the cold war unleashed a white nationalism at home and abroad that justified and reestablished racial violence and hierarchies.[6] Nearly two decades before Reverend Martin Luther King, Jr., associated America's racial and class inequalities with its wars, black pacifists, rights activists, soldiers, and veterans correlated the violent rhetoric and practices of anti-communism to the violence against integration and anti-colonialism. Their critical consciousness drew on pacifist, anti-colonial and racial justice struggles that predated World War II, but it acquired momentum in the late 1940s and 1950s as the inequities of the draft compelled a growing population of young black men into military occupations and wars against other people of color while they experienced violence, terror, and resistance to their calls for full citizenship. Their experiences in the overlapping wars between 1948 and 1960 shaped the nonviolent philosophy that became integral to the civil rights movement, and they challenged ideas that associated full citizenship with blacks' participation in an integrated battlefield. By the 1960s, the majority of African Americans agreed that U.S. militarism and the wars that it engendered were inimical to their pursuit of a racial justice based on human dignity and freedom.

Many African Americans hailed Truman's order as a civil rights victory, but the Army insisted that the mandate for "equality of opportunity" did not mean an integrated military. After the president signed the order, General Omar Bradley, who was Army Chief of Staff, announced that the service with the largest number of black troops did not intend to heed the order. Until Americans abandoned segregation, he did not expect the army to change. Southern newspapers applauded Bradley's intransigence and linked racial integration of the military with the specter of communism and the black vote. The *Montgomery Advertiser* described the order as "raw and repugnant." Other Southern newspapers characterized Truman as "grandstanding" for "the Negro vote which seems to be swinging to the Wallace-Communist progressive banner in some areas."[7]

The president's committee charged with ensuring "equality of opportunity" in the military pressed the services to integrate. Grudgingly, the navy announced plans for gradual integration, but commanders removed the few black officers and limited blacks' enlistment. The new air force resolved to have full integration completed by the start of the new decade. The army repeatedly resisted the committee's requests, and after months of negotiations, the Secretary of the Army agreed to remove the racial quotas established during World War II in exchange for the retention of all-black units. The committee, which included Urban League director Lester Granger and *Chicago Defender* editor John Sengstacke, watched with dismay as the president accepted the compromise. On the eve of the Korean War, the only visible integration in the Army could be found in Northern recruiting offices.[8]

Despite evidence gathered since the war in the Philippines, Army officials argued that black men were unfit for combat, and white soldiers refused to serve alongside them. Under the new Selective Service Act, commanders none-theless trained troops in segregated units for diverse combat positions. Some commanders of all-black units ensured that their troops were equipped and trained like white units, but because the Army's "Negro policy" rested on the rhetorical and ideological claims of black men's inferiority, other black troops were not equally trained or outfitted for combat. In July 1950, the U.S. Army went to war in Korea nearly as segregated as it had been at the end of World War II.[9] Black men now had the "right to fight," or rather, the "obligation to serve," but they entered combat under horrible conditions made worse by segregation.

The all-black 503rd Field Artillery landed in Korea in early August without enough ammunition. The battalion then moved north to aid another all-black unit. What Private Charles Rangel and others in his unit saw next startled them. "Three truckloads of GIs—dead GIs—stacked up just like wood, in their uni-forms. And they were black." Minimally trained for combat, Rangel and the other men in his company realized the entire division lacked preparation for the extreme weather, mountainous terrain, and tactics of the North Korean mili-tary. Along with other artillery units in the Eighth Army Division, the 503rd spent the next months struggling to gain ground against the much larger North Korean army. For his all-black unit, the situation was deadly, as they often found themselves without adequate equipment or information. By the fall his unit had enough ammunition, but their World War II–era automatic rifles froze in the severe cold.[10]

Observers reported that the military had an inadequate number of troops and insufficient supplies. Correspondents described "GI's scrounging for food."[11] Others reported the inadequate equipment. Veteran war correspon-dent Marguerite Higgins characterized the Army's lack of preparation as a "long retreat" where the "raw, young" recruits were shocked by what they found in battle and suffered from "bugout fever." She "saw young Americans turn in battle, or throw down their arms, cursing their government for what they thought was embroilment in a hopeless cause." Unable to use the outdated tanks and bazookas, and without enough ammunition, the troops pulled back and retreated.[12] The regiments in the Eighth Army Division arrived from Japan, but the units lacked heavy artillery and not one had an armor company. The troops' frequent and rapid retreats exacerbated the Army's equipment short-ages.[13] Reporters assigned from the black weeklies observed similar difficulties across the units, regardless of race. James Hicks wondered why the Army did not "hold" against the troops they considered inferior in every way.[14]

Hicks praised the largest of the all-black units, the 24th Infantry Regi-ment, but he soon expressed caution. The regiment was "hit hard" by the "staggering" casualties and "this crack regiment is continually being sent into the line without vital equipment necessary for combat." These problems, he charged, appeared months before the war began. He discovered that "the enlisted men from a headquarters company chipped in their own money to fix equipment. Hicks discovered that many, possibly all, of the black units lacked parts for jeeps and had too few weapons. His concerns continued "because the 24th Regiment is currently being judged on its performance, the lack of vital equipment notwithstanding." Officers accused the 24th of leaving equipment to the enemy. Company commanders were later told that no new equipment was to come since the regiment "had carelessly used it and allowed it to get away." Hicks learned that the 24th had been in combat longer than the other units and like the other units, it "had been run off," leaving equipment behind.[15]

Some soldiers understood that their participation in combat signaled progress to many black readers, but they also considered the particular conditions they faced on the battlefield the consequences of their segregation. Unlike white units, the men did not rotate out of combat, and many regiments fought without relief, beginning in late July and continuing through the start of the bitter winter. When Curtis Morrow's unit arrived into the 24th as replacement troops, he realized he was there to die so that the white units could retreat.[16] Poorly supplied, their shoes disintegrated and they bound their feet with rags and ropes until new ones arrived weeks later. When the temperatures dropped, the men fought without jackets and gloves. Charles Armstrong and his unit "lived like bandits. [We] didn't get much sleep. Sometimes we had rations, other times we had to eat what we could find." At one point, the men caught and barbecued a pig stolen from a Korean farm.[17]

Despite these conditions, black soldiers persisted. An assistant platoon sergeant in the 24th, Robert Yancy faced his work with precision and diligence, yet he found many things unequal for the segregated regiment. Commanders sent the men as the first units into combat and they went with the worst equipment.[18] The men felt other inequities. Black troops carried all their own gear, equipment, and weapons up and down the mountainous terrain. In contrast, South Korean civilians carried the equipment and supplies for the white troops.[19] Yancy was not alone in making this assessment. Eighteen-year-old Curtis Morrow and the other men took pride in how they conducted their patrols and ambushes, but they became discouraged by the limited food and outdated equipment. The men knew that their commanders scrutinized them more and considered them "unfit for the fight" because of their race.[20]

The segregated work of killing created an individual and collective critical consciousness, and the men's responses to combat changed. Most troubling, whole black companies were killed and many black soldiers suffered repeated injuries.[21] Experienced soldiers complained about the inadequate and outdated equipment and uniforms; they detested the inexperienced white officers who expressed contempt for the black men, and they despised the segregation and the racist language used to describe them and the enemy.[22] Ivory Perry questioned the shooting and killing of "somebody I don't know nothing about, never had any conflict toward." His fear for his safety under horrific conditions of battle, along with the sleep deprivation, cold, and disease, eroded how he understood himself and others as human beings.[23] James Milton Harp, a gunner in the 231st Field Artillery, took pride in his ability to handle the guns. He and others in his unit "blew up anything," comforted that "he did not see the face of the enemy." When he did, he had enough, especially fighting to stay alive. "I didn't want any more part of it." For Curtis Morrow and other men in his segregated unit, the experience of racism mixed with fear, repulsion, and glory on the battlefield generated a deep resistance to the work of killing. He wondered if the young Korean and Chinese men whom he killed were really his enemy. "What the hell had we black people ever done to them that merited such inhumane treatment?" That soldiers killed many more civilians than enemy troops added to the distress.[24]

Within weeks after the United States entered the war, the NAACP received reports that the army had charged black soldiers with cowardice. Other soldiers sent disturbing accounts about their mistreatment from white commanders. The overwhelming majority of these complaints came from soldiers in the Army, all assigned to segregated units in Korea. James Hicks corroborated these charges, describing the poor conditions on the battlefield, including shortages of equipment, food, and warm clothing. He witnessed black soldiers pulled out of the foxholes, then "shackled" and transferred to Tokyo. Each of the men received a hastily conducted court-martial. After weeks of watching white and black troops retreat, Hicks suspected that army commanders were embarrassed by the army's disarray, yet only black troops faced excessive charges, inadequate counsel, and lengthy prison terms. Several received life sentences. The Army court sentenced Lieutenant Leon Gilbert, a company commander who refused to advance under the terrible conditions, to death.[25]

With information forwarded by Hicks and the accused soldiers, the NAACP sent Thurgood Marshall to investigate. He interviewed several men from each company of the 24th and from every battery of the 159th. In Pusan, Korea, he went through 118 complaints filed in the 25th Division "from all types of offenses." He determined that commanders disproportionately charged black soldiers with cowardice and disobeying orders.[26] The accused and convicted men reported how white soldiers and their units repeatedly retreated. Earlier, Hicks had described how he and others witnessed whites' flight and he "steadfastly claimed that the entire U.S. Army in Korea was running in face of enemy fire." Yet few white troops were arrested out of the foxhole, court-martialed in less than fifty minutes, and sentenced to life in prison.[27]

Aware of the military's problems on the battlefield, Marshall focused on the procedures that were used to try and sentence the thirty-six men. The men's trials occurred in haste and some lasted no more than fifty minutes. An experienced lawyer, Marshall insisted "[c]ounsel did not have time to prepare defense for the men who were rushed from the fox holes to trial." Many of the men did not testify at their own hearings, or give vital information to their lawyers. He was disturbed by the repeated use of "nigger" by some white officers and the aspersions cast against black troops more generally. Marshall managed to have the sentences dramatically reduced for twenty-one soldiers. The military dropped charges against four men with lengthy sentences; and Gilbert's life sentence was reduced to five years.[28]

Marshall departed Korea just as General Matthew Ridgway, the new commander of troops in Korea, called for the integration of combat units. Troop shortages on the battlefield forced some commanders to integrate their units as early as the previous fall. By the early spring, 1951, some black officers commanded integrated units in the Eighth Division. L. Alex Wilson, the war correspondent for the *Chicago Defender*, returned to the United States in December and told radio audiences how he witnessed integration on the battlefield.[29] "The Korean War has done more to wipe out Jim Crow in the Army than any other campaign," Wilson determined. "Negro and white GIs during the grave crisis in Korea—the first armed showdown between American democracy and communism—have made liars out of bigoted politicians." "War," he declared, provided the "purgative [for] race hate among comrades on the front lines."[30]

Despite the eagerness to draft blacks for military labor, however, Americans resisted integration elsewhere. *Defender* columnist Willard Townsend argued that the war put black Americans—"the loyal American Negro"—in a "difficult position." Should they back segregated America, or communist Russia? The answer, he concluded, depended on white Americans' response to segregation, since the communists had long denounced it. "The Dixiecrats and their fellow travelers must give up the luxury of racial bigotry or find the darker races of the world united under the banner" of communism. Black Americans, Townsend implied, should take their cues from native people's response to colonial oppression in Asia, where a "seething resentment" grew against racial, economic, and political exploitation.[31]

Unlike World War II, when many prominent left-leaning African Americans gave assent to the war—in many cases, because they had seen that war as a way to end imperial control of black nations—a substantial list opposed the Korean War. W. E. B. Du Bois and Charlotta Bass, editor of the *California Eagle*, who had both been active members of the Council of African Affairs (CAA)—the leading organization devoted to anti-colonialism—during World War II, now denounced the Korean War. African American luminaries from academia to the arts aligned themselves with international peace movements. Paul Robeson—who had been chairman of the CAA during World War II—held a series of peace rallies, which precipitated intense backlash from the Truman administration and mainstream civil rights organizations. Undaunted, Robeson and many other African Americans, including jazz musician Charlie

Parker, singer Marian Anderson, and sociologist E. Franklin Frazier, signed the World Peace Appeal of 1950.[32]

Other African Americans countered this rising dissent and insisted that the war was against the "Red Menace" and not a "race war." They represented African Americans as "loyal" Americans. As they distinguished themselves from "colored communists," they also argued that democratic nations needed to end racial segregation. If some African Americans found communism attractive, Walter White and other mainstream civil rights leaders argued, it was because of racism in the United States. Racial equality and full citizenship, they stressed, would diminish, if not extinguish, the "Red Menace."[33] Depictions of communists as the "Red Menace" originally described the Soviet Union's actions in Eastern Europe, but by 1950 the term became associated with Asians and the Korean War. Racial stereotypes from World War II reinforced these associations. African Americans who supported anti-colonial struggles, such as Du Bois, Bass, and Robeson, found themselves targets of these racialized claims.[34]

Despite mainstream civil rights activists' attempts to disassociate their struggles from communism, anti-integrationists successfully linked African Americans who insisted on their rights and agitated for integration to communism and political perversion.[35] Walter White hoped to deflect these associations by demurring to Truman's foreign policy and confining the NAACP's focus to domestic civil rights. Du Bois, who had returned to the association during World War II, linked domestic discrimination with anti-colonialism and the global struggle for human rights. He accused White of harnessing the association to "the reactionary, war-mongering colonial imperialism of the present administration." Du Bois's remarks created controversy, and White used the furor to dismiss him.[36]

Du Bois helped organize the international Peace Information Center and launched a seemingly improbable senate campaign in New York, where he described civil rights as the pursuit of peace.[37] For Du Bois, the problem of the twentieth century remained the injustice of the color line, but this inequality now included the grievous imbalance between the poor and the wealthy.[38] The FBI arrested Du Bois after he wrote "An Appeal" to ban nuclear weapons in 1950. Photographs of the handcuffed eighty-three-year-old intellectual appeared in newspapers across the United States. Officials seized his passport, closed his office, and barred him and others from attending the peace congresses held over the next half-decade. After Du Bois successfully fought the government's efforts to jail him, he began a cross-country speaking tour, attracting thousands in each city.[39] In his keynote address to the Progressive Party Convention in early July 1952, he described the United States as "the greatest warmonger of all history." He urged white Americans to join blacks and "demand the end of this senseless war in Korea. The American Negroes are declaring that war destroys civil rights, lowers wages and stops housing."[40]

Peace activism swelled around the world, but many African Americans who had participated in the international peace movement found that their efforts were considered subversive as the talk of war reverberated through nearly every American institution. "It is practically impossible to hold a mass meeting for peace or to say a word for peace," Du Bois observed. The suppression of anti-war activism resulted in peace becoming synonymous with "'Communism' and 'Communism' is attributed to every vile or evil object." Now, he concluded, "Communism is regarded as a 'cause' of Peace" and U.S. officials used the threat of peace "to fulminate for a vaster army, atomic and hydrogen bombs, and universal military service."[41]

African Americans who opposed the Korean War and America's militarism were hounded and silenced. The government confiscated Paul Robeson's passport in 1950 after he praised the Soviet Union's anti-racism and denounced the war.[42] The government targeted journalist, peace activist, and New York communist Claudia Jones; a Trinidadian, she became the only black woman to be tried, incarcerated, and deported. As Du Bois noted, speaking for peace made one a criminal, but the popular association of civil rights with communism meant that black antiwar activists invited charges of treason. Other black writers and intellectuals on the Left felt pressured to renounce communism and to distance themselves from peace activism. Many chose self-imposed silence about politics, a practice that poet Langston Hughes began in 1950 and continued for the next decade and a half.[43]

The NAACP—leaving behind its World War II support for the Council of African Affairs—distanced itself from the black Left's critique of American foreign policy and, instead, presented an image of an America determined to shed its violent and racist past. Returning to the NAACP in 1949 after a year's hiatus, White used his yearly "Progress Report" to tell "the story of America, particularly on the race issue," and refute "Soviet Propaganda," which used the nation's racial violence to agitate for communism. He ignored the escalation in violence against blacks and the dozens who were murdered and assaulted. Instead, he focused on blacks' gains in the military, employment, housing, education, and voting. For many African Americans, including William Patterson, director of the radical Civil Rights Congress (CRC), White's efforts to refute the cumulative and dismal statistics about racial violence, restricted voting rights, and high unemployment appeared dangerous at best.[44]

The CRC issued a report that documented the widespread and systematic violence against African Americans' political and economic rights to demonstrate how segregation and the violence it engendered against them met the United Nation's definition of genocide. *We Charge Genocide* documented the deliberate suppression of blacks' political participation and their exclusion from many sectors of the labor market. The CRC charged that Southern governors, including Georgia governor Eugene Talmadge and South Carolina governor Strom Thurmond, mobilized this racial violence into the new Dixiecrat movement by equating the assault on black political rights with civic virtue. Each year, the CRC argued, the United States through "consistent, conscious, unified policies of segregation, discrimination and violence" created the conditions for the deaths of 32,000 African Americans.[45]

Presented to the UN just months after the start of the Korean War, the CRC's petition linked "domestic genocide" against African Americans to U.S. wars. The organized and widespread violence against those who worked for integration and blacks who claimed their rights as citizens resembled U. S. wars against nations who argued for self-determination. "White supremacy at home," the petitioners charged, "makes for colored massacres abroad. Both reveal contempt for human life in a colored skin. The lyncher and the atom bomb are related." The petitioners concluded that the surge in murders, beatings, burnings, rapes, and false imprisonments of African Americans between 1947 and 1951 correlated "almost in direct ratio to the surge towards war." Many anti-integrationists were also ardent anti-communists, black critics noted, and the organized defense of segregation trained a generation to kill abroad.[46]

Alarmed that the CRC report might undermine blacks' support for anticommunism and the newly desegregated military, Roy Wilkins, White's assistant in the NAACP, asked prominent African Americans to refute the report. Boxer Sugar Ray Robinson insisted "America provides opportunity for everyone, regardless of race, creed, or color." Noting African Americans' subterranean resistance to the war, the CRC persisted. Paul Robeson spoke and wrote about the escalating abuse against blacks at the polls, the attacks in the streets, and the murders. The NAACP counteracted by emphasizing the ties of the CRC and the peace movement to communism. After Walter White wrote an article for *Ebony* diagnosing Robeson's support for the Communist Party as a sign of mental instability, his wife Eslanda Robeson sent a rebuttal to the magazine, arguing that "Negro leaders go out of their way to insist that American democracy, with all its faults, is the best there is and therefore we must all fight if need be die for it. Since most of the *faults* and few of the *benefits* of this democracy apply directly to Negroes, these Leaders find themselves in the very strange position of insisting that Negroes fight and die for the faults of our democracy." *Ebony* ignored her response and instead her article appeared in Bass's *California Eagle*.[47]

The "revitalizing powers" of the integrated battlefield proved doubtful to the increasing numbers of black men in the military and they went beyond the CRC association between segregation in the United States and its wars elsewhere to challenge the long-held argument that their participation in the military advanced their freedom struggles at home. These men insisted that "ordinary people, both colored and white" did not "make these wars." Resisting the rhetoric that wars made democracy, black soldiers correlated "the homeless victims of war" in Korea with the assaults on African Americans in

Mississippi and Florida. "These people," one soldier observed on behalf of his unit in Korea, "are like us, the victims of hate and deceit."[48]

Their communities continued to feel the immediate impact of the integrated draft. The Selective Service Act of 1948, amended during and after the Korean War, encoded myriad class and racial inequalities. Blacks' exclusions from draft boards across the South and minimal appointment to boards elsewhere meant that their communities had higher draft rates. Blacks' limited access to employment meant that they enlisted at twice the rates of whites. Over the next decade, the nation's need for war labor, blacks' constricted access to labor markets, and the class and racial inequalities of draft policies pulled and impressed poor black men into the military in disproportionate percentages and rates.[49]

For young black men, the escalation in the draft portended not simply a U.S. readiness to battle Communists, but endless participation in war. The peacetime military was a myth. By mid-decade, the Pentagon ordered one-and-a-half million soldiers and sailors to sixty-three places in Europe, Latin America, the Caribbean, Asia, and Africa, where they participated in occupations, wars, interventions, and skirmishes. Beguiled by the Army's tales of adventure and mobility and anxious to escape poverty, Walter Dean Myers joined other black soldiers sent into combat hidden from view. What he had hoped would be an escape "from the dangers of the street" became "numbing years. After years of learning to kill efficiently, all the poetry of war left me upon my first scent of decaying flesh."[50] Yet black weeklies during and after the Korean War largely ignored how the work of war emphasized killing other colored people. Instead, African Americans read about the glories of war, how black men used their machine guns with expertise and advanced civil rights. These were good race men, a cadre for black dignity, and *Ebony*'s favorite success story.

The silence about war's violence did not go unchallenged as a new generation of black correspondents and anti-war intellectuals documented how U.S. wars impacted other oppressed people. Articles by William Worthy, a conscientious objector during World War II, linked the rising American imperialism and violence in Asia with the anti-integrationist violence against African Americans. His articles about the horrors of combat countered the popular characterizations of the Korean War as blacks' march to full citizenship. After Worthy went to Korea, he traveled to China, the Soviet Union, and Cuba and then wrote about how the United States intended to use its wars and military occupations to salvage European military and economic imperialism: the federal government took away his passport.[51] Worthy concluded that the United States' intention to salvage European imperialism would plunge the American people into protracted wars.[52]

As Walter White declared that the Korean War had killed Jim Crow, Worthy insisted that black Americans needed to focus on the events unfolding in Southeast Asia. He informed readers that the French colonial efforts had failed, but America now provided diplomatic support, money, equipment, and advisors to

Vietnam's oppressive pro-Western leaders. He warned that America's support for the seven-year-old war in Indo-China "was a dirty war" and a "colonial prelude to a World War III of color." The mainstream press, he insisted, persuaded ordinary Americans that these efforts stemmed communism. President Eisenhower's foreign policy, Worthy observed, was "based on the need for America to obtain profitable foreign markets and raw materials to sustain her economy." This "mineral diplomacy" meant "a million and a half soldiers, airmen, sailors, and marines in 63 lands overseas, and American military advisory groups in 34 foreign countries."[53] In a conclusion that was both prescient and chilling, in 1954 Worthy predicted that the United States would insist that Vietnam could be lost to the communists. A war there, he noted, would be fought between an endless supply of soldiers and guerillas, where there would be "no real battle lines."[54]

The non-aligned nations that met in Bandung, Indonesia, in April 1955 presented African Americans with a political paradigm that went beyond war. The three thousand delegates who arrived to discuss "racialism and colonialism" included more than a dozen African American journalists, including William Worthy, Richard Wright, and *Chicago Defender* journalist Ethel Payne. The conference occurred in the wake of the shrill anti-communist rhetoric from the newly formed White Citizen's Council that linked its outrage over the Supreme Court decision to integrate schools with American's wars against communism.[55] The gathering demonstrated a new and collective political power as Asian and African nations called for self-determination and the right to settle their own problems without interference from either the West or the Soviet Union. As Penny Von Eschen has noted, the conference "not only had world-wide ramifications," but "Bandung and nonalignment created an alternative to viewing global politics through the prism of the Cold War and helped to create a new vocabulary for critiquing American policies."[56] African Americans assessed how some of these new nations emerged out of armed struggle, while others had mounted persistent and effective nonviolent campaigns for independence.

Africans' and Asians' call for political rights, dignity, and freedom from violence articulated at Bandung continued to reverberate for African Americans as they encountered organized and violent resistance to their appeals and demands for equal rights. The home front vigilantism in the South had been particularly virulent in the years after World War II. Violence flared and expanded further during the Korean War. The Citizen's Council, first organized in the summer of 1954 by Robert Patterson, a former World War II paratrooper and an extreme segregationist from Mississippi, grew rapidly and attracted prominent politicians, including Senator James Eastland, business owners, and newspaper editors. Within a year, the Citizen's Councils spread to other states in the South and included moderates participating in the denunciation of the *Brown* decision. These organizations used economic pressure, intimidation, and threats against blacks and whites. They overtly and openly supported vigilante violence and shared members with the Ku Klux Klan and other violent anti-integrationist organizations. In Mississippi, the economic pressure and violence targeted African Americans, many of whom were veterans, as they sought to register to vote. George Lee, a minister, organized the Belzoni Branch of the NAACP, and was the first African American in the county to get his name on the voting list. After a rally at the end of April 1955, he was fatally shot while driving home. The only witness disappeared.[57]

In a country already galvanized by these murders, the lynching of fourteen-year-old Emmett Till in late August 1955 generated an immediate response from the black press and a mobilized black America. With support from the NAACP, Mamie Till Bradley had her son's body returned to Chicago because she wanted "the whole world to see what they did to my boy." Twin images, one of the smiling teenager, the other of his mutilated corpse, appeared side by side in the popular *Jet* magazine. Maybe the trial would end with the acquittal of the murderers as others had ended, but black America intended to put the violence of the Jim Crow South on display.[58]

Two weeks after their arrest, J. W. Milam and his half-brother Roy Bryant went to court in a trial that lasted four and a half days. The defense lawyers described Milam and Bryant as war heroes and ordinary men defending Bryant's wife, Caroline, from the "aggressive talk" of the black teenager visiting from the North. Milam had received a field promotion from a private to a lieutenant in Germany during World War II; Roy Bryant had fought as a paratrooper in Korea.[59] Milam's lawyer, John Whitten, was a veteran, and veterans from twenty-one states reportedly sent money to support the two defendants. At the start of the trial, Whitten described Milam as a "good soldier" who "did not leave the battlefield."[60] The all-white and all-male jury returned a not guilty verdict after sixty-seven minutes of deliberation. Reportedly the jury sent out for ice cream before they delivered their decision to the judge.[61]

The short trial adjudicated in a segregated courtroom and deliberated by an all-white male jury made the violence of Jim Crow visible as an organized war against integration.[62] With bravado, Milam and Bryant later recounted to journalist William Bradford Huie how they murdered the teenager. For Milam and Bryant, Till was not just a sexual predator, but a purveyor of a dangerous integration. Milam described how he pistol whipped the boy, just as he had pistol whipped Germans. He was not sorry he "killed a niggah who gets out of place."[63] Huie did not see the murder as premeditated, but for Milam, murdering Till appears to have been another battle in the war against integration.

After Till's murder, anti-integrationists presented their massive resistance as a war for democracy, but African Americans did not concede. In December 1955, civil rights activists, black nationalists, veterans of Asian and European wars, and pacifists mounted a boycott against segregation on the Montgomery, Alabama buses. Activists pulled community organizations into the new

Montgomery Improvement Association (MIA); the name of the new organization indicated the links between local and global struggles for freedom. E.D. Nixon, a key organizer, had belonged to the Universal Negro Improvement Association (UNIA), served as president of the Montgomery NAACP, and headed the local Brotherhood of Sleeping Car Porters. Joanne Gibson Robinson, a professor at Alabama State College, and Rosa Parks, who launched the bus boycott after her refusal to yield to the Jim Crow laws, belonged to the influential Women's Political Council (WPC). Parks had served as the secretary of the Montgomery NAACP since 1943 and she led the branch voter registration drive and youth workshops, which she organized in the 1940s. In 1955 she became secretary of the Alabama State Conference of NAACP branches. Months before her arrest, Parks and other women in the WPC had discussed how defiance of the bus segregation might instigate a federal case.[64]

Community organizations created by military and civil rights veterans infused the mass boycott with a nascent nonviolent character. World War II veteran Rufus Lewis organized the voting efforts for men and women who served in World War II and the Korean War; he worked with former veterans to coordinate the car routes needed for daily transportation. Church members provided funds, meeting spaces, phones, cars, and drivers. These complicated plans were worked out each night in the churches where working-class black men, women, and their children gathered to pray and testify. The support for the new young pastor of Dexter Avenue Baptist Church, Reverend Martin Luther King, Jr., to lead the MIA demonstrated, again, how these community ties could create a new organization that was immediately effective.[65] But the powerful origins of the MIA also created a pastiche of ideologies and tactics, which included armed self-defense, passive resistance, and defiance, a practice launched after the *Morgan* decision and used in anti-apartheid struggles in South Africa.[66]

Watching the events unfold, James Farmer and William Worthy, both pacifists and members of the Fellowship of Reconciliation and the Congress of Racial Equality, tracked the MIA's use of nonviolence in the day-to-day actions. Farmer and Worthy argued that someone with experience in the philosophy and tactics of nonviolence should go to Montgomery. Bayard Rustin was the foremost authority in nonviolence. Now executive director of the War Resister League, Rustin agreed, seeing it as an opportunity to connect his antiwar activism with the racial justice movement. He found a community cobbling together the raiment of nonviolence with communal traditions of self-defense. As members in the MIA faced bombs, threats, assaults, and terror from anti-black organizations and the local police, they increasingly used mass direct-action nonviolence. At the same time, Rustin learned that after Reverend Martin Luther King, Jr., received numerous threats, the community organized armed men into shifts for round-the-clock protection. "This is like war," one guard told Rustin. Surprised by the arsenal in many blacks' homes, including

King's, Rustin nonetheless discerned the community's receptiveness to the philosophy and tactics of nonviolence.[67]

Rustin helped write *Speak Truth to Power* for the American Friends Service Committee (due to his conviction for homosexual activity in California, his name did not appear as a co-author), but his articulation of nonviolent direct activism became integral to the document's authority. Once in Montgomery and working daily with King, Rustin helped calibrate indigenous practices of resistance with the ideology and tactics of a nonviolence that were both local and international. The efforts of black Montgomerians, Rustin observed, "would be a nonviolent protest, not a boycott as the former put forth a philosophy and not simply an action with a finite goal. [Nonviolence] would permeate the entire community culture." Whereas previous black struggles against segregation were linked to U.S. wars abroad, this victory would be "Victory Without Violence." In this struggle, African Americans eschewed the language of battle and war that had characterized earlier struggles that occurred in the midst of wars abroad.[68]

This community-based challenge to segregation nurtured indigenous behaviors into a collective critical consciousness about the efficacy of nonviolence. Through workshops they learned that how they dressed, walked, and surrendered en masse could disarm their attackers. They learned how collective and nonviolent tactics turned individual and passive resistance into direct and mass action. They created forums for consciousness-raising where art, music, and oral practices advanced and sustained the movement. When Rustin first arrived, he witnessed the mass meetings where the men and women who were arrested each day, after they withstood the violence with nonviolence, arrived and testified about their experiences. These were peace warriors returned from the frontlines of struggle and they "became symbols of courage." In these meetings the congregations used prayers to affirm a familiar religious and philosophical commitment to nonviolence. These prayers became forums for the community to gain a heightened awareness of the connections between their protests in the segregated South and anti-colonial struggles. King and others then gave lectures about the success of nonviolent mass action used elsewhere, including India and South Africa.[69]

When Reverend Martin Luther King described the Montgomery bus boycott to end segregation as part of the global struggle by the oppressed against colonialism and imperialism, he displayed a critical consciousness influenced by Rustin's analyses of nonviolent direct action as radical action used elsewhere in anti-colonial efforts. Rustin witnessed thousands of African Americans in daily challenges to racial violence and economic oppression, much of it invisible to whites. Now acting as a community in radical protest against local and national racial oppression, the MIA confronted the violence used by the local Citizen's Council and police with defiant nonviolence. King compared the enormous effort by governments to sustain these systems of oppression and the people's efforts to end them. He repeatedly called attention to the unchecked violence, threats, and intimidation that blacks in Montgomery confronted daily from whites determined to maintain their control and by local and state authorities determined to defy federal law.[70]

The nonviolent mass action incited violent retaliations from the Citizen's Councils and other anti-integration resistance. While many of these anti-integrationists denounced civil rights legislation imposed by the federal courts as an invasion akin to the Civil War, others considered the South as the epicenter of the anti-communist struggle. Anti-integrationists tied black activism for civil rights of any sort to communism, and, in turn, anti-communism legitimized new forms of violence against activists. Richard M. Weaver, a conservative intellectual, described integration as communism, and "[t]he Communists are skilled enough in warfare" and threatened to impose "racial collectivism" and "obliterate" "our historic constitutional structure."[71] The rhetoric and practices of anti-communism included fears of "outside agitation," which vilified blacks who belonged to the NAACP or any other organization calling for integration. The charges of the menacing black rapist used to justify vigilantism in the early twentieth century morphed into charges against the menacing black radical, an image that encapsulated the black teenager "with new ideas" from the North and the black veteran claiming the right to vote. Anti-communism endorsed a racial violence that was far more open, widespread, and legitimized by the racialized language, tactics, and philosophy that informed wars abroad.

The 1957 standoff in Little Rock, Arkansas, accelerated this violent and massive resistance to integration across the South, and many African Americans debated the need for armed troops to halt the resistance to civil rights laws. After Eisenhower removed the integrated 101st Airborne and no longer showed a willingness to use federal power to enforce judicial orders or protect black citizens from violence, many African Americans called for self-defense. "They could have integration in one minute," Louis Armstrong said, "if they'd just give the Negroes something to protect themselves with. Just give them an even chance. Then watch them cowards haul out of there."[72] As the danger and reprisals continued into the late 1950s and as anti-colonial struggles in Africa became armed struggles, many African Americans agreed, though few openly called for organized black resistance. Instead, they quietly organized their guns to protect their homes and families.[73] In some cases, individual and collective acts of self-defense had diminished some violence. After activist and veteran Robert F. Williams and others in the Monroe, North Carolina, NAACP had an armed confrontation with the Klan in 1957, they did not see any further public displays of its terror.[74]

Even so, many African Americans considered nonviolent direct action the more effective tactic. The activists committed to this philosophy and tactics were typically well informed about the collective nonviolent actions of people elsewhere engaged in anti-colonial and freedom struggles. They were typically radical pacifists, veterans, and civil rights activists. And they sought new forms of organizations and leadership that built and perpetuated progressive and revolutionary movements for social change. African Americans saw the Montgomery bus boycott as different from passive resistance and one that demonstrated a new radicalism akin to that in anti-colonial struggles. Gandhi's methods against colonialism in India and against apartheid in South Africa and the nonviolent, direct-action campaigns that Kwame Nkrumah, the new president of independent Ghana, led against the British appealed to many African Americans.[75]

Just as those who called for black self-defense measured their strategies through the prism of the anti-colonial struggles in Asia and Africa, and saw violence as a corrective—albeit unfortunate corrective—to colonialism, those who pursued nonviolence considered the tactics and philosophy from anti-colonial successes in India and Ghana. As Bayard Rustin noted, "preparation of the weapons of wars" abroad and "the development of policies of intimidation" at home were related. He and others proposed mass nonviolent resistance, demonstrations, strikes, boycotts, noncooperation, and civil disobedience to confront violence in their own communities and to stop invasions and end wars.[76] These advocates intended to use nonviolence as a social revolution against racial injustice and economic exploitation that would also alter American society. Over time, they imagined that the nation would end international conflict and profoundly shift the nation's relationship to the international community. Nonviolence created radical social change, they argued, not simply because of its techniques and tactics, but because it also advocated a way of life with implications for the local and international. In their construction, mass nonviolence had the potential to be as revolutionary as armed self-defense. William Worthy argued that African Americans' nonviolent efforts for full citizenship made them "custodians of American democracy."[77]

As some imagined a democracy without violence, increasing numbers of poor black men faced the draft or the pressure to enlist. Writer James Baldwin refuted the prevailing belief among the civil rights elite that the integrated military benefited blacks. He argued that black Americans' continued "fight for the right to fight" yielded little, and instead led to "one's murder" and to one's role as a "murderer."[78] Assessing the menace that black people faced in ghettoes during the Korean and Vietnam wars, Baldwin concluded America "does not know what to do with its black population now that blacks are no longer a source of wealth, are no longer to be bought and sold and bred like cattle." Young black men, he observed, especially perplexed the nation for they "pose as devastating a threat to the economy as they pose to the morals of young white cheerleaders. It is not at all accidental that the jails and the army and the needle claim so many."[79]

As a massive coalition of civil rights, labor, and veterans' organizations successfully pressed for the integration of the military in the half-decade between

World War II and the Korean War, another cadre of black veterans, pacifists, and racial justice activists argued against war as tens of thousands of black men entered the military. By the 1960s, the idea of combat as a "right" and a declaration of black citizenship, and the military as "equal opportunity," no longer retained its rhetorical and organizing power for civil rights struggles as it had in the period between 1940 and 1955. Many African Americans considered their disproportionate presence in the military and combat as evidence of their political and economic inequality in American society. In a new introduction to *We Charge Genocide*, William Patterson noted that "the increasing use of blacks as [an] armed gendarme to force America's murderous brand of democracy upon foreign peoples" compelled them to unite in the struggle for peace.[80] Two decades after mainstream civil rights leaders insisted that the integrated battlefield was essential to blacks' citizenship, the majority believed their participation in war thwarted their struggles for freedom and racial justice. On the eve of the Vietnam War, a considerable percentage of African Americans rejected the logic of militarism and war as integral to their concepts of equality, racial justice, and freedom.

Notes

1. "New Army Upsets South's Traditions," *Ebony,* Vol. 9 (September 1954), 16–20.

2. Roi Ottley, *No Green Pastures: The Negro in Europe Today* (New York, 1951), 1; Walter White, *How Far the Promised Land?* (New York, 1955), 96, 102–103.

3. Harry C. Truman, "Executive Order 9981," *Documentary History of the Truman Presidency: The Truman Administration's Civil Rights Program*, Dennis Merrill, ed. (New York, 1996), 741; "Pertinent GI Questions," *Baltimore Afro-American* August 4, 1951, 4.

4. William Worthy, "Korean Debacle Bound to Open Eyes of US GIs," *Baltimore Afro-American*, August 22, 1953.

5. William Worthy, *Our Disgrace in Indo-China* (Cambridge, Mass., 1954), 5.

6. For a definition of an antiwar racial justice, see Barbara Lee, "Gender, Race, and Militarism: Toward a More Just Alternative," in Barbara Sutton, ed., *Security Disarmed: Critical Perspectives on Gender, Race and Militarism* (New Brunswick, 2008): 56-64.

7. Quoted in William C. Berman, *The Politics of Civil Rights in the Truman Administration* (Columbus, 1970), 118 and 119.

8. Morris J. MacGregor and Bernard C. Nalty, "The Fahy Committee," *Blacks in the United States: Basic Documents, Volume IX* (Wilmington, Del., 1977); "The Air Force Goes Interracial," *Ebony,* Vol. 4 (September 1949), 15–17.

9. Harry C. Truman, "Executive Order 9981," *Documentary History of the Truman Presidency: The Truman Administration's Civil Rights Program*, Dennis Merrill, ed. (New York, 1996), 741; Bernard C. Nalty, *Strength for the Fight: A History of Black Americans in the Military* (New York, 1986); Richard M. Dalfiume, *Desegregation of the U.S. Armed Forces* (Columbus, 1969).

10. Charles Rangel, *And I Haven't Had a Bad Day Since: From the Streets of Harlem to*

the Halls of Congress (New York, 2007), 62–63. Women attached to combat units in Iraq and Afghanistan have made similar complaints. See Meg McLagan, *Lioness* (Docudrama, 2009).

11. "Retreat Held Rout," *New York Times*, July 5, 1950, 2.

12. Marguerite Higgins, "The Terrible Days in Korea," *Saturday Evening Post,* August 19, 1950, 26–27, 110–112.

13. Max Hastings, *The Korean War* (New York, 1987), 20.

14. James Hicks, "Army Passes Buck," *Baltimore Afro-American*, August 26, 1950, 1–2;

15. James Hicks, "24th Hit Hard," *Baltimore Afro-American*, August 19, 1950, 1, 19.

16. James Hicks, "Fight or Die," *Baltimore Afro-American*, August 12, 1950, 19; Curtis James Morrow, *What's a Commie Ever Done to Black People?: A Korean War Memoir* (Jefferson, 1997), 3.

17. "Charles Armstrong," Yvonne Latty and Ron Traver, ed., *We Were There: Voices of African American Veterans from World War II to Iraq* (New York, 2005) 58.

18. "Robert Yancy," *We Were There*, 69–70.

19. Selika Marianne Ducksworth, "What Hour of the Night: Black Enlisted Men's Experiences and the Desegregation of the Army During the Korean War, 1950–1," (Dissertation, Ohio State University, 1994), 115–116.

20. Morrow, 44–45.

21. James Hicks, "24th Quickly Learns New-Style Fighting," *Baltimore Afro-American*, August 5, 1950, 1; Morrow, 63–65; 71–89.

22. Lyle Rishell, *With a Black Platoon in Combat: A Year in Korea* (College Station, Texas, 1993), 40–41.

23. Morrow, 9; Lipsitz, *A Life in the Struggle*, 53–55. Quote is on page 53.

24. Gregory H. Winger interview with James Milton Harp, May 16, 2003, Veterans' Oral History Project, Library of Congress; Morrow, *What's a Commie Ever Done to Black People?*, 12; Morrow, 64.

25. James Hicks, "Courts Martial Hasty," *Baltimore Afro-American*, February 24, 1951, 1–2; Juan Williams, *Thurgood Marshall: American Revolutionary* (New York, 1998), 170.

26. Thurgood Marshall, *Report on Korea: The Shameful Story of the Courts Martial of Negro GIs* (New York, 1951), 13.

27. James L. Hicks, "Courts Martial Hasty," *Baltimore Afro-American*, February 24, 1951, 1–2; Hicks, "Courts Martial Hasty," *Baltimore Afro-American*, February 24, 1951, 1–2; Blair, 445.

28. Marshall, *Report on Korea*, 13–15; quote on 16.

29. "L. Alex Wilson to Air Korean War on Radio," *Chicago Defender*, December 2, 1950.

30. Mathew Ridgway, *Soldier: The Memoirs of Mathew Ridgway* (New York, 1956), 192–193; Leo Bogart, ed., *Project Clear: Social Research and the Desegregation of the United States Army* (New Brunswick, 1991); L. Alex Wilson, "Bombs, Brass, and Brotherhood: Integrations Is the Test by War in Korea," Chicago *Defender*, February 3, 1951, 1.

31. Willard Townsend, "Columnist Says Negro Has Stake in South Korean War," *Chicago Defender*, August 19, 1950, 7.

32. Brenda Gayle Plummer, *Rising Wind: Black Americans and U.S. Foreign Affairs, 1935–1960* (Chapel Hill, 1996), 104.

33. Says Red Propaganda Misses Mark in Korea," April 25, 1953, *Chicago Defender*, 12;

"Case of the Exiles," *Chicago Defender* October 10, 1953, 11; White, *How Far the Promised Land*, 24–25.

34. Bill V. Mullen, *Afro-Orientalism* (Minneapolis, 2004), 64–68.

35. Jeff Woods, *Black Struggle Red Scare: Segregation and Anti-Communism in the South, 1948–1968* (Baton Rouge, 2004), 49–52.

36. Quoted in Penny Von Eschen, *Race Against Empire: Black Americans and Anticolonialism, 1937–1957* (Ithaca, 1997), 118.

37. W.E.B. Du Bois, "No Progress Without Peace," from the *National Guardian* October 4, 1950, reprinted in W.E.B. Du Bois, *Newspaper Columns by W.E.B. Du Bois*, Herbert Aptheker, v. 2, 1945–1961 (White Plains, N.Y., 1986), 873.

38. W.E.B. Du Bois, "I Take My Stand," in *The Oxford W.E.B. Du Bois Reader*, Eric Sundquist, ed. (New York, 1996), 469; W.E.B. Du Bois, "U. S. Needs No More Cowards," from the *National Guardian*, October 25, 1950; reprinted in W.E.B. Du Bois, *Newspaper Columns by W.E.B. Du Bois*, Herbert Aptheker, v. 2, 1945–1961 (White Plains, N.Y., 1986), 874 (quote) and 878–879.

39. W.E.B. Du Bois, "There Must be a Vast Social Change in the United States," *National Guardian*, July 11, 1951, 884 and fn. 882.

40. W.E.B. Du Bois, "We Cry Aloud," *National Guardian*, July 10, 1952; includes keynote address to the Progressive Party Convention, 892; 894.

41. Du Bois, "The World Peace Movement," *Against Racism: Unpublished Essays, Papers, and Addresses*, Herbert Aptheker, ed. (Amherst, 1985), 238.

42. Arnold Rampersad, *The Life of Langston Hughes,* Volume II (New York, 1986), 186–195; 209–221; Robbie Lieberman, "'Another Side of the Story': African American Intellectuals Speak Out for Peace and Freedom During the Early Cold War Years," *Anticommunism and the African American Freedom Movement*, Lieberman and Clarence Lang, eds. (New York, 2009), 17–50.

43. Carole Boyce Davies, *Left of Karl Marx The Political Life of Claudia Jones* (Durham, 2007); James Smethurst, *The Black Arts Movement: Literary Nationalism in the 1960s and 1970s* (Chapel Hill, 2005), 29–38; Bill V. Mullen and James Smethurst, *Left of the Color Line: Race, Radicalism, and Twentieth-Century Literature of the United States* (Chapel Hill, 2003), 1–12; and Mary Helen Washington, "Alice Childress, Lorraine Hansberry, and Claudia Jones: Black Women Write the Popular Front," in Mullen and Smethurst, *Left of the Color Line*, 183–200.

44. Civil Rights Congress, *We Charge Genocide*, 3; Pettis Perry, *White Chauvinism and the Struggle for Peace* (New York, 1952), 6–7; Gerald Horne, *Communist Front?: The Civil Rights Congress, 1946–1956* (Rutherford, 1988), 163–181.

45. *We Charge Genocide*, xiv; 125–126.

46. *Ibid.*, 7–8.

47. Quoted in Martin B. Duberman, *Paul Robeson* (New York, 1989), 395; Kenneth Janken, *White: The Biography of Walter White and the NAACP* (New York, 2003), 319–321;

48. "Men of the 857th, "Pertinent GI Questions"; and George F. Baynham, "Hear Our Lord Amen?" *Baltimore Afro-American,* August 4, 1951, 4.

49. Kimberley L. Phillips, "War! What is it Good For?: Conscription and Migration in Black America," in *Repositioning North American Migration History*, Marc Rodriguez, ed. (New York, 2004), 265–283.

50. Walter Dean Myers, *Bad Boy: A Memoir* (New York, 2001), 200–201.

51. Davies, *Left of Karl Marx*, 147–158.

52. William Worthy, *Our Disgrace in Indo-China* (Cambridge, Mass., 1954), 5–6; on Worthy's work as a war intellectual in the late 1950s and 1960s, see Peniel E. Joseph, *Waiting 'Til The Midnight Hour: A Narrative of Black Power in America* (New York, 2006), 44–51.

53. William Worthy, "Of Global Bondage," *The Crisis* 61 (October 1954), 469.

54. Worthy, *Our Disgrace in Indo-China*.

55. Kathleen Currie, Interview with Ethel Payne, August 25, 1987; and September 8, 1987, Women in Journalism, Washington Press Club, 63–84, www.wpcf.org/oralhistory/payn.html; Von Eschen, 167–172; Richard Wright, *Color Curtain*, in *Black Power: Three Books from Exile: Black Power, The Color Curtain* and *White Man, Listen!* (New York, 1957), 437–440; Hazel Rowley, *The Life and Times of Richard Wright* (Chicago, 2001), 462–468. Cary Fraser, "An American Dilemma: Race and RealPolitik in the American Response to the Bandung Conference, 1955," in *Window on Freedom*, 115–137.

56. Von Eschen, 173.

57. "NACW Calls for Probe of Mississippi Killing," *Baltimore Afro-American*, July 2, 1955, 20; David T. Beito, *Black Maverick: T. M. Howard's Fight for Civil Rights and Economic Power* (Urbana, 2009), 108–110. In December 1955, Courts was shot. See James Hicks, "Mob Shoots Leader," *Baltimore Afro-American*, December 3, 1955, 1.

58. "NAACP Urges U.S. Action in Miss. 'Reign of Terror,'" *Baltimore Afro-American* September 17, 1955, 14.

59. "'Were Never into Meanness' Says Accused Men's Mother," Memphis *Commercial Appeal*, September 2, 1955, in *The Lynching of Emmett Till: A Documentary Narrative*, Christopher Metress (Charlottesville, 2002), 34–37; Gene Roberts and Hank Klibanoff, *The Race Beat: The Press, the Civil Rights Struggle, and the Awakening of a Nation* (New York, 2006),

60. Metress, 37–45.

61. Sam Johnson, "Jury Hears Defense and Prosecution Arguments as Testimony Ends in Kidnap-Slaying Case," *Greenwood Commonwealth*, September 23, 1955, reprinted Metress, 99.

62. Ruth Feldstein, *Motherhood in Black and White: Race and Sex in American Liberalism* (Ithaca, 2000), 86–110.

63. Metress, *The Lynching of Emmett Till*, 246; Roberts and Klibanoff, 101–102.

64. Aldon D. Morris, *The Origins of the Civil Rights Movement: Black Communities Organizing for Change* (New York, 1984), 51–55; Steven Hahn, *The Political Worlds of Slavery and Freedom* (Cambridge, 2009), 149–150.

65. Reverend Martin Luther King, Jr., *Stride Toward Freedom*, reprinted in *A Testament of Hope: The Essential Writings and Speeches of Martin Luther King, Jr.*, ed. James M. Washington (New York, 1986), 425–427; 438–450; Bayard Rustin, "Montgomery Diary," in *Time on Two Crosses: The Collected Writings of Bayard Rustin,* Devon W. Carbado and Donald Weise, eds. (San Francisco, 2003), 58–65.

66. Christopher B. Strain, *Pure Fire: Self-Defense as Activism in the Civil Rights Era* (Athens, 2005), 36–48; Rustin, 58; John D'Emilio, *Lost Prophet: The Life and Times of Bayard Rustin* (Chicago, 2004), 237–246.

67. Rustin, 58.

68. Rustin, 58. For the account of Rustin's work in writing Chapter Four of *Speak Truth*

to Power, see D'Emilio, 219–222; "Speak Truth to Power: A Quaker Search for an Alternative to Violence," www.quaker.org/sttp.html.

69. Rustin, 60.

70. King, "Nonviolence and Racial Justice," in *A Testament of Hope: The Essential Writings and Speeches*, 7–8; William Worthy, "Worthy Finds Montgomery is Moscow," *Baltimore Afro-American*, March 6, 1956; and "Tale of Two Cities," *Baltimore Afro-American*, March 20, 1956; and "None Are So Blind," *Baltimore Afro-American*, October 30, 1956, 11.

71. Richard M. Weaver, "Integration is Communization," *National Review*, July 13, 1957, 67.

72. "Satchmo Ready to Take Golden Horn to Russia," *Los Angeles Times*, October 11, 1957, 5.

73. Charles B. Strain, *Pure Fire: Self-Defense as Activism in the Civil Rights Era* (Athens: University of Georgia Press, 2005), 7.

74. Julian Mayfield, "Challenge to Negro Leadership: The Case of Robert Williams," in *Reporting Civil Rights; American Journalism, 1941–1961, Part One* (New York, 2003), 558.

75. Forman, 105.

76. "Speak Truth to Power: A Quaker Search for an Alternative to Violence," www.quaker.org/sttp.html.

77. Scott H. Bennett, *Radical Pacifism: The War Resisters League and Gandhian Nonviolence in America, 1915–1963* (Syracuse, 2003), xv–xvi; D'Emilio, 223–248; William Worthy, "Worthy Views Group as Custodians of Democracy," *Atlanta Daily World*, May 8, 1957, 6.

78. *Ibid.*, 458–459.

79. James Baldwin, *No Name in the Street*, Reprinted in *The Price of the Ticket: Collected Non-Fiction, 1948–1985* (New York, 1985), 517.

80. William Peterson, "Foreward," *We Charge Genocide* (New York, 1970), viii–xi.

{ INDEX }